Holy Ground, Healing Water

NUMBER TWENTY FOUR
Environmental History Series
Dan L. Flores
General Editor

DONALD J. BLAKESLEE

Holy Ground, Healing Water

CULTURAL LANDSCAPES AT WACONDA LAKE, KANSAS

TEXAS A&M UNIVERSITY PRESS
College Station

Manufactured in the United States of America

First edition

This paper meets the requirements of ANSI/NISO Z39.48-1992 (Permanence of Paper).

Binding materials have been chosen for durability.
∞

LIBRARY OF CONGRESS CATALOGING-IN-PUBLICATION DATA

Blakeslee, Donald J., 1943–
Holy ground, healing water : cultural landscapes at Waconda Lake, Kansas / Donald J. Blakeslee.—1st ed.
p. cm.—(Environmental history series ; no. 24)
Includes bibliographical references and index.
ISBN-13: 978-1-60344-210-7 (cloth : alk. paper)
ISBN-13: 978-1-60344-211-4 (pbk. : alk. paper)
ISBN-10: 1-60344-210-3 (cloth : alk. paper) 1. Indians of North America—Kansas—Waconda Lake—Antiquities. 2. Indians of North America—Kansas—Waconda Lake—Social life and customs. 3. Excavations (Archaeology)—Kansas—Waconda Lake. 4. Waconda Lake (Kan.)—Antiquities. 5. Waconda Lake (Kan.)—History. 6. Waconda Lake (Kan.)—Description and travel. 7. Landscape protection—Kansas—Waconda Lake. I. Title. II. Series: Environmental history series ; no. 24.
E78.K16B55 2010
978.1'23—dc22

2010003554

IN MEMORY OF JACK BLAKESLEE AND F.C. LEWIS

CONTENTS

LIST OF ILLUSTRATIONS

LIST OF TABLES

ACKNOWLEDGMENTS

THERE IS NEVER enough room to credit all of the people who have contributed to a volume like this. Still, there are a few that I would be ashamed not to mention. They are: Bob Blasing and Bill Chada of the Bureau of Reclamation, Craig Miner from the Department of History at Wichita State University, Mary Nelson in the Special Collections at Ablah Library, and all of the librarians at the Kansas State Historical Society.

Holy Ground, Healing Water

1. Introduction

WHEN WE FACE the past, we pick out from the endless string of days certain ones to mark the passing of one era and the beginning of another. Sometimes we remember the precise day—the fourth of July in 1776—sometimes just the year—1066 or 1492. I would like to offer a new date for consideration: July 6, 1870. On that day, a Mr. Charles DeRudio paid two hundred dollars to the clerk in the land office in Junction City, Kansas, and under the provisions of the Preemption Act, he obtained ownership of the SE1/4 Section 25, Township 6 South, Range 10 West. This is on the north bank of the Solomon River in north-central Kansas.

On the face of it, this was a very mundane event. Settlers from all over the eastern United States and from a growing number of European countries had been obtaining title to land in the West for decades. And it was not unusual for someone to pay the two hundred dollars; the Preemption Act had been around for nearly three decades by the time Mr. DeRudio laid down his cash. By 1870, claims under the Homestead Act were certainly more common, as they required cash payments of only nineteen dollars. Instead, the claimant had to live on and work the land for five years, making improvements to it.

When we look more closely at the date, the significance of the exchange becomes clearer. Euro-Americans had been trying to settle the area around Mr. DeRudio's land since 1864. But natives of the region, Pawnees and then Cheyennes, Arapahos and Sioux, defended their territory fiercely. The years 1867 and 1868 had seen raids on the Saline, Solomon and Republican rivers, in which some settlers were killed, others kidnapped, their cabins burned and their livestock slain or taken. After 1870, however, raids were reduced to isolated nuisances, and natives were no longer an enemy to be feared but a rarity and the subject, when seen, of idle curiosity.

It is true that the people who survived the raids did not soon forget the fear and hatred that reigned in the 1860s, but they were soon far outnumbered by newcomers who had no direct experience of the hostilities. For 1870 marks the beginning of a renewed wave of settlement that soon pushed far west of the forks of the Solomon—all the way to the plains of Colorado.

So 1870 was not just any year, at least in this area. And Charles DeRudio was not just another settler.[1] He was Lieutenant Charles C. DeRudio, commander of Company G of the Seventh Cavalry. His military career in the United States began in 1864 when he joined the Union Army as a private in the Seventy-Ninth Highlanders New York regiment. For bravery he was later promoted to second lieutenant and assigned to the Second U.S. Colored Troops regiment, stationed in Florida. Then in 1869 he was assigned to the Seventh Cavalry under George Armstrong Custer at Fort Riley, Kansas.

But this was DeRudio's second career, or, rather, his second life. He was born Carlo Camillo di Rudio, son of Count Ercule di Rudio and Contessa Elisabetta de Domini on their estate about forty miles north of Venice, a region then under the control of the Austrian Empire. As a young man, he became a revolutionary, fighting with Calvi against Austrian domination and then with Garibaldi against the French and the Papacy. Always on the losing side, he had to flee Italy and ended up in Paris, where he fought on the side of the revolutionaries against Louis Napoleon. Once again he had chosen the losing side, and once more he fled, first back to Italy and then to London.

There he became involved in an assassination plot against Napoleon III. When the assassination attempt (in an opera house in Paris) failed, the conspirators were brought before a court of law. Two of the four (or five, according to di Rudio) were sentenced to death, while di Rudio and one other man were sentenced to life imprisonment on Devil's Island. He escaped from the island prison and made his way temporarily back to England only to take his final refuge in the United States.

Apparently, Carlo Di Rudio, now calling himself Charles DeRudio, regaled the members of the Seventh Cavalry with stories of his earlier escapades. In so doing, he drew the ire of Custer, who brooked no competitors for fame and glory. As a result, DeRudio apparently became aligned with Captain William F. Benteen, who had little use for Custer.

Jumping ahead in time for a moment, DeRudio fought at the battle of the Little Bighorn and managed to survive. He was with Major Marcus Reno's unit at the beginning of the battle but became separated from it early in the fighting and spent a day and a half hiding in the woods on the opposite side of the river from Reno's defensive position on the bluff top. DeRudio's account of his part in the battle was published on the front page of the July 30, 1876, edition of the *New York Herald.* One suspects that Custer rolled over in his grave. DeRudio remained with the Seventh Cavalry and was promoted to captain in 1882. He retired in 1896 and died in 1910.[2]

Returning to the fighting in Kansas in the 1860s, DeRudio was with a detachment from Fort Zarah on the Arkansas River under the command of Captain Benteen. They rode north to the Solomon Valley in the wake of the raid that occurred in August 1868. En route, they chased a group of Cheyenne warriors for ten miles or so, and in so doing they unknowingly caused the Cheyennes to abandon two young captives, Maggie and Esther Bell, who were later rescued. In 1869 and again in April 1870, Lieutenant DeRudio and Company G were stationed on the north bank of the Solomon in the vicinity of his claim.

So the transfer occurred at a significant point in time—when the land was permanently wrested from native control—and the new owner was by no means out of place in the frontier population: immigrant, nationalist, would-be assassin, escaped felon, and soldier.

On top of all this, the piece of land was not just any quarter section. It was the land that contained Waconda Spring, a Native American religious shrine. This was a large mineral spring that flowed from the top of a travertine mound. The native peoples considered it to be a spot where it was possible for humans to communicate with the animal spirits that lived in the underworld, and it was sacred to all of the nations of the region. Apparently it was a place where no fighting was supposed to occur.

It is clear, however, that Lieutenant DeRudio did not choose this quarter section because he shared Native American religious beliefs or even respected them. Instead, a mineral spring was a chance to make money. In the years that followed, a company was formed to try to make salt from the waters of the spring, but that venture never came to fruition. Then water from the spring was sold as a cure for various ailments. Later still, a spa grew up on the site and remained in use until the federal government bought the land when it created Waconda Lake. In 1870, then, the meaning of the landscape changed, along with concepts of ownership. Although native nations contested control of the region, no one owned the land until DeRudio claimed it under the new regime that he helped to establish. Thereafter Waconda Spring was seen as an economic resource rather than the home of powerful spirits.

This book deals with the landscape around Waconda Spring, not primarily as a physical or even an ecological entity, but as a cultural and historical force. People invest the land and features of the landscape with meanings particular to their own cultures and their own histories. And those meanings have force in everyday events; they mold history and culture. Today, many of those meanings have faded, and landscapes have tended to lose their force because we have divorced ourselves from them. We are an indoor nation now, linked to the world more frequently through electronic means than through direct experience. Only a lucky few get to spend significant amounts of time with their boots on the ground, experiencing their environment directly rather than driving through it.

Today, the Solomon River valley is a pretty ordinary place. The landscape is dominated by Waconda Lake, built by the Bureau of Reclamation for flood control, irrigation, water supply, and recreation. The region around it is farming country that does not loom large in the nation's imagination and certainly not in that of the larger world. Yet it was not always so, and July 6, 1870, marks a turning point, a change in inherent meaning, a new way of looking at the land.

In the nineteenth century, the Great Plains of North America was considered one of the most romantic spots on the face of the earth. All sorts of people braved hardships and danger (or, in later years, traveled with a modicum of luxury) to visit them. There was Paul Wilhelm, Duke of Württemburg, in the 1820s; Charles Augustus Murray, from a noble Scottish family, in the 1830s; Maximilian, Prince of Wied-Neuwied, also in the 1830s; Sir St. George Gore in the 1850s; and Grand Duke Alexis of Russia in the 1870s.[3] Painters dramatized the landscape, and writers eulogized it: Samuel Seymour in the 1820s, and George Catlin, Karl Bodmer, and Alfred Jacob Miller in the 1830s provided indelible impressions of life on the plains through their art,[4] while writers such as John Treat Irving, Washington Irving, Friedrich Wislizenus, and Joseph Nicollet, all in the 1830s, did the same in words.[5]

Yet today Americans consider this one of the most boring spots they can imagine. That is, they do so when they think of it at all. Even its natives tend toward an inferiority complex, imagining that life on one of the coasts or in the mountains or just about anywhere else must be more interesting. In Cawker City, Kansas, at the center of the region discussed in this book, the biggest tourist attraction (other than Waconda Lake) is "The World's Largest Ball of Twine." It competes with "The World's Largest Hand-dug Well" in Greensburg and even with another "World's Largest Ball of Twine" in Darwin, Minnesota.

Part of the problem is that modern-day Americans spend most of their time indoors, and even when they are outside, most residents of the plains end up spending their time in the cultivated places, among orderly rows of corn or milo, in spaces sliced by section-line roads and power lines. There is very little romance to be had, nor much in the way of adventures to be experienced.

This book seeks to look back from the humdrum present through the romantic haze of the nineteenth century to an older landscape, one that is more wonderful by far than what the modern imagination can conceive. It is the cultural landscape of the original inhabitants, people who carried no inferiority complex about the land that was their home. They created trails that led to sacred sites, to natural resources, and to the villages of friend and foe alike. One of these thoroughfares, the Pawnee Trail, influenced the Euro-American history of the region well into the nineteenth century.

The Pawnee Trail ran past two very different sacred sites. One was Waconda Spring, an enormous spring issuing from the top of a hill. Even to the secular mind, it was an extraordinary thing, a pool a hundred feet in diameter sitting at the top of a hill rather than on low ground, and occasionally overflowing the brim and running down toward the river. For the native peoples of the region it was also a giant lodge, with the pool of water in the place where a smokehole should be. The residents of the lodge were the spirits that animated the species of land animals. And the pool was a giant mirror that on clear nights drew the spirits of the stars—that is, their reflections—down to earth.

Nearby was a different kind of sacred site, one created by human effort. It was the figure of a giant serpent carved into the earth. Exactly what its purpose was and what ceremonies were conducted there we do not know, but it was probably created by the ancestors of today's Wichitas, who made similar monuments elsewhere.

Finally, we will turn from the native landscape to the late nineteenth and early twentieth century, when the connection between people and the land had not been severed by modern luxuries such as air conditioning, central heating, and the ubiquitous blandness of television. This was another time in our own cultural tradition, when the landscape was not just something to be traversed or to be exploited, when special places allowed people to establish contact with the world of the intellect and of the spirit. At that time, there were special places in our own cultural landscape that have now fallen into disuse. Lincoln Camp and Waconda Spring are two of them. We will trace their history to their ultimate destruction in the modern era.

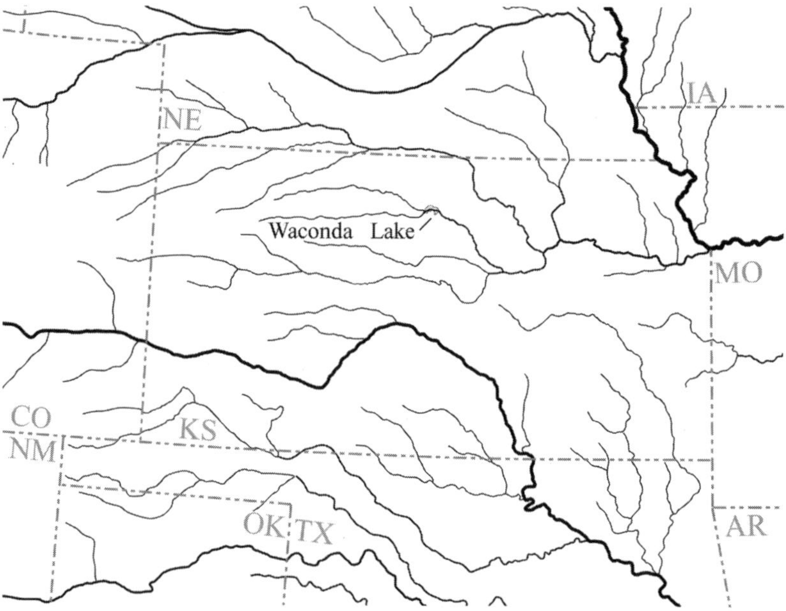

FIGURE 1.1 Location of Waconda Lake (map by author).

This book is the result of an archaeological survey of the federal land around Waconda Lake, a Bureau of Reclamation reservoir in north-central Kansas (Figure 1.1). My students from Wichita State University and I surveyed the land around the lake and reanalyzed the collections from excavations that were done before the lake waters rose to cover many of the sites there. We found a good many sites but knew that others, including Waconda Spring, had been covered by the waters of the lake. Indeed, except at the very headwaters of the lake, most of the ground where one might expect to find ancient sites was flooded. Many of the sites we did find were old farmsteads, and all of them had been bulldozed after the land had been purchased for the lake, in order to remove safety hazards. The same had been done to structures at Lincoln Camp, which had been the site of a Civilian Conservation Corps (CCC) and prisoner-of-war camp. The Sage site, a figure carved into a ridge top south of the lake, had been partially destroyed by farm activities long before we recognized it as a feature created by humans. Another site was quite simply invisible. It was the Pawnee Trail, a native trail that ran down Limestone Creek, crossed the river and continued south across the Blue Hills. Because it was a route followed only by pedestrians and horsemen, there were no wheel ruts that cut through the sod, making portions of the trail visible today. In contrast, the most readily visible aspect of the cultural landscape around the lake was the old fence lines, made from limestone and strung with barbed wire. They were everywhere, and we also found some of the quarries where the fence posts had been cut from the top of the Greenhorn formation.

Once the survey was complete, it was my job to analyze and report the findings, both for professionals and for members of the general public. One set of prehistoric sites, farmsteads that had been occupied between about AD 1000 and 1250, stood out. They had been the focus of investigations by the University of Nebraska when the reservoir was first being constructed. Collections from the sites, most of which are now under water, were transferred to Wichita State University, and I wrote a monograph about them that addressed the interests and concerns of professional archaeologists.[6]

This volume, in contrast, is intended for the general public as well as professionals, and it addresses all of the sites at Waconda Lake, regardless of age or cultural affiliation. They are a mixed bag, but all of them have something to tell us about how people relate to landscapes that they have modified and have imbued with meaning.

2. Native Americans at Waconda Lake

THE NATURAL LANDSCAPE around what is now Waconda Lake began to take form deep in geological time, long before humans came on the scene. All of the bedrock in the region is Cretaceous in age, dating to about one hundred million years ago, but within that time frame there is an east-to-west progression from older to younger deposits. The land to the east is marked by knobby hills that are capped by deposits of Dakota sandstone (Figure 2.1a). The sand was deposited by rivers that fed a great delta at the edge of an ancient continent. In the spots where the hills are today, the sandstone became tightly cemented with iron oxides, inhibiting erosion. At Waconda Lake, the Dakota Formation is overlain by shales and limestones, called the Greenhorn Formation, that are somewhat younger in age. These formed on the bed of a shallow sea that rose over the former delta and covered all the center of what is now North America. When these rocks were later exposed, the flat-lying limestone proved to be more resistant to erosion than the shale, and the flat-topped hills and ridges are underlain with limestone deposits, while the slopes are composed of shale (Figure 2.1b). The topmost layer in the Greenhorn Formation is an eight-to-twelve-inch-thick bed of hard limestone called "the Fencepost limestone" for reasons discussed in chapter 6. Given its geologic position, it outcrops at the ends of the ridges near the lake and is covered with only a fairly thin mantle of soil.

Still farther west, more ocean-bed deposits, called the Niobrara Formation, overlie the Greenhorn Formation. These include the Smoky Hill Chalk Member, which erodes readily, forming the badlands of the Smoky Hill River valley, including Castle Rock (Figure 2.1c). The Smoky Hill chalk became important to the early human occupants of the region because in spots it contains a chippable kind of stone called Smoky Hill jasper. It was especially important because the limestone of the Greenhorn Forma-

FIGURE 2.1 Landforms near Waconda Lake: a. Smoky Hills developed on the Dakota sandstone; b. flat-topped ridges that developed on the Greenhorn Formation; c. badlands that developed on the Smoky Hill chalk (photographs by author).

tion do not contain any chippable stone. To the east, the nearest sources of stone for making points and other chipped tools was the Flint Hills, some eighty miles away.

Long after the seabeds had formed, the uplift that produced the Rocky Mountains began, and as soon as the mountains began to rise, they also began to erode. The uplift ensured that the streams that formed flowed from west to east, and over time they carried millions of tons of sand and gravel, completely covering up whatever earlier landscapes were present, filling and eventually overflowing the stream valleys, covering even the uplands with alluvial deposits called the Ogallala Formation. The vast tilted plain that resulted reached from the Rockies eastward to the Flint Hills.

When the uplift came to an end, the forces of erosion continued to work on the sheet of alluvium. On the eastern side, where rainfall was relatively frequent, erosion began cutting into the Ogallala Formation, creating the valleys seen today, while leaving remnants of the Ogallala gravels on hilltops. This eroded region is known today as the Dissected High Plains, and it includes all of the land around Waconda Lake.

Natural modifications to the landscape have continued to the present day. During the last twelve thousand years, changes in climate have driven modifications in the alluvial fill of the stream valleys. There have been cycles of erosion and deposition that have removed sediment and then deposited more, deepening and then refilling the valleys.[1] At the same time, vegetation has changed as well. Pollen and other studies have shown that during the last ice age, the vegetation of the region was far different from what it is now. Cool summer temperatures reduced evaporation and allowed trees to grow on the uplands. There were stands of spruce with a grass and sage understory. Rapidly rising temperatures at the end of the ice age quickly killed off the spruce, but oak and elm may have grown along the stream banks. Reduction in the amount of shade from trees probably improved the food available to grazing animals.

The animal communities that lived in the ice-age landscape were profoundly different from the modern ones. There were herds of mammoths, mastodons, giant bison, camels, and horses. There were also two species of peccaries (New World pigs) and two species of giant ground sloths. There were even giant beavers (up to 480 pounds) and giant armadillos. There was also the stag moose, a deer-like animal that looked like a bastard cross between a moose and an elk, an animal with a large body, long skinny legs, and ornate antlers. The great size of many of these animals has led to use of the general term "megafauna" to describe them.

Along with the giant herbivores came large predators, including saber-toothed cats the size of modern lions but armed with canines so large and thin that they grew special sockets for them in their lower jaws. Also from the cat family were jaguars larger than those of today, and the American lion, which was also larger than the modern African lion. Then there was the short-faced bear that had enormously long legs that enabled it to run down its prey, and the dire wolf with large, bone-crushing jaws and teeth.

There were smaller animals as well, and these occurred in a pattern that simply does not exist today. Animals such as the snowshoe hare and the arctic shrew lived in the same areas as rodents that today live no farther north than Mexico. Paleontologists call animals in this situation "disharmonious fauna." Since the natural ranges of northern animals are limited by summer heat and the ranges of tropical animals by winter cold, the implication is that ice-age Kansas had an equable climate with relatively cool summers and temperate winters.

—Paleoindian Period

Although it is generally accepted that humans came to the Americas from Asia, the date of their arrival has been the subject of decades-long debate.

The earliest widespread incontrovertible evidence—the complex called Clovis—dates to about 11,300 radiocarbon years ago or 11,000 BC. A long series of earlier sites have been proposed, and most of them rejected. Today a few widely scattered sites are given serious consideration as evidence for a pre-Clovis occupation: Meadowcroft Rockshelter in Pennsylvania, Monte Verde in Chile, and La Sena in Nebraska.

The latter site, located fairly close to Waconda Lake—in Frontier County, Nebraska—has been very carefully investigated.[2] It consists of the skeletal remains of a single, aged, male mammoth that has been dated to about 18,400 radiocarbon years ago (ca. 21,000 calendar years). The skeleton of this animal had been dismembered, and the largest and strongest bones—those of the legs—had been broken open, while the most fragile bones were intact. Nothing in the deposits indicated how this might have happened by natural means, and given that the bones appear to have been broken by being struck at high speed by a hard object such as a rock, the investigators concluded that humans may have been involved.

No spear points or stone tools of any sort, not even a rock suitable for breaking the bones, have been found, however. The investigators suggest that the animal may have already been dead when humans came on the scene and that they broke open the leg bones to remove the rich marrow. Large flakes of bone taken from the legs may have been used to further butcher the animal. They also suggest that fine-grained loess—the wind-carried dust that mantled the landscape at the time—may have limited access to chippable stone, necessitating the use of bone for tools.

Regardless of whether or not there were people in the Americas prior to Clovis, that complex offers the earliest readily interpretable evidence for the lifeways that allowed people to adapt to the Great Plains at the end of the Pleistocene. Radiocarbon dates from 10,900 to 11,400 years ago come from many sites on the high plains and adjacent areas of the Southwest. We happen to be lucky that modern arroyos in the region have cut into Clovis-aged deposits, and the bones of large animals that mark many of them draw attention.

Clovis appears a few thousand years after the continental glaciers had begun to melt, but more moisture was available then on the Great Plains than is the case today. Herds of megafauna, including mammoths and the giant ancestor of modern bison, still roamed the grasslands that were emerging from the ice-age forests. Trees were probably still more widespread on the High Plains than they are today; there is evidence for their presence at the Twelve-Mile Creek site in western Kansas as late as 10,300 years ago.[3]

All of the archaeological evidence indicates that the people who left the Clovis remains were efficient hunters of large game. Mammoth is the most common animal in Clovis sites but the spectacular size of mammoth bones may have affected the sample of discovered sites. Giant bison is second,[4] while horse, camel, bear, and rabbit have also been found, but never in large numbers. It is likely that Clovis people ate plant foods as well, but no tools used primarily for such foods have been reported.[5]

The role of humans in the extinction of the megafauna has been debated for decades. The issue is the timing of the events. Many species seem to have become extinct at the same time that the Clovis sites appear. If humans were present long before Clovis, it is difficult to understand why humans would have caused a sudden burst of extinctions thousands of years later. If Clovis peoples were the first ones on the continent, on the other hand, an overkill hypothesis becomes more plausible.[6] Thus it is possible that human hunters contributed to the extinctions and in so doing, changed the environment fundamentally. It is equally possible that the rapid environmental changes at this time had the greatest impact, with the previous environment literally disappearing.[7] There are no modern equivalents to the disharmonious fauna of the last ice age, and increasingly cold winters and hot summers may have made it impossible for some species to survive. The appearance of new species other than humans may also have contributed to the die-off.

A recent new hypothesis is that a comet smashed into the continental glacier in North America, causing the extinctions of various animal species and almost causing an extinction of the human population.[8] The absence of a crater is explained by the comet having hit ice, causing instantaneous melting and an influx of fresh water into the Atlantic. There was such an influx, but it had been explained previously as the result of meltwater gradually building up until it overflowed a barrier, which was quickly eroded. Some Clovis sites are marked by a dense black layer that in this scenario is the result of widespread fires produced by the impact.

All of the Clovis sites on the Plains appear to be the result of very short occupations, but evidence suggestive of winter storage of frozen mammoth meat at the Colby site in Wyoming implies the use of longer-term camps during the winter.[9] The presence of high-quality stone from distant sources at many sites is taken as evidence for long-distance travel, and the stone tool inventories in the sites is appropriate for highly mobile populations.

Caches of large bifacially flaked pieces of stone, points, and other pieces of stone, such as the Busse cache in western Kansas, are interpreted as raw material supplies. The only burial of Clovis age on the Plains is at the Anzick site in Montana. It contained an impressive cache of complete and partially finished points accompanying an infant burial.[10]

While we can see evidence for travel, it is not possible to project the native trails of the Historic period back to Clovis times. The landscape was different then, and water was more readily available than it is today, and water was an important consideration when laying out the trails. Thus potential routes of travel, which require regularly spaced water sources, were more numerous in Clovis times than they were after temperatures rose. We do not know that the trails used in later times were already being traveled, but more potential trails were available in the Clovis era than later.

We also cannot say whether any of the sacred sites of the Historic period were in use this far back in time. We cannot project back beliefs known from the Historic period to such an early age; to do so would be to deny the possibility of change through time. We have plenty of evidence for profound cultural changes after the Clovis era, and we have little evidence so far for Clovis-age sacred places in North America. The single instance documented to date is the Powars II site in Wyoming.[11] A slope stained red by naturally occurring hematite (an iron oxide) has yielded so many Paleoindian spear points that it is obvious that they had been left as offerings by prehistoric visitors. In fact, in 1995 Dr. George Frison led a small group of archaeologists to the site, and while we were there, I saw the late Stan Ahler pull a point from the slope.

Following Clovis are several archaeological complexes identified by distinctive styles of thin-based points: Goshen, Folsom, Midland, Plainview, and others (Figure 2.2). The earliest is the Goshen complex, best known from the northwestern Plains.[12] It is suspected to be transitional between Clovis and Folsom, the next well-studied Paleoindian complex. Folsom—and the closely related Midland—is less widely distributed than Clovis and is found primarily in the Plains and the adjacent portion of the Southwest. At the time it appeared around 10,900 radiocarbon years ago, the climate was still more moderate than today, with more moisture availability. By this time, mammoths had become extinct, and the bison (still larger than the present-day species) was the primary game animal. The Folsom complex dates to the Younger Dryas, a 1,300-year-long period beginning about 12,800 years ago when the climate of at least the Northern Hemisphere reverted to glacial conditions. The Younger Dryas appears to have had a very rapid beginning and a similarly rapid end, when the climate reverted once again to a warmer regime in as little as seven years.[13]

FIGURE 2.2 Paleoindian points: a. Clovis, b. Agate Basin, c. Plainview, d. Folsom (courtesy Peter A. Bostrom, LithicCastingLab.com).

The stone items in the Folsom tool kit were clearly designed for ease of transport, and awls, needles, bone points, and bone disks have been reported.[14] As with Clovis, Folsom sites often contain tools made from stone that outcrops hundreds of miles from the sites. As is the case with Clovis, however, the evidence for long-distance travel is not tied to direct evidence for the use of particular trails.

Bison kills, butchering spots, and camp sites have been reported, along with winter habitations.[15] The bison kills were usually small-scale events, sometimes with only partial butchering of the carcasses.[16] The Cooper site in western Oklahoma is a well-reported example.[17] That site has clear evidence for hunting ritual, as does the Lake Theo site.[18] At the Cooper site, there are three layers of bison bone corresponding to three bison kills separated in time by at least a few years. At the base of the second layer of bone was an older bison skull, apparently pulled from the first deposit. It was situated pointing down the arroyo and had a lightning bolt painted on its nose in red ocher.[19]

At around 10,500 BP, a different series of Paleoindian complexes appear, marked by points that are less extensively thinned but are purposefully narrowed at the base.[20] The basic difference suggests that these points were placed in a socketed rather than split foreshaft. Otherwise, the way of life changed only gradually, with the development of more sophisticated forms of bison hunting. The Jones-Miller site in eastern Colorado is a good example. It appears to have been a bison pound—a corral into which a herd was driven. It is especially notable for the evidence of hunting ritual, including a center pole, bone whistle, miniature point, and butchered dog skeleton.[21]

At the same time as these "classic" Paleoindian complexes from the High Plains, there was a somewhat different tradition farther east, which is best known from a series of sites in the Medicine Creek valley.[22] These appear to be related to the Dalton complex of the Eastern Woodlands, and the complexes found on the Plains may have used the forested river valleys more than the uplands. The sites in the Medicine Creek valley contain more small-game remains than those of bison, but this may reflect the necessity of staying in one spot to quarry stone, as that valley contains excellent exposures of Smoky Hill jasper.

The Paleoindian sequence on the Plains ends with the appearance of a point style called Allen or Frederick. These are thin-based points with distinctive fluting patterns, and do not appear to derive directly either from the early thin-based points of the High Plains or from the Dalton-like points found farther east. This complex, which dates to before eight thousand radiocarbon years ago, may represent a reoccupation of the Plains in a wet interval.

In our investigations at Waconda Lake, we did not find much evidence from the Paleoindian period, and we did not expect to do so. It is not in a region where much Paleoindian material is found, for reasons of geomorphology. In his investigation of the area, David May found sediments of Paleoindian age exposed in a cut bank of the Solomon River barely above the midsummer water level.[23]

Nevertheless, the University of Nebraska recovered fragments of two Paleoindian points (Folsom and Scottsbluff) from a much later site, 14ML5. Thinking that the points may have been found by the residents of the later site when they were digging storage pits, we dug two deep tests at the site but found no buried cultural deposits. We also investigated the cut bank of Oak Creek adjacent to the site, hoping to find an exposure of Paleoindian-age sediments. This also proved unsuccessful, as the stream had deposited alluvium there subsequent to the occupation of the later site.

—Archaic Period

The Archaic period begins with the onset of the Altithermal climatic episode, a period of higher temperatures and reduced moisture availability on the Plains. Ephemeral water sources dried up, and the area that could support bison herds was much reduced. Although it has been argued that the area covered by the short grasses that bison favor may have expanded, classic studies of the drought of the 1930s show that total available forage would have been reduced to a small fraction of the former amount.[24] Two recent studies found no evidence of Altithermal-age points in collections from the High Plains of western Kansas.[25] Since the portions of the collections they analyzed that derived from the uplands came mostly from blowouts in sand dunes, the absence of evidence for any Altithermal-age specimens suggests that the uplands were not used, even in wet years. The only reliable water sources would have been some springs and the rivers that flow eastward from the Rocky Mountains. Without knowing the extent to which the dry climate lowered the level of groundwater, we cannot say how far east one would have had to go to find reliable springs. The Spring Creek site on Red Willow Creek in Nebraska is an Altithermal camp that lies at a longitude west of Waconda Lake,[26] so it is quite possible that there were both water and people in the vicinity of Waconda Lake. Spring Creek stands alone in the regional record, however, and I wonder if the date from the site (on tiny bits of charcoal recovered from six different pits) is correct.

Several studies suggest that few trees would have been available, and forage on the hills and ridges may have been very sparse. In southeastern Nebraska, trees on uplands died off except for an occasional oak, and the same was true for trees along the stream banks except for willow. At Muscotah Marsh in northeastern Kansas there was almost no arboreal pollen between 8000 and 5000 BP, while the Cheyenne bottoms of central Kansas were also relatively dry, without the mudflats created by periodic flooding.[27]

Another factor affecting the archaeological record was the widespread erosion that occurred during the Altithermal. Sparse plant cover could not protect slopes from erosion during the occasional spring and summer thunderstorms, and studies conducted all over the central United States point to dramatic amounts of erosion that destroyed many sites and covered others deeply, leaving little for the modern archaeologist to find.[28] If people were present on the High Plains, however, one would expect that they would have left the occasional artifact on the uplands where erosion could not have acted so dramatically.[29]

The deep erosion and the changes in vegetation produced a landscape that was far different than it is today. Long-distance travel, if it occurred, would have been restricted to the valleys of the major rivers flowing from the Rockies—the Canadian, Arkansas, and Platte—and the likely trails would have had to cling closely to the riverbank through regions where

FIGURE 2.3 Archaic Period points: a. Logan Creek, b. Duncan, c. Uvalde, d. Montel (photographs by author).

springs no longer flowed. In contrast, historic trails tended to lie at a distance from the rivers, to avoid the many arroyos and stream crossings that a river route usually involves. North-south routes of travel that cut across the east-flowing river valleys might have been possible, and the Pawnee Trail described in chapter 3 could have been in use.

After the Altithermal, one finds a stark contrast between the archaeological records for eastern and western Kansas. In the Flint Hills and Osage Plains of the eastern part of the state, sites are plentiful, and both Middle and Late Archaic complexes have been defined. The Munkers Creek, Vermillion, Chelsea, El Dorado, and Walnut phases have been defined,[30] even though many of the sites are fairly deeply buried in stream terraces. In the west, there are points similar to those of the McKean complex of the northwestern Plains (Figure 2.3), but there have been no substantial investigations of Archaic sites there, and no post-McKean complexes have been defined. The western sequence, so far as it is known, appears to be quite different from that in the eastern part of the state; for instance, the numerous axes and adzes found in the east are missing in the west. At the present time, we do not know where the line between the two different patterns should be drawn. We also do not have a good idea of the ages of many of the point styles that were in use there.

The post-Altithermal populations of the state appear to have had a broad-based diet, although McKean peoples to the north seem to have hunted bison frequently. In Kansas, a wide range of animal remains are found in the excavated sites, along with rock-filled hearths and grinding stones that would have been appropriate for processing vegetable foods. Adair reports the recovery of seeds of goosefoot, smartweed, sunflower, bulrush, marsh elder, and grape, along with walnut and hickory shells.[31] Although no botanical evidence for domestication appears until the very end of the Archaic, the presence of numerous adzes and axes in Middle Archaic sites in the eastern part of the state may be a hint that slash-and-burn horticulture was practiced. Adair concludes, from her knowledge of the ethnobotany of the Southwest and Eastern Woodlands, that "a broader distribution of cultivated plants, including the native cucurbits, marsh elder, and goosefoot in Plains Archaic sites would not be surprising."[32]

We did not find any Archaic sites during our survey around Waconda Lake, but John Reynolds[33] tentatively assigned the Range Mound, a stone-filled burial mound in Glen Elder, to the Archaic, given that it contained no pottery. Mark Latham encountered a single Archaic site in his survey of the Glen Elder locality.[34] It was exposed in the side of a trench silo, and it is likely that Archaic sites are seldom encountered because they are usually buried below the depth disturbed by plowing.

Burial mounds, by their very nature, are sacred sites. But we do not have any direct evidence that the Archaic-period residents of the region considered any natural features of the landscape to be sacred places. It is not until the next time period that we have even indirect evidence for such a belief system.

What we do have is fairly spectacular evidence for long-distance communication. At Waconda Lake, it takes the form of marine shell beads found in Range Mound. Jim Feagins reanalyzed the artifacts from the site and reports disk-shaped beads and beads made from the shells of *Theodoxus luteofasciatus* and *Polinices uber*. Both of these species of marine gastropod live both in the Gulf of California and along the Pacific coast of Baja California, reaching as far north as San Diego. These species also occur as far south as Peru, but the most likely point of origin is either in the Gulf of California or the Pacific coast of Baja California.[35] I suspect that the disk beads were made from the columella (central spire) of whelks or conchs, probably from the Gulf of Mexico or even the Atlantic Ocean.

The Range Mound is far from unique for this time period. Burial sites all across the central portion of the country, far distant from any ocean, contain ornaments made from marine shells. This pattern lasts through subsequent periods, up to the Late Prehistoric, with marine shells scarce or absent in habitation sites but consistently present in burials. Clearly the beads or the shells from which they were made had deep religious significance. The shell ornaments are indicative of exchange relationships that stretched across the continent,[36] and their presence hints at the use of long-distance trails.

—Early Ceramic Period

The Early Ceramic period is marked by the widespread appearance of pottery, by traces of horticulture, and by use of burial mounds in the eastern part of the state. While there are a few hints of what is called Early Woodland (1000 BC to AD 1) in eastern Kansas, pottery becomes widespread only around the time of Christ. This is not to say that there are no sites of the Early Woodland period; we merely assign them to the Archaic because they lack pottery.

The earliest well-defined Woodland complex in Kansas is Kansas City Hopewell in the northeastern part of the state.[37] It is called Hopewell because it shares a variety of traits, including ceramic decoration, with Middle Woodland sites in Illinois and other parts of the Eastern Woodlands. Similar pottery is found in association with distinctive Middle Woodland (Snyders) points at least as far west as Manhattan.[38] In the southern half of Kansas, similar Middle Woodland ceramic decoration is found as far west as the Arkansas River valley, with sites near Augusta, Wichita, and Cheney Reservoir. Points of Woodland age are very common all across Kansas (figure 2.4).

The system of cultural interaction that produced the similarities between Kansas City Hopewell and other Kansas sites with complexes in

FIGURE 2.4 Early Ceramic points: a. Snyders, b. Gibson, c. Marcos, d. Darl (photographs by author).

the Eastern Woodlands provides our first strong hint for the use of specific trails and sacred sites that continued in use into the Historic period. Hopewellian sites in Ohio and elsewhere have yielded artifacts made of meteoric iron. While most of the iron has corroded to the point that it is impossible to measure the levels of trace elements reliably, two objects from sites in Ohio have been shown to be made of iron from the Brenham meteorite that landed near Greensburg, Kansas.[39] The spot where the meteorite fell in many pieces (called a strewnfield) lies along a trail that was in use in the early Historic period. Most often called the Black Dog Trail in southeastern Kansas, it crossed the Arkansas River near the little town of Oxford and continued west on the divide between the Ninnescah and Chikaskia rivers, passing by Greensburg and continuing on to the Arkansas River in the vicinity of Kinsley, Kansas. To the east, the trail left Kansas at present-day Baxter Springs and crossed Missouri near its southern border before swinging north to reach the Mississippi opposite the mouth of the Ohio River. Thus, in the Historic period there was a native trail that provided a direct route between the Brenham strewnfield and the Ohio River, a trail that might well have been in use in Hopewellian times.

Furthermore, near the strewnfield is a site that meets the criteria (discussed in chapter 5) for a sacred site. The Star site has a high hill, a trail, a cliff with water at its base, an opening to the underworld, and (for the region) a fine growth of trees. It contains rock art that relates directly to the Brenham meteorite, including the figure of a man holding a star in his hand.[40] The rock art at this site is probably considerably younger than the Hopewellian period, however, as the rock face on which it is carved is soft and easily eroded. Any depictions made by Hopewellians would be gone by now.

Nevertheless, there is other evidence suggesting that the combination of traits that marked sacred sites in the Historic period may have been recognized in Hopewellian times. There is a huge amount of obsidian in one Ohio site that has been traced primarily to Obsidian Cliff in Yellowstone Park.[41] Hundreds of oversized, flaked, obsidian artifacts were found in one mound at the Hopewell site, and piles of flaking debris, apparently from their manufacture, were found in an adjacent mound. Obsidian Cliff has the same set of features as the Star site and other sacred sites recognized by the Pawnee in the Historic period. Obsidian from this site (and iron from the Brenham meteorite) may have been deemed appropriate for the manufacture of ritual objects because it came from a sacred place.

In Kansas, non-Hopewellian Early Ceramic period sites are common, and most of them appear to date to the Late Woodland, after AD 500 or so. This was the time when the bow and arrow was introduced in this region, and tiny, corner-notched Scallorn points are common in Late Woodland sites.

In the area around Waconda Lake, Late Woodland sites can be assigned to the Keith complex.[42] While most Keith dates fall into the Late Woodland, some are of Middle Woodland age, and the use of ceramics may have begun here around AD 200. The lifeway that has emerged from the few investigations of Keith sites indicates that hunting and gathering remained the dominant form of subsistence. The primary defining characteristic of Keith pottery is the use of calcite mixed with the clay, but there are sites in the central part of Kansas that contain both calcite-tempered and sand-tempered sherds. We do not yet know whether these sites reflect sequential occupations by two different groups or the use of two temper types by a single group. In fact, we do not know why Keith peoples used calcite to temper their pottery. One possibility is that the burned and crushed calcite particles were a source of ions that prevented the clay from shrinking excessively during drying and firing. If so, the use of calcite may simply reflect a preference for a regionally available material that, being composed of crystals, was more easily crushed than limestone, another potential source of positive ions.

During the University of Nebraska investigations at Waconda Lake, a little Early Ceramic material mixed in with later remains was recovered from site 14ML8, under the present-day dam. The director of the project, Preston Holder, preferred to concentrate on the Middle Ceramic remains around the lake, so this early lead was not pursued. When we examined the collections from the site, we found the excavations there—in a historic farmyard—revealed deposits that were badly mixed, so that separate analysis of the early materials is not possible.

During our survey of the land around Waconda Lake, we tested one Early Ceramic site. It is 14ML534, located on an erosional remnant that rises above the river terrace on the south side of the lake. When we surveyed this little hillock, we discovered some shell beads on the western slope. We tested the site with a series of two-meter squares, hoping to find some useful information on the period, as sites other than those of the Middle Ceramic had been ignored during the University of Nebraska investigations. What we found, however, was a mystery at first. There were very few stone tools but a large number of mussel shells. Sometimes these were scattered, but more often they were lined up in curving rows, stacked horizontally. Eventually, we discovered a row at the edge of a curving zone of dirt that differed in color from the rest of the deposit, and we could see that the rows had been created by rodents that had completely reworked the deposits at the site. When they encountered shells while digging their burrows, they pushed the shells to one side, creating the rows from what had been a thin scatter of shells. The dirt in most of the burrows was no different in color from the surrounding soil, but a few contained the reddish dirt from the subsoil at the site.

Because this discovery indicated that the site had been thoroughly disturbed since it was laid down, we abandoned the excavations. The scarcity of stone tools indicated that the occupation had been very short, and the lack of undisturbed context meant that we would be able to learn very little from further excavation. Analysis of the mussel shells by Charles Cope, however, gave us one insight. He reported that the species present all preferred a still-water environment, and examination of an aerial photo of the site showed that there once was an oxbow lake in an old meander of the river just north of the hill. Apparently the people who created the site had not had much luck obtaining other food the day they visited this spot, and made do with the little mussels gathered from the pond (freshwater mussels are very chewy and pretty much devoid of flavor).

The shell beads that we recovered from the site were the most interesting part of the assemblage. What we found on the surface were disk-shaped beads, but in the test excavations we recovered some cylindrical beads made from the columella of a conch or whelk. Close examination showed that the disk-shaped beads had broken off from the ends of the cylindrical specimens, and the natural curvature of the shell in all of the disk beads showed that they all had the same origin. We did not find any evidence of human bone at the site, even though later research (see below) revealed that marine-shell disk beads from this time period are almost always found in burial contexts. It may be that the disks found here all became separated from the cylinders after the shell had been made fragile by acids in the soil.

In addition to the Range Mound, references in the field notes for the excavation of 14ML1 suggest that there had once been a burial mound adjacent to that (much later) site. There are also burial mounds on the bluff tops on the south side of the river just downstream from Glen Elder Dam. Unfortunately one of them has been bulldozed to open up a bit more farmland, leaving a pyramid-shaped pile of rocks next to a fence line.

May's geomorphological work shows that Early Ceramic age sediments exist within half a meter of surface of the widespread Kirwin terrace. Thus if this locality had a substantial population in Early Ceramic times, there should be some visibility of cultural remains, similar to the situation at

Medicine Creek.[43] A few specimens of Early Ceramic age occur in the University of Nebraska collections from Middle Ceramic sites, but they are rare. If there were numerous Early Ceramic sites over most of the reservoir area, then the numerous pits dug by the later people should have exposed more Early Ceramic material. Instead, what material that does occur is either near the dam and the mounds downstream from it (14ML8) or at the very upper end of the reservoir (14OB27). Mark Latham (personal communication), during his survey of the Glen Elder locality, learned of a substantial cluster of Woodland sites a short distance upstream from where we worked. They have the potential of revealing much about the lifeways of an Early Ceramic community in this part of the state.

—Middle Ceramic Period

The University of Nebraska excavations in the 1960s concentrated on sites of this time period (figure 2.5), and the reports of that work generated a good deal of discussion. My reanalysis of the Middle Ceramic period has been published elsewhere. It provided a complete revision of the

a b c

FIGURE 2.5 Middle Ceramic points: a. Washita, b. Harrell, c. Huffaker (photographs by author).

classification of the sites and new insights into how the people of that time period made a living and organized their societies. A series of radiocarbon dates suggest that the new pattern was established at Waconda Lake shortly after AD 1000 and lasted for about 250 years.[44]

During this time period, the valleys of the major creeks that flow into Waconda Lake became filled with the remains of farmsteads wherever springs provided water and there was good (silty loam) soil with hardwood timber.[45] At these spots, the people built substantial square to rectangular houses with sod roofs and extended entryways. The houses were large enough to hold extended families. They also had outside work areas with hearths, storage pits, and (probably) roofed arbors. There is evidence to suggest that two teams of people built most of the houses, even the ones that could have held only a single family.[46]

That fact is one of several that point to the existence of communities made up of these scattered farmsteads. Another is the clustering of different house styles within the locality. In one spot the houses are definitely rectangular; in another they are trapezoidal. At the same time, there is a subtle but similar pattern in the pottery they made. In one spot they put the decoration on the top of the lip, in another on the outer edge of the lip. And finally, one burial ground was found in the 1960s that contained too many bodies to have come only from the adjacent farmstead and that contained pottery that also did not come from just one spot.[47]

The evidence recovered from the farmsteads suggests that they were occupied year-round,[48] in contrast to the villages of the historic nations of the region that were abandoned twice a year when the people went on long-distance bison hunts. The fact that residence was year-round meant that the local large game was quickly hunted out, and large animals do not occur frequently in the food remains. Instead, the bones of just about every kind of animal present in the environment do occur, including mollusks, fish, reptiles, amphibians, and birds, along with small mammals. Some of these are clearly the remains of garden hunting—keeping the fields as clear of pests as possible. The most frequently encountered bones are those of the rice rat, an animal that appears to have spread from its natural habitat in the southeastern states when gardening became common.[49] They were eaten along with the products of the gardens—corn, squash, beans, sunflower seeds, and marsh elder—and wild plant foods such as prairie turnip, fruits, and nuts.

The gardens appear to have been planted in hardwood groves in which some of the trees were killed by girdling them (chopping through the bark all around the circumference) and the undergrowth burned off. Digging sticks and hoes with blades made from the shoulder blades of bison were the main horticultural tools. There is no evidence that fertilizer was used, and the people had to create new gardens when the soil fertility was exhausted, perhaps every five years or so.[50]

This way of life probably had a greater impact on the environment than any of the previous ones. Slash-and-burn farming generates a series of abandoned gardens that provide for a succession of plants and animals. Goosefoot, wild sunflowers, and other seed-bearing plants would have been common. The rice rat probably lived on weeds in these abandoned fields while also raiding the fields that were still in use. As time passed, the number of such pests would have grown, and when crops in the garden began to fail because of lower soil fertility, the rodents may have been hunted purposefully.[51]

Following this occupation of the Solomon Valley, a new people arrived from the east. Under the present-day town of Glen Elder are the remains of one of the sites of these people whose remains we call the White Rock phase.[52] There is absolutely no evidence of any interaction between these people and the prior inhabitants, and the latter may have left a generation or two before the newcomers showed up, at least in this part of Kansas.

The newcomers derived ultimately from the region east of the plains, in Iowa, Wisconsin, or Minnesota. Their archaeological remains are classified as part of the Oneota Tradition, and sites of that tradition spread widely in the fourteenth century. The sites that eventually show up in Kansas are called the White Rock phase.[53] Analysis of the remains from the Glen Elder site suggest that it was a large hunting camp, occupied by a hundred people or more.[54] Arrow points, end scrapers (tools used to clean the inner sides of large animal hides), and other tools all differ somewhat from those of the earlier people, and the pottery is distinctly different.

Thus rather than being permanent residents, at least in the vicinity of Waconda Lake, we have a new use of the region—as a hunting ground for people whose villages lay at great distances. This adaptation is reflected in the material remains, particularly the stone tools. For the first time in the prehistory of the region, the bulk of the tools seem to have been quarried from bedrock sources rather than gathered from surface exposures. This probably reflects the time pressures inherent in moving a large group of pedestrians for long distances while keeping them fed. A small group can move leisurely, hunting and gathering as they go and stopping to look for chippable stone. A large group cannot sustain itself readily from the resources that happen to be found en route, and under these circumstances, a quick visit to a bedrock source that can provide all the stone they need makes sense. Another reflection of long-distance travel is the reappearance in the White Rock sites of the combination of large bifacially flaked blanks and true blades (long, narrow flakes) that marked Clovis assemblages.

The White Rock hunting camp at Glen Elder contained a set of stone tools that reflects the emphasis on bison hunting. Triangular points, blade knives, and end scrapers dominate the assemblage, and the wear on the blades and end scrapers suggests that they were used to manufacture parfleches, rawhide containers that were used to carry the products of the hunt back home. Large, stone hammer heads (called "grooved mauls" by archaeologists) may have been used to turn bison jerky into a powder called pemmican, which could be packed tightly into the parfleches. They could also have been used to smash open leg bones to obtain marrow.

The only tools found in White Rock sites that do not relate directly to bison hunting are bison-scapula hoes. These are agricultural tools, and their presence in the sites, has led most archaeologists to interpret White Rock phase sites as villages, but Oneota villages farther east have a much higher density of pits and artifacts than White Rock phase sites. In the Historic period, documentary evidence demonstrates that Kansa and Osage people planted crops, not only in their hunting camps, but also along the trails that they took to the hunting grounds.[55]

How long Oneota-tradition people continued to hunt in north central Kansas is not clear. It cannot have been very long, as the number of White Rock phase sites is quite limited. Nevertheless, the pattern of large-group, long-distance bison hunts continued into the Historic period.

—Late Ceramic Period

After the White Rock phase disappears, there are two main archaeological complexes in Kansas. In the western part of the state, sites of the Dismal River aspect, attributed to Apaches, are found from Great Bend west into Colorado. All of the identified sites appear to fit into a narrow time frame, between AD 1675 and AD 1725, but Apaches appear to have been on the High Plains as early as the time of the Coronado expedition, 1541. At any rate, the people that Coronado's chroniclers call the Querecho have traditionally been identified as Apaches.

This leaves more than a century in which there probably were Apaches living in western Kansas, and the appearance of sites of the Dismal River aspect. The latter are identified by the presence of a distinctive kind of thin-walled pottery, and the Apaches appear to have learned pottery making from the residents of the northernmost pueblos of New Mexico. Earlier

FIGURE 2.6 Late Ceramic Fresno points (photographs by author).

ceramic sites are not as readily identified. At any rate, the Apache occupation of the region came to an end in the 1720s, when Comanches drove them south and west. There were plenty of Apaches in Kansas in 1724, when the French explorer Bourgmont made a treaty with them. Bourgmont described the Apaches he met as growing some corn and squash, making pots, and trading every spring with Spaniards who came out onto the Plains for that purpose.[56] These Apaches were gone when the Mallet brothers (French traders) crossed the state in 1739. The single piece of Apache pottery found so far at Waconda Lake is described in chapter 4.

"The Great Bend aspect" is the name given to the sites of the protohistoric Wichitas in Kansas. The Wichitas were never a politically unified tribe the way some others were; there were no tribal chiefs or tribal council that we know of. Instead, they were a set of allied but independent bands, and this seems to be reflected in their archaeology. There are three main clusters of Great Bend village sites—one in Rice County, one in the vicinity of Arkansas City, and another at Marion. There is a fourth, smaller one near Augusta. Each of these site clusters seems to have exploited its own territory, as the kinds of stone used to make tools are different in each (figure 2.6).

Judging from their material culture, the ancestry of the Wichitas lies primarily to the south of Kansas, with the exception of a few earlier complexes in the southern part of the state. The various bands may have come north at different times, with the people who created the Pratt complex near the town of the same name being the first. Most of them continued to reside in Kansas until the beginning of the eighteenth century, when enemies armed with guns drove them south, first into Oklahoma and then into Texas.[57]

The Wichita bands supported themselves with a combination of maize agriculture and bison hunting. Their farm fields were located on low ground next to large rivers, and there they grew corn, beans, squash, and sunflowers. They grew enough to trade with their non-agricultural neighbors such as the Kiowas and Comanches. Bison hunts took place at some distance from the villages. When Coronado arrived in Kansas, he encountered Wichitas from Rice County or MacPherson County near present-day Larned; they were traveling west to hunt buffalo.[58]

The stone tools in Great Bend sites make it clear that the protohistoric Wichitas were traveling long distances. Sites in the vicinity of Marion, Kansas, in the Flint Hills, contain huge numbers of artifacts made from stone that came from northeastern Oklahoma and Missouri, in spite of the fact that local stone was readily available. In contrast, sites in Rice County contain large numbers of tools made from stone that came from northwestern Kansas and even the panhandle of Texas. Only the stone tools from Great Bend sites in southernmost Kansas, which are situated in the immediate vicinity of excellent quarries, are dominated by local stone.[59] In all likelihood, travel from the villages to distant sources of stone was along the same trails documented in the Historic period.

Great Bend hunting camps are widely distributed in eastern Kansas.[60] They are identifiable from pieces of Great Bend pottery and from some of their distinctive stone tools. These sites indicate clearly that eastern Kansas and part of western Missouri were controlled by the Wichitas at the beginning of the Historic period. No study has yet been done to determine how much of western Kansas they may also have controlled, but the villages along the Little Arkansas River and Cow Creek in Rice County have tools made from stone from both northwestern Kansas and northern Texas.

At Waconda Lake we tested one Great Bend camp, but all of the cultural material there had been disturbed by plowing. The pottery we recovered was tempered with the same fine sand as the pottery found in villages in Rice County, and since those sites contain significant amounts of Smoky Hill jasper from the area west of Waconda Lake, it is likely that the area around the lake was part of their hunting territory. The Sage site, described in chapter 5, appears to be an icon carved by Great Bend people to mark their territory.

All of this has some interesting implications regarding the arrival and territory of the Pawnees. In the late eighteenth century, when the distribution of Pawnee villages and the extent of Pawnee hunting territory became clear, there was a Pawnee village on the Republican River at the mouth of White Rock Creek, and the South Band Pawnees claimed northern Kansas west of the Flint Hills as their hunting territory. Indeed, a South Band village in Nebraska contains huge amounts of stone from the northern Flint

Hills, while the village of another band has Smoky Hill jasper from northwestern Kansas or southwestern Nebraska.[61]

The shift in territories may have taken place after the Wichitas abandoned their Kansas homeland at the beginning of the eighteenth century. There appears to have been a major realignment of tribal territories farther north near the end of the seventeenth century,[62] and there is no clear evidence of Pawnee villages in central Nebraska until well into that century. All this makes the identification of the Harahey—a group mentioned in the Coronado narratives and usually identified as Pawnees—quite problematic. Similarly, the identity of the Guas who killed Father Padilla somewhere in Kansas in 1542 cannot be Kansas (i.e., Kaws) because the Kansas (and the related Osages, Omahas, and Poncas) did not arrive in the region until the seventeenth century. At least that is my reading of the radiocarbon dates reported in Henning and Schermer.[63]

3. Tracing the Pawnee Trail

THERE ONCE WAS a network of Native American trails that crisscrossed the Great Plains. These pathways in turn were a segment of a much larger web that covered the North American continent. Most of the trails were old in 1492, and features that they shared made them important to later travelers. Explorers, traders, and army expeditions all followed them, and by channeling movements of people the trails had a profound influence on the early Euro-American history of the Plains.

Unfortunately, there have been few comprehensive studies of Native American trails, and memories of many have faded. Myer's catalog of trails in Tennessee is a notable exception.[1] He provides a detailed account of dozens of trails in that state and summary descriptions of many in the surrounding region. In contrast to his encyclopedic approach, studies of native trails on the Great Plains have tended to be region-specific,[2] limited to a single portion of a trail,[3] or even site-specific.[4]

What I will do here is make available full information on one trail and place it properly in what is a very rich historical context. To this end, in this chapter I will discuss the nature of native trails on the Plains and the features associated with them. In so doing, I will be using information gathered since 1984. In that year Bob Blasing, one of my students at Wichita State University, encountered evidence for a native trail in a survey of the upper portion of the Deep Creek valley in east-central Kansas. Our discussions of the significance of his find convinced both of us of the research potential of such trails. A subsequent survey at Wilson Lake, Kansas, located a portion of the Pawnee Trail. The report of that survey (Blakeslee, Blasing, and Garcia 1986) provided then-current information on the trail, but only limited numbers of the report were printed, and the data it contained have faded into the foggy realm of seldom-cited archaeological contract reports.[5] Partly to introduce these data to a larger audience but also to correct some errors and to add new data, the Pawnee Trail is described here.

The system of trails that covered North America was not accidental in nature but developed over the millennia from the needs of the native peoples and from their intimate knowledge of the landscape. Knowledge of the terrain allowed them to link potential campsites with easily traveled roads, and their home villages with needed resources. Through knowledge of their land, they were able not only to avoid difficult routes but to use camps that provided for most or all of their needs. Campsites were located in spots that provided the necessities of life, and the trails sometimes provided resources as well. Finally, the trails themselves led to places the travelers intended to go: other villages, hunting grounds, quarries, shrines.

The uses to which trails were put determine much about them. They were used, of course, for hunting, and in the early Historic period on the Plains, hunting expeditions could involve whole villages marching together over hundreds of miles. The Pawnee bands of central Nebraska went to northwestern Kansas and western Nebraska to hunt,[6] while the Osages who lived in western Missouri and eastern Kansas traveled west beyond the Arkansas River to southwestern Kansas and western Oklahoma.[7]

Trade and intertribal visits took groups, small and large, sometimes short and sometimes enormous distances.[8] The Pawnee visited annually with Wichita bands living in Kansas, Oklahoma, and Texas, while one Kiowa band from Oklahoma and Texas regularly visited the Crow in Wyoming and Montana.[9] Some intertribal visits were formal and involved hundreds to thousands of people, but other informal visits could be made by single individuals and families.[10]

Warfare was another reason for travel. The term "warpath" is part and parcel of our stereotype of Native Americans, but the warpath in seasons of peace was also the route of the hunt, commerce, and religion. Only the larger war parties tended to use the trails away from home, however, as a small group could be spotted easily and overcome while traveling a widely known route. Migrations probably also followed old trails, but our evidence for this is scanty. Recent studies of migrations have shown that the travelers were likely to have been moving along known paths into previously known territory.[11] That the route called the Old North Trail links the new homeland of the Comanches in the southern plains with the old one in Wyoming is probably no accident.

Two uses for trails that are not part of the common image of Native Americans are pilgrimages and boundaries for tribal territories. The landscape of the Native Americans was not merely secular but included holy places, just as our own does. Shrines where ceremonies were conducted, where healing could take place, where individuals could communicate with the spirits of the sky world or the underworld, were scattered across the land. People could and did travel to them regularly, sometimes individually, sometimes in large groups. The Pawnees, for instance, recognized a series of "animal lodges," places where the spirits of various animal species dwelt beneath the ground, and where direct communication with them was possible.[12] The origins of important ceremonies were connected with these spots,[13] and each of the animal lodges whose location is known today is associated with a trail by which the Pawnees traveled to it.

Trails were also used as territorial boundaries, but our knowledge of this use is woefully limited. We do have brief mention of a peace treaty at which the Omaha, Ponca, Arikara, Cheyenne, and Ioway people agreed on hunting territories,[14] and we have also later accounts from a land claims case of the Omaha territory that resulted from that treaty.[15] All of the witnesses from the Omaha nation described their traditional territory in terms of a set of trails that created a loop encompassing most of northeastern Nebraska. These were the trails they usually followed on their bison hunt, and the land that lay within the loop was theirs. One witness mentioned the use of figures outlined in stone as additional markers.[16]

—Features of Native Trails

The uses for trails determine both the features found along them and the routes they follow. Water was both a necessity and a hindrance for all travelers. Drinking water had to be available every day or at least every other day,[17] as Native Americans did not have containers with the capacity of water barrels. In prehistoric times, they were limited to what they could carry on their own backs or what they could pack on their dogs, and water is extremely heavy. It was only in 1853 that the Cheyenne learned from the Kiowa the trick of making a large-capacity water bottle from the skin and hoof of the lower leg of a mule.[18] The resulting container had to be carried on horseback.

Trails thus featured springs, creeks, lakes, and water holes, and most major trails provided water at the end of each day's travel. Thus the accounts of the Coronado expedition reported that while his Wichita guides steered him in August 1541 from central Kansas to New Mexico across the arid high plains, "they led us by watering places and among the cattle and over good road."[19]

While streams provided water to drink, stream crossings were a nuisance to the traveler. They involved climbing up and down steep slopes and vertical banks, beating through thick brush, getting wet, and, except for at the smallest streams, packing and unpacking any burden-bearing dogs. It should be no wonder, then, that native trails led to the best fords across major streams and, whenever possible, along the divides between streams. When Kansa guides led Etienne de Véniard, Sieur de la Bourgmont, west into central Kansas in 1724, it should be no surprise that they took him to the Rocky Ford crossing of the Kansas River.[20] Similarly, we should not be surprised to learn that trail after trail took to the high dividing ridges between streams. By following these, the traveler could avoid crossing all but the major rivers, and the same rock formations that created the ridges often provided rocky fords where the ridge was cut by a river. As Bob Blasing has pointed out, it is possible to follow the crest of the Flint Hills from the Arkansas River in Oklahoma to the Platte River in Nebraska, and to have to cross only the Cottonwood and Kansas Rivers.[21] At both crossings, the same resistant bedrock that created the ridge also provides a fine ford.

Two early Euro-American travelers on the Plains describe the advantages of routes along the divides. One is Charles Augustus Murray, who in 1835 accompanied a Pawnee band on their summer bison hunt. He said: "The 'dividing ridge' of a district is that which, while it is as it were the back-bone of the range of which it forms a part, heads at the same time all the transverse ridges, whether on the right or left-hand and thereby spares to the traveler an infinity of toilsome ascent and descent."[22]

Murray came by this knowledge the hard way. Having lost the last of his Pawnee guides, he was forced to lead his small party of greenhorns out of the Plains. Without a guide, they quickly ran into trouble: "Never since we entered the prairies of the west, had we been entangled in such a labyrinth of steep, irregular, and broken ridges as those which obstructed our progress when we attempted to leave the course of the stream. As soon as one height was attained, another and a higher arose before us. In the ascent the packs slipped over our mules' and horses' tails; in the descent, over their necks and ears."[23] It is little wonder that Murray concluded, "The first quality in a guide through an unknown range of rolling prairie, is having a good and quick eye for hitting off the 'dividing ridge.'"[24]

The other early writer to describe the advantages of routes that follow divides is Colonel Richard Irving Dodge. He wrote, "The line or ridge separating the waters of two streams not uniting with each another, is called a 'principal divide.' In very many parts of the plains the sides of ravines are so extremely precipitous that crossing them is out of the question, and all travel must either be along the 'bottoms' or along the 'divides.' The 'bottom,' though comparatively level, is almost always scored by a ditch which, winding from one precipitous side to the other, necessitates innumerable crossings; and, as its banks are generally steep, immense labor is required to make a wagon road. Sometimes a 'bottom' is so narrow and broken that it is impossible to follow it. The 'divide' on the contrary, is nearly always comparatively unbroken level, and offers a good, though sometimes exceedingly crooked, route."[25]

Major trails did sometimes follow stream valleys rather than divides, but these seem to have been major streams, the valleys of which provided fairly unbroken stream terraces for easy traveling. In most such cases, the trail tended to be on the north side of the stream.[26] The south-facing slope of the north side was freer of trees and brush than the damper, north-facing slope on the south bank.

Only Louis Burns argues that Native Americans did not use divides for long-distance travel: "In our research, we have frequently encountered statements to the effect that Osage trails followed the highlands. Facts do not support such statements which are obviously based on Euro-American backgrounds. Euro-American trails generally followed the highlands because they used wheeled vehicles."[27]

Burns is wrong. Apparently he reached his conclusion based on his study of Osage trails in eastern Kansas and Oklahoma—trails that the Osage used to travel west to hunt bison. The position of their nineteenth-century villages in a region where streams flow north to south necessitated that they travel across stream valleys for the most part and use tributary stream valleys as means of access to the main valleys. Even so, portions of many of their trails did follow divides. The whole western end of the Black Dog Trail, arguably the most famous of the Osage trails, followed the upland ridge between the Ninnescah and Chikaskia rivers.

The best trails provided multiple resources for the traveler. Springs at the heads of creeks are to be found near the crests of divides. Major fords are often associated with water holes.[28] These water holes and other good sources of water often featured edible plants, fish, shellfish, and other game. Some water holes also were located in groves of trees that provided both fuel and shelter for the traveler. The importance of these in the relatively treeless Plains cannot be underestimated.

Other resources were to be found at salt marshes, where both salt and game were easily obtained. Quarries for useful stone lie along some trails and were themselves reason for the development of a trail. Blasing found small quarries along the trail that followed the crest of the Flint Hills.[29] A much larger set of quarries is to be found farther south along the same trail, on the Kansas-Oklahoma border. These provided the high quality Kay County or Florence A chert, pieces of which can be found in archaeological sites all over Oklahoma and Kansas.

—Man-made Features

Other trailside features were created by the travelers themselves. They include villages, camps, burials, cairns, stone figures and intaglios, and possibly patches of vegetation. In combination with the natural features of the landscape that influenced the course of the trails, they made travel along the trails a relatively comfortable and culturally rich experience. Unfortunately we do not know how many places along the trails were used to educate the young.[30] But we do have an account by Timothy McCleary from the northern Plains that gives an impression of how travel through such a cultural landscape was experienced:

> The two of us headed north from Crow Agency, Montana, on an early fall afternoon. As we traveled, I recalled the mental map of the trip provided to me by Mr. Gros Ventre. To the east were the two prominent buttes that he said was the site of a desperate yet successful stand and charge by the Apsáalooke war leader Homosexual Dog and his men against an overwhelming number of Lakotas. Mr. Gros Ventre had told me that the Apsáalooke refer to this area as *Bishkawataash Ammikáshkuluua,* "Where Homosexual Dog Was Chased Downhill"; local Anglos call it Squaw Buttes. We then passed Square Hill and Pronged Points.
>
> The territory was still familiar to me through Mr. Gros Ventre's recollections. He had mentioned the Island of Pines, and then the Spotted Rimrocks. There was the prominent butte near Forsyth, Montana, with the auspicious name of *Búattaaile,* "Coyote's Penis." Every butte, bluff, and coulee had its Apsáalooke name and story. It was a comfortable drive, a chance to place the oral landscape I had heard about into terrain I could see.[31]

In the case of major villages, it is difficult to decide which came first, the trails or the villages. Trails would grow outward from major villages, but villages also were purposefully situated on major trails for the advantages they provide. Not only is it difficult to determine the age of a trail and thus to determine whether it might be associated with a particular prehistoric site, but the features of the landscape that might lead to the development of a trail, such as water, timber, and useful stone, are the very factors that might influence the location of a village. For instance, the best place on a riverbank to locate a large village is beside a good ford. Otherwise the land and resources available to the village residents would be cut in half by an impassible stream. As we have already seen, however, a good ford is likely to be associated with a trail. Thus villages and trails may be associated because the village was placed on a trail, because the trail grew up from the patterns of travel of the village residents, or because both trail and village locations were responses to features of the natural environment. Blasing provides an illustration of the relationship between the locations of historic Kansa villages and camps on the one hand and the trails of eastern Kansas on the other.[32]

Other sites were clearly the product of existing trails. For instance, in 1839, Dr. Friedrich Wislizenus traveled along what would become the Oregon Trail. In southeastern Nebraska, his little party came to the junction between two Pawnee trails (including the trail called *the* Pawnee Trail below). There he found the skeleton of a camp—several hundred dome-shaped wigwam structures of interlaced poles, lacking only the covers needed to turn them into shelters.[33]

In 1859, J. R. Mead found war lodges along the Pawnee trail on Spillman Creek, south of Waconda Lake. He describes them merely as "shelters of fallen wood" located in thickets.[34] They were the kind of temporary shelters made by members of small war parties, hidden in thickets for protection. We know from other descriptions that they were conical in form like a tipi, but made with many timbers in order to make them relatively bulletproof.

Sometimes the archaeologist can associate camps with trails through the presence of exotic goods in the sites, goods that traveled down the trail. In 1991, I found at a quarry site in Apache Canyon on the west side of the Llano Estacado a spot where a prehistoric traveler had dumped the contents of his pouch in order to fill it with blanks from the quarry of the local quartzite. Lying among large spalls of the quartzite was a cluster of small, utilized flakes of Alibates dolomite and Tecovas jasper, types of stone from the far side of the Llano. Connecting the sources of these kinds of stone with Apache Canyon is a trail that runs past Garcia Lake and eastward down Tierra Blanca Creek.

Pictographs and petroglyphs are often associated with native trails, especially at stream crossings where there are rock exposures. The Mountain Branch of the Santa Fe Trail, for instance, features petroglyphs at every stream crossing, clear evidence that it had been used by Native Americans long before William Becknell and the others followed it to Santa Fe.[35]

Individuals using the trails sometimes suffered accidents or attacks by enemies, or merely sickened and died before they reached their destinations. Often they would be buried adjacent to the trails, in spots that their relatives might continue to visit for years if their regular travels took them along those trails. We have a clear account of this for the Omahas.[36] Beside the Pawnee Trail on the terraces on both the north and south banks of the Saline River, there are rock-covered burial mounds.[37] The remaining burial mounds in and around that project domain are all on the ends of high ridges, making it likely that the burial mounds on the low ground are in true association with the trail.

Common features along Native American trails are cairns, often of stone but sometimes of sod or even wood. The cairns had multiple functions. Some marked the locations of the trails themselves. These tend to be found in areas that lack natural landmarks by which travelers could otherwise guide themselves. In 1706, for instance, Juan de Ulibarrí encountered sod cairns marking the trail to El Cuartelejo in the featureless high plains of western Kansas.[38] Such trail markers were necessary even along heavily traveled routes because huge herds of bison could and did cross the trails, effectively erasing all evidence of prior human travel.[39]

Other cairns marked trail exits or places where particular resources could be found. This turned out to be the nature of most of the cairns found by Blasing in the Deep Creek drainage. Rather than being on the trail itself, they were located near the ends of subsidiary ridges where they could be seen from the trail. When Blasing went from the trail to the cairns and continued beyond them he found stone quarries and campsites.[40] Similarly, a set of cairns I have visited on a trail along Cherry Creek in northwestern Kansas mark the site of a good spring. Still other cairns marked entry points onto trails. Such is the case on the south side of the Saline River at Wilson Lake. A series of cairns there mark the mouths of canyons that provide good passage to the trail atop the divide.[41]

Cairns also functioned as shrines,[42] some resulting from travelers tossing a stone atop a pile as a prayer of thanks for having survived a particularly dangerous passage. A prominent example of this are the multiple cairns along the aptly named Bad Pass Trail in Montana.[43] Sometimes cairns even functioned as mail drops, with passersby placing mnemonic devices to indicate a message to friends who might be following them.[44]

Still other trail-associated features are stone outline figures and intaglios. In the Omaha Land Claims case, Louis LeRoy, a Ponca, was asked by the attorney for the United States about a sign supposedly erected by the Poncas asserting their claim to some of the land that was also used by the

Omahas. The attorney intended to elicit information about a handwritten sign on a board erected in recent times, but the witness replied in terms of the creation of a "stone buffalo on the ground" that he had been told about.[45] The only such figure known for the state of Kansas is the Penokee man, located on the upper South Solomon River west from Waconda Lake. An intaglio, or figure cut from the sod of a hillside (in essence, a reverse bas-relief), is located at the lake and is reported below.

Certain patches of vegetation may also be human-made features associated with Native American trails. In the Deep Creek drainage, Blasing noticed papaw trees outside the previously reported range, apparently in association with branches of the Flint Hills Trail where it ran down various draws to the Kansas River.[46] At Wilson Lake, every trailside rock-shelter seemed to be associated with edible plants, but we could not prove that they were the result of human occupation of the shelters. It is easy to imagine, however, that human use of a trail could result in the propagation of useful plants either by accident or by design.

—Origins of Native Trails

In spite of all of this clear evidence for human use of the trails, they were often mistaken for game trails, and there is a persistent historic myth that asserts that the Native American followed game trails and that his trails were then followed by frontiersmen, to eventually grow into modern highways. While frontiersmen often followed native trails and these routes sometimes became modern highways, the first link in the chain of use is simply not true. The origins of the native trails lie in human, not animal, behavior.

The myth of the solitary native following game paths was not demolished by the firsthand experience of thousands in the way the Great American Desert idea faded like a mirage from the minds of settlers in the supposedly desolate waste. Instead, the trail myth lives on. For instance, I was taught in high school that the first Euro-American settlers in Kentucky followed the "Great Buffalo Trace," a road carved through the mountain passes by hundreds of generations of migrating buffalo. The truth of the matter is that buffalo were extremely rare east of the Appalachians, and bison bone is not found in the prehistoric archaeological sites there. Furthermore, bison did not migrate regularly over large distances, especially over mountain ranges. The "buffalo trace" was a native trail that led to the hunting grounds of Kentucky where some bison herds could be found.

How then did the myth arise that certain cross-country trails were carved out by animals and followed only later by natives? More particularly, how did the idea come about that native trails on the plains were bison trails first? The answers lie in our own intellectual history. They include the biblically based belief that humans in the New World must have a short history, while the animal occupants have been here since the Creation. It also involves the basic assumption of nineteenth-century natural theology—that humans can read God's wisdom by observing the natural world. It was associated, in the case of the Great Plains, by the former belief in an annual bison migration from the Llano Estacado of Texas to the plains of Canada and back. Finally, it involves a few grains of truth in that game trails and native trails did often coincide at stream crossings and other select spots.

Animals do frequently create trails that look like footpaths. Cattle do, bison do, and deer do. Most of these trails, however, are short, and in spite of many assertions to the contrary, they do not always provide the best route between any two points that they happen to connect. Where there is only one feasible route between two adjacent points, the game trail, if there is one, will necessarily follow it. But the wanderer who trusts game trails for guidance across unknown territory will be led halfway into an otherwise impenetrable thicket as often as to water. Apparently the people who repeated the idea that game trails are the best routes of travel had little outdoor experience.

They had in its stead the belief, at least initially, that Native Americans, as descendants of Adam, must have arrived in the New World long after the Creation, in one version as the Lost Tribes of Israel. In this historical framework, game trails obviously preceded native trails. With the development of natural theology it was but a short leap to the conclusions that animal trails are perfectly designed routes of travel and that humans, of course, learned the routes from the animals.

The facts are that the natives were here as early as the elk, and that they preceded the modern form of bison by thousands of years. While the first Native Americans may have followed trails carved out by the mammoths and mastodons they hunted, those trails would have faded after the extinction of the giant beasts.

Game trails do sometimes lead to water, they lead to salt licks, and they lead to fords across streams. For instance, Colonel Dodge learned from plainsmen that for twenty-five years bison herds crossed the Arkansas River primarily at five spots: at the mouth of Walnut Creek, the Pawnee Fork, Mulberry Creek, the Cimarron Crossing, and the mouth of Big Sand Creek.[47] All of these spots were also crossing points of native trails and later were crossing points associated with the Santa Fe Trail.[48] They all coincided at the natural fords of the river.

One can see, then, how the idea began that native trails followed buffalo trails. Bison, however, like cattle, create trails only when they travel single file, and they travel in that fashion only when they are moving to water. "To their watering places they form narrow paths, over which they leisurely move on, one behind the other. A buffalo region is crossed by such paths in every direction."[49] Native trails, however, were somewhat broader. "Indian roads are usually recognizable by the marks of their tent poles, fastened at one end on either side of their pack horses, and trailing on the ground with the other."[50] This pattern preceded the use of horses in the Historic period; in the Plains sign language the sign for dog represents the tent poles dragged by this original pack animal.[51]

At other times, bison travel in a broader front. Just how observers of bison movements who sometimes saw them in a band twenty to fifty miles wide[52] managed to retain the idea that they generated the narrow native trails is hard to imagine. When moving in large groups, bison travel in wide columns; when feeding, they fan out in order to find grass. Bison trails, therefore, occur only near water, around obstacles or in narrow gaps in an otherwise impassible landscape.

In other places, the movement of bison herds tended to destroy rather than to create trails. In 1806, when Zebulon Pike was following the trail of a large Spanish army through central Kansas, he lost the trail where a large bison herd had effectively erased it. The Spanish army, in turn, was following the Pawnee Trail.[53] Thus a trail that was in use every year and that had been traveled by a large army shortly before Pike arrived was obscured by the movement of (apparently) a single herd.

In the nineteenth century, many travelers across the Plains developed the idea that the bison herds migrated from one edge of the grassland to the other every year. This myth grew from repeated observations of large bison herds crossing their main routes of travel. Since the latter were east-west trails, the only bison movements that could cross them would have to be more or less north-south ones. Thus the nature of the Euro-American travel helped to create the Euro-American picture of bison movements.

Lack of serious thinking about the matter also helped. How such postulated north-south bison movements could have generated the many east-west native trails is not explained. The more accurate modern understanding of bison movements is that there were localized herds that had seasonal rounds of travel. In the coldest winter weather on the northern plains, the herds headed in whatever direction would take them to the shelter of trees.[54] In the summertime in North Dakota, there was an east-to-west movement as the ponds east of the Missouri River dried up.[55]

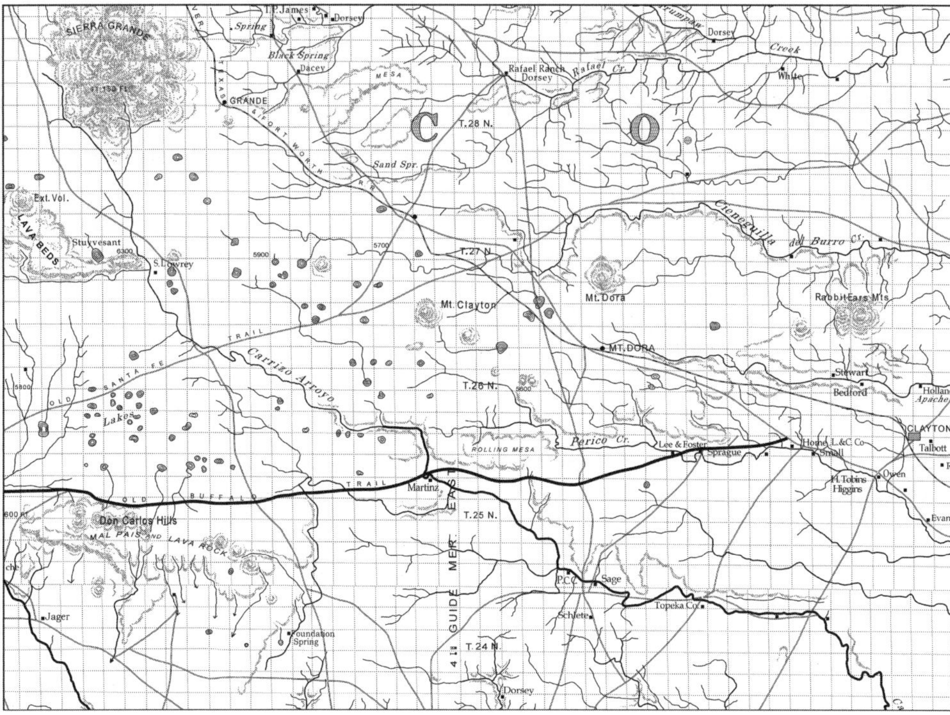

FIGURE 3.1 The Colfax and Mora land grant map. A route called "Old Buffalo Trail" is highlighted. In spite of the name, it was not a buffalo trail but a wagon road to Buffalo Spring (from an original print owned by author).

The cross-country trails, then, are native trails. The "Old Buffalo Trail" of the 1889 map of Colfax and Mora counties, for instance, runs from Peck, New Mexico, to near Clayton, a distance of some forty-five miles (Figure 3.1). It actually continued eastward to the XIT Ranch headquarters at Buffalo Spring at the northern edge of the Texas Panhandle. The name of the spring probably is the source of the name for the trail given on the map; it certainly was not from herds of bison passing single file from town to town. Neither is the Pawnee Trail, which stretches some 185 miles from Fort Kearney in the north to Fort Zarah in the south, the creation of an annual military expedition of bison. Both were created by humans.

—Eyewitness accounts

We have only a few firsthand descriptions of native trails on the Great Plains. Most often a writer who mentions following a native trail does not bother with a physical description. Wislizenus, cited above, is one exception. Another is Louis Henry Morgan, who visited the Plains in 1859, while conducting research on Native American kinship systems: "All over the prairie we came upon native trails. They are usually horse trails which consist of two, three, four and sometimes five parallel paths deeply worn in the ground. Three paths are the most usual number."[56]

The presence of fresh travois tracks enabled C. A. Murray to distinguish what sort of party had traveled along the trail: "A war-party leaves only the trail of the horses, or, of course, if it be a foot party, the still slighter tracks of their own feet; but when they are on their summer hunt, or migrating from one region to another, they take their squaws and children with them, and this trail can always be distinguished from the former, by two parallel tracks about three and a-half feet apart, not unlike those of a light pair of wheels: these are made by the points of the long curved poles on which their lodges are stretched, the thickest or butt ends of which are fastened to each side of the pack-saddle, while the points trail behind the horse."[57]

He also reported the differences between various kinds of campsites found along the trails: "It requires no great experience or observation of native life to enable a prairie traveler to distinguish a mid-day from a night camping-place; in the former he will often find some cut branches under which the party had sheltered themselves from the heat of the noon sun; in the latter, generally some scraps of charred wood, or round marks in the grass, showing where fire had been."[58]

Detailed eyewitness accounts of natives using the trails are few. One of the most complete is by Alexander Henry, who participated in a Hidatsa expedition to a Cheyenne camp in 1806:

> In the front was Le Borgne's [an Hidatsa chief] brother, attended by Two Crows [another chief] on his left, holding out the stem [of a peace pipe], and a war chief on his right, supporting the American flag on a long pole. These three great men advanced ten paces; 40 Big Bellies immediately followed and formed abreast, singing and shaking their rattles. To the right and left of these, and somewhat in the rear, two parties of thirty men each, filed off, singing in the same manner. In the rear of those, again, but in the middle line, was formed another party of 40 young men, also singing. The center of these four squads was a vacant space, into which we were desired to form abreast, in company with some of the most respectable old men. Behind them and us came small parties of tens, twenties, and thirties, singing and shouting at intervals. The women brought up the rear.[59]

Native trails included both major trails and minor ones, and major trails sometimes had multiple routes. In the Historic period, when whole bands or nations united for bison hunting expeditions, the resources along a single trail were often inadequate to serve all of the people. Whenever possible, the villages or bands involved would travel along separate but parallel routes located only a few miles apart. Weltfish records this pattern for the Pawnee nation in the nineteenth century.[60] Major trails also split into several alternative routes at stream crossings. Blasing recorded an instance of this on the Flint Hills Trail, which split to follow several draws down to the Kansas River crossing.[61] Reeves reports two parallel trails along the front of the Rocky Mountains in Montana, one used during warm weather and another, closer to the mountain front, that was used during the cold season when travel on the open plains was dangerous.[62]

The tendency of major trails to split and recombine, much like the course of a braided stream, led some observers to conclude that there were no trails per se, only broad zones of travel. Thus J. R. Mead wrote of the Pawnee Trail: "They had no defined path to follow, but kept to a general course about 15 degrees west of south and east of north within a strip of country a mile or more in width."[63] This is only a partial truth, however, that pertains only to portions of the route. In most places there was a clearly defined path; in others, more or less parallel trails.

With this understanding of the nature of native trails, we can turn to the specifics of a single trail. It is the Pawnee Trail, which crosses Waconda Lake at about the midpoint of its route between the Great Bend of the Arkansas River and Grand Island on the Platte.

—Naming the Trails

Before describing the Pawnee Trail, it is necessary to define it. Native Americans created many trails, but they seem not to have named them. The Pawnees used many trails, and several have been called "the Pawnee Trail" by Euro-Americans. The very same trails, however, were used by other nations as well. To complicate matters further, each trail joins with others, so that the point at which a given trail ends is moot. Some trails have been given different names for various sections of their route, and if that were not confusion enough, the names given by Euro-Americans to some trails changed through time. Thus a section of the Old Traders' Trail from the Platte River in western Nebraska to the Arkansas in eastern Colorado became known as the Fort Wallace–Fort Lyons Trail after the

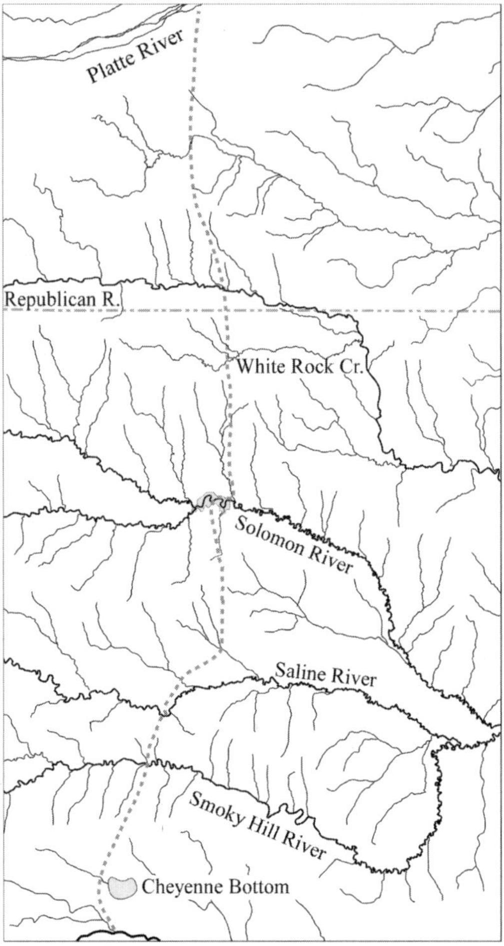

FIGURE 3.2 The Pawnee Trail ran between the Platte and Arkansas rivers. In the early historic period, it was used by the South Band Pawnees during their annual bison hunts.

military posts came into use. Similarly, what had been an unnamed Kansa trail in northeastern Kansas came to be called Sublette's Trace after 1827, only to later become a part of the Oregon Trail.[64]

I propose the policy of using a single name for a trail between major rivers and for a trail that follows a single stream. It is also reasonable to use, whenever possible, the name for a trail that is recorded most frequently in the literature. Thus the Pawnee Trail (Figure 3.2) is the trail that ran from Grand Island on the Platte River to the Arkansas River at Great Bend. Native trails continued north from Grand Island and south from Great Bend, but these should have different names. Similarly, the Pawnee Trail intersected others that followed the major streams that it crossed, such as the Platte River Trail, the Smoky Hill Trail, the Saline River Trail, et cetera.

—The Pawnee Trail

Beginning at the north end, the Pawnee Trail heads south from the Platte at one of the numerous fords of that stream a few miles northeast of Doniphan, Nebraska. Gene Weltfish, who did ethnographic work among the Pawnees, mentions a traditional camping spot at this point.[65] From there, it ran past Ayr, Nebraska, where the Mallet brothers mistook the Little Blue River for a tributary of the Platte because the trail crosses the stream at a point where it flows to the north.[66] This section of the trail is mentioned in a history of Adams County, Nebraska.[67]

The trail crosses the Republican River at the little town of Guide Rock, which was named for a sacred site of the Pawnees described in chapter 6. Pa:hu:ru' (the rock that points the way) labeled a narrow rock outcrop that was used as a landmark on the trail. It was part of a complex of features also called Pa:hu:ru' by the Pawnees. That complex included a high hill, a much smaller earth-lodge-shaped mound, a spring, and the trail itself. This was one of the "animal lodges" sacred to the Pawnees, a place where human supplicants might obtain sacred power from the animal spirits of the underworld.[68]

From this spot, the trail ran south to White Rock Creek, just west of the town of Burr Oak, Kansas. At this spot, there is a high loess hill on the south bank, one of the landmarks that gave a name for the creek, which originally was called White Mound Creek. Another such mound lies downstream, just southwest of the town of Lovewell, near a Republican Pawnee village at the mouth of the creek. In 1739, the Mallet brothers, discussed in the next chapter, called this stream the White Hills River.[69]

Directly south of the white hill, the trail intersects tributaries of Limestone Creek, which flows south to the Solomon River just below the dam that creates Waconda Lake. Part of our efforts during the survey of the federal land there was directed toward determining the exact route of the trail in the vicinity of the project domain. This effort was successful and has led to the correction of some errors in the original description of the trail in the Wilson Lake report.

One such error involves what is certainly the standard depiction of the Pawnee Trail in the historic literature: the Frémont map of 1845. John

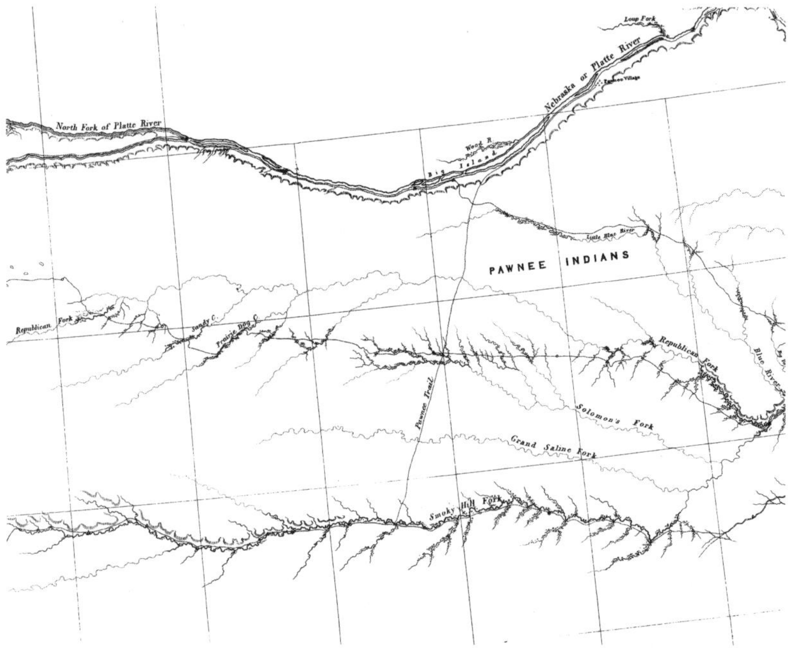

FIGURE 3.3 The Frémont map showing a Pawnee trail. The route shown is actually a line connecting segments of three trails that Fremont had encountered on his various expeditions (map by author).

Charles Frémont had made two expeditions across the plains prior to 1845, and the map (Figure 3.3) summarizes his knowledge of the West as of that date. It shows a "Pawnee Trail" running in a south-southwesterly direction from the "Big Island" on the Platte River, across various streams to the Smoky Hill River.

The map is detailed only along the routes that Frémont had traveled: portions of the Republican and Solomon rivers, and the Smoky Hill. The courses of streams in areas he had not explored are inked in only lightly to indicate uncertainty. The map shows the trail crossing the Solomon River a short distance below what appears to be a major fork and just above the mouth of a northerly tributary. In 1986, using these features and the proportions of the map as a guide, we concluded that the fork was in fact the fork of the Solomon and the tributary stream was Limestone Creek.[70] This conclusion turns out to be correct for the Pawnee Trail but not for the Frémont map.

During the course of the work at Waconda Lake, I projected the Frémont map onto the U.S.G.S. 1:500,000 state base map for Kansas in order to determine the precision of the Frémont map. This process demonstrated two things: that the proportions of the Frémont map were incorrect and that the trail he drew was very misleading. Frémont compressed the distances between streams significantly, but the detail with which he drew their courses where he crossed them allowed me to identify them anyway.

When I drew his version of the trail on a modern map on which I had recorded other trails, it became clear that Frémont had recorded several native trails during his various expeditions. Assuming that they were a single trail, he had simply connected the dots to draw his map. The trail he recorded near the Solomon was on Cedar Creek, about twenty-five miles upstream from Waconda Lake. That trail, rather than connecting with the one coming from Grand Island, actually ran northwest, not northeast as Frémont drew it. The Cedar Creek trail was used by the Omahas on their last bison hunt in 1876.[71] The trail encountered on the Smoky Hill was a third one that did not connect directly with the other two.

Fortunately, local informants and archaeological sites allowed us to map the Pawnee Trail at Waconda Lake. Three local residents offered independent but mutually supporting evidence. As a child, Mr. Dale LaDow was told of lodge poles visible at one spot along Limestone Creek, on the family farm east of the old highway crossing. Family traditions also mentioned Sioux traveling along the creek at that point. He drew a little sketch that showed this point east of the Winn homestead.

Mr. Gerald Dubbert, a local landowner who had been the primary informant for the University of Nebraska crews in the 1960s, also had information that also indicated a trail on Limestone Creek. He said that a Mr. Winn had homesteaded land there because he had been advised to do so by Black Kettle, the Cheyenne chief. According to this story, Black Kettle told Winn of a major spring that never went dry during the summer nor froze during the winter. The directions he gave Mr. Winn involved traveling along the Solomon River to the mouth of Limestone Creek, then going up Limestone Creek to the spring. That is, he told him to follow the Solomon River Trail to Limestone Creek and to ascend the Pawnee Trail to the spring. Interestingly, J. R. Mead, who wrote the first article on native trails in the plains, described the Solomon River Trail as ascending the river only to this point and the Saline River Trail only to Spillman Creek.[72] In both cases, the points in question are where the east-west trails intersected the north-south Pawnee Trail. There is good reason to believe, however, that both of the east-west trails continued upstream beyond the Pawnee Trail.

The third informant was John McClure, a member of the Kansas House of Representatives. He grew up on a tributary of Limestone Creek and knew the countryside intimately. He told me of a major site near the mouth of Limestone Creek, where the Pawnee Trail would have intersected the Solomon River Trail, and of many other sites along the Limestone. Thus it turned out that our original interpretation of the Frémont map—that the Pawnee Trail ran down Limestone Creek—was correct, even though the map was not.

The trail reached the Solomon River in the vicinity of the village of Glen Elder. This is the location of Glen Elder Dam, and on the bluff above the dam is site 14ML1, a hunting camp of the White Rock phase.[73] On the far side of Limestone Creek is another large site reported by John McClure. Also nearby is the Range Mound, a rock-filled burial mound of the Archaic period.[74] Across the river and downstream from the dam are three other rock-filled mounds at the ends of ridges. If any low-lying burial mounds like those at Wilson Lake once existed here, they have been covered by the lake.

About three miles upstream from Glen Elder Dam is Waconda Spring, now covered by the waters of the lake. Like Guide Rock, it was one of the sacred animal lodges of the Pawnee and was sacred to other nations as well. It is described in chapter 7. There is a local tradition that when various nations came to visit the spring, they would camp on the south side of the river. The camp or camps are also under water, but we did find two sites on the south shore of the lake. These are long, linear scatters of flint chips, burned rock, and mussel shell that are very similar to trailside scatters I have seen elsewhere in Kansas and Oklahoma. They appear to mark the primary route of the trail south from the river, although it is likely that there was a trail crossing where the dam now stands and perhaps in other places as well.

Two miles south from Waconda Spring and one-quarter of a mile west is another site. It is an intaglio carved into the end of a high ridge. The Sage site, 14ML561, was found during our survey of the federal land around the lake. It is reported in chapter 8.

Farther south, on Walnut Creek, Gerald Dubbert showed me an old trail crossing. Wagon wheel ruts are still visible at this spot on his brother's farm, where early settlers appear to have used the old native trail. Mr. Dubbert was curious about the crossing, as he had not been able to figure out why the trail ran as it did. He had assumed that it was merely an historic wagon road, and while he could see that it could have come from Glen Elder to the east, he did not understand why it ran to the south-southeast after crossing the stream rather than west to the next town.

The answer lies to the south in the high, arid hills that border the Solo-

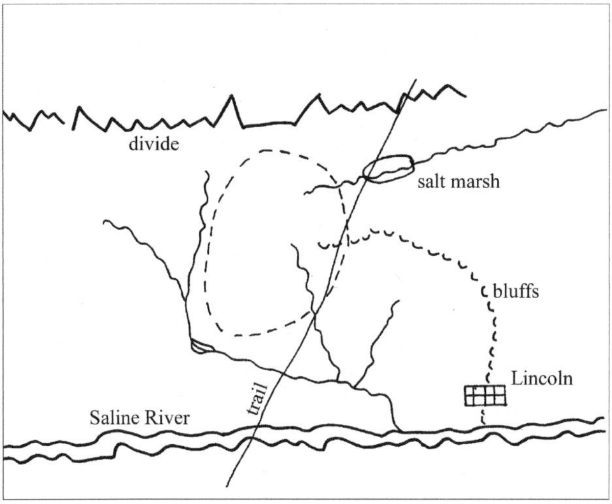

FIGURE 3.4 J. R. Mead's sketch of the Pawnee Trail. This schematic drawing was made by the hunter and trader J. R. Mead for a friend, many years after he had hunted along the Solomon River (courtesy Kansas State Historical Society).

mon River on the south. In this region, the General Land Office surveyors recorded only a single source of water, a spring at the head of Salt Creek. It is the only source of water between Walnut Creek and the Spillman Creek crossing twenty miles to the south. The spring is of fresh water, although, as its name indicates, Salt Creek eventually flows through a salt marsh.

To the south, on Bacon Creek, a tributary of Spillman Creek, the General Land Office surveyor recorded a segment of the trail and an associated Pawnee campsite. A crew from Kansas State University recorded sections of the trail between the spring and the campsite, and they recorded the camp as well. In 1991 they visited our field camp at Downs, Kansas, and discussed their survey in Lincoln County. I drew for them the likely route of the trail along the divides between the spring and Bacon Creek. Later they were able to confirm its location using a small plane. In one spot, the trail was precisely on the divide as predicted. In another, it diverged from it somewhat to take advantage of a good ford.[75]

The general course of the trail in the vicinity of the Solomon River to the Saline is shown on a map sketched by J. R. Mead (Figure 3.4). This rather schematic representation led us to postulate the existence of two branches of the trail in 1986.[76] Subsequent work has shown that, except for the immediate vicinity of the Saline River, there is only one trail. Part of the confusion arose from an apparent name change in the Spillman Creek system. Both the Mead map and the General Land Office map show Bacon Creek as Spillman Creek. Mead, who named Spillman Creek, referred to this branch simply as the east fork of Spillman Creek.[77] His information, plus the fact that I had not yet found the spring at the head of Salt Creek, led us to read the Mead map incorrectly.

At the camp on Bacon Creek, the trail turned west to the crossings of Wolf Creek and the Solomon River in the vicinity of Wilson Lake dam. We had found cairns and burial mounds in this spot during our survey of Wilson Lake in the mid-1980s.[78] In 1985 Bob Blasing interviewed a former landowner, who took him to the point where the trail ran down to the north side of the Saline River. It was at a spot now called Rock Town, upstream from the dam. The trail is no longer visible at that point, but on the south side of the river there are cairns at the mouths of canyons that lead the traveler back to the main trail on the divide.

The course of the trail through a "narrow rocky defile" was described in 1835 by Charles Augustus Murray (see chapter 4). From there the trail ran over high ground to the Smoky Hill River at the mouth of Beaver Creek, south of Dorrance, Kansas. At this point in 1861, James R. Mead recorded the name of an early French trader. This too is described in detail in chapter 4.

The trail then ran up the west side of Beaver Creek to its head on the divide between the waters of the Kansas and Arkansas drainages. It then descended to the Arkansas River, crossing Deception Creek, Blood Creek, Walnut Creek, and the Little Walnut in the process. South of the river, a trail continued south all the way to the Great Salt Flat in Oklahoma. The upper portion of this trail shows up on a map of Fort Zarah sketched by Adolph Hunnius in 1867.[79] It also shows up on a much earlier map, drawn in 1602 by a Wichita who the Spanish called Miguel.[80] I propose that this southern extension of the Pawnee Trail be called Miguel's Trail in his honor. This map shows the trail running south past one *salina* or salt flat (now the Quivira National Wildlife Refuge) to another on an east-flowing river (the Great Salt Flat on the Salt Fork of the Arkansas in Oklahoma).

4. The Pawnee Trail in Regional History

THE FAR-REACHING INFLUENCE that native trails have exerted on the course of the history of the continent has gone largely unrecognized. The truth is that European settlers entered a landscape that had been modified for millennia by Native Americans. That landscape affected much of their behavior from the time that Pilgrims in Massachusetts planted their crops in old native fields[1] until well into the nineteenth century. Native trails largely determined where people went and where important events occurred. From the first explorers following native guides to long-distance traders hunting for customers, Europeans first moved along native trails, then adapted them for their own use as emigrant roads, railbeds, and cattle trails. Military expeditions moved along them, battles were fought beside them, and military posts were erected on them. Later came trading posts, towns, and ranch headquarters, all of which took advantage of the already existing routes of travel and their associated resources.

The Pawnee Trail was as important to its region as any other was. It saw its share of explorers, traders, merchants, and vagabonds. Fort Kearney was built near its northern terminus, with Fort Zarah at the southern end. William Allison also had a trading post at the latter point, where the Pawnee Trail crossed the Santa Fe Trail. The following are some of the important early travelers who used it—Euro-Americans whose behavior was influenced by the native landscape.

—Pedro de Villasur, 1720

In 1719, Spain became aware of a threat to her New Mexico frontier. An expedition led by Antonio de Valverde, governor of New Mexico, learned from El Cuartelejo Apaches of French intrusions into Spanish territories.[2] The expedition was told of two French and Pawnee or Jumano (Wichita) forts on a large river. To investigate the threat, Spain sent another expedition from Santa Fe, headed by Pedro de Villasur, lieutenant governor of New Mexico. It included forty Spanish soldiers, some colonials, and seventy Apache allies.

Documentation of the route of the expedition is extremely scanty. We do know that Villasur stopped at the place called El Cuartelejo, an Apache ranchería on Ladder Creek in Scott County, Kansas. To get there, Villasur may have retraced the route of Governor Valverde's expedition of the previous year, which reached eastern Colorado, or he may have used the route taken by Juan de Ulibarrí in 1706 directly to El Cuartelejo.

Villasur picked up his Apache allies and, one assumes, Apache guides who led him along the swiftest route to the Pawnee villages in central Nebraska. To get there from El Cuartelejo, all they had to do was to go east to the Smoky Hill River, then down that stream to where Wilson Lake now lies, then north along the Pawnee Trail (Figure 4.1). As it happens, the only

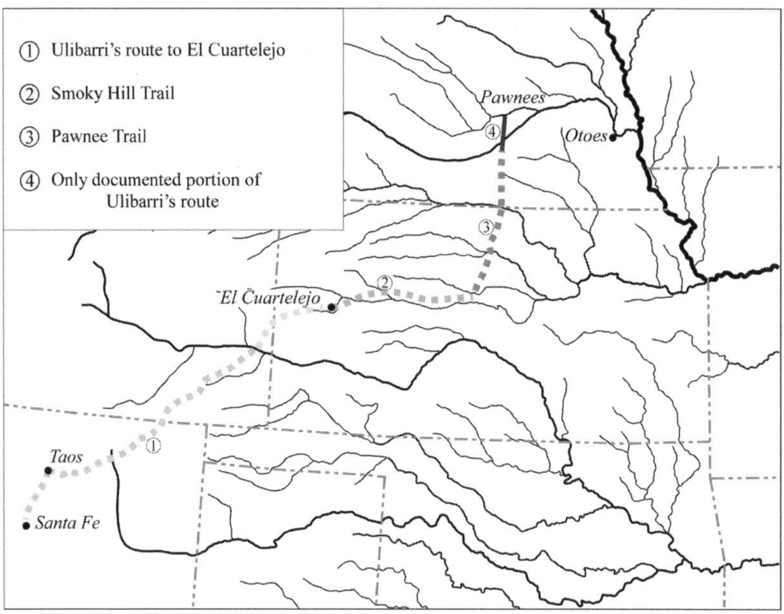

FIGURE 4.1 Projected route of the Villasur expedition. For the first part of the trip, he would have followed the route Valverde took the previous year. This would have taken him nearly to El Cuartelejo, an Apache settlement. From there, he would have followed the Smoky Hill Trail to its junction with the Pawnee Trail. The surviving page of the expedition journal has him on the Pawnee Trail at the Platte River crossing (map by author).

FIGURE 4.2 The Segesser painting of the Villasur massacre. This extraordinary depiction of the battle was apparently drawn shortly after the event by an Indian artist in New Mexico (courtesy Palace of the Governors Photo Archives [NMHM/DCA], 184800).

surviving page of the diary of the expedition picks up the story at the Platte River crossing of the Pawnee Trail.[3] From there the Spaniards went north and east to the Loup River and then down its north bank, only to retreat to the junction of the two rivers.

Here the diary ends, for on the morning of August 12, 1720, a combined Pawnee and Oto force surprised the Spanish camp and overwhelmed it, killing all but a handful of the Spaniards. The terror-stricken survivors, with the help of their Apache allies, made their painful way back, first to El Cuartelejo and then to Santa Fe. This devastating defeat was one of the pivotal historic events in Plains history; it broke Spanish power for decades and allowed French penetration of the Plains to continue. In a serendipitous accident of preservation, a painting of the attack, made by a native artist in New Mexico, happened to survive (Figure 4.2). Today it is in the Museum of New Mexico in Santa Fe.[4]

The story may not end there, however. While examining the collection from site 14ML1 (in the town of Glen Elder) made by the University of Nebraska in the 1960s, we came across a strange little rim sherd. It was so different from all of the others that had been found around the reservoir that at first I thought it was something of Euro-American manufacture, perhaps a piece of skeet. Closer examination showed that it was pottery tempered with mica. At that point, because I knew that some Apache

FIGURE 4.3 Ocate micaceous sherd found at Glen Elder, Kansas (courtesy U. S. Bureau of Reclamation, Nebraska–Kansas Office; photograph by author).

pottery was mica-tempered, I called James Gunnerson at the University of Nebraska State Museum. Jim had spent years investigating Apache sites on the High Plains, and I hoped he might be able to identify what we had. After I had begun describing the sherd, Jim interrupted to complete the description accurately. With just a partial description, he realized it was a rim of Ocate micaceous, a type of pottery made by Jicarilla Apaches from about AD 1720 to 1750 (Figure 4.3). Could it have been dropped by one of Villasur's Apache allies? While the proposal may seem far-fetched, the Apaches did not stay in this region long after Villasur's debacle. They were already being pressed hard by Comanche raiders, and they were gone by the time the Mallet brothers passed through in 1739 (see below).

—The Mallet Brothers, 1739

The French government sponsored expeditions onto the Plains both before and after Villasur's defeat. Nevertheless, the first successful French expedition from the east to Santa Fe was conducted by an independent band of French Canadian entrepreneurs headed by the brothers Pierre and Paul Mallet.[5]

Without native aid, it too would have foundered. Using old and inaccurate geographical information, the Mallets tried to reach Santa Fe by ascending the Missouri River. They were in South Dakota before friendly Arikaras turned them around. Buying horses in an Omaha village in northeastern Nebraska, they followed a series of native trails, first down the eastern side of Nebraska, then up the Platte to the Pawnee villages on the Loup.

From there they headed south, crossing the neck of land from the Loup to the Platte and then continuing down the Pawnee Trail.

In spite of the fact that the documentation of the Mallet journey route is scanty in the extreme, the few details in the surviving account place them on the Pawnee Trail. As they entered what is now Kansas, they recorded names for the rivers on which they camped. They were the Côtes Blanches (White Hills), Aimable (Friendly), des Soucis (River of Worries), Kans (Kansas), and à la Flèche (Arrow) Rivers. Of these, the *Kans* is readily identified as the Smoky Hill, the main fork of the Kansas River, which was already known to the French by that name.

Once this identification is made, the other streams are readily identified. The River of the Arrow is the Arkansas, and the name applied by the Mallets seems to be a variant of Flint River, the name by which it was known to most of the Plains nations. In Pawnee, the word *tahu:ru* translates as flint, arrowhead, and arrow.[6] The Mallets' use of it hints that they might have had a Pawnee guide during this portion of their trip. At minimum, they had explicit directions from the Pawnees whose villages they had visited.

Counting back from the Smoky Hill River, the River of Worries turns out to be the Saline River. The name may reflect the enormous numbers of rattlesnakes found near the trail crossing. In 1835, Charles Augustus Murray traveled down one of the little canyons that led to the crossing from the south. He later wrote, "I never should have believed it possible that so many rattlesnakes could have assembled together as I saw in that ravine."[7]

The stream crossed by the Mallets prior to the Saline should be the Solomon, and the one before that White Rock Creek. Their name for the latter, White Hills River, is probably a translation of another Pawnee name, for in the nineteenth century the same stream was recorded as "White Mound Creek" on General Land Office survey maps. As mentioned in the previous chapter, there are two prominent white loess hills on the banks of this stream.

This leaves the Aimable or Friendly River as the Solomon. It is possible, but by no means demonstrable, that the name is an indirect reference to the sacred spring on its bank. Waconda Spring was sacred not only to the Pawnee but to other nations such as the Omaha and the Kansa. Perhaps the name is a reference to the truce expected between nations when visiting the sacred site. We know that various nations made pilgrimages to more than one Pawnee sacred site.[8] If so, it is analogous to the "Land of Peace" around the catlinite pipestone quarry on Jonathon Carver's map of the Sioux country.[9]

From the Arkansas River, the Mallets continued on other trails to Santa Fe. Just south of the river, they followed Miguel's Trail south to the Black

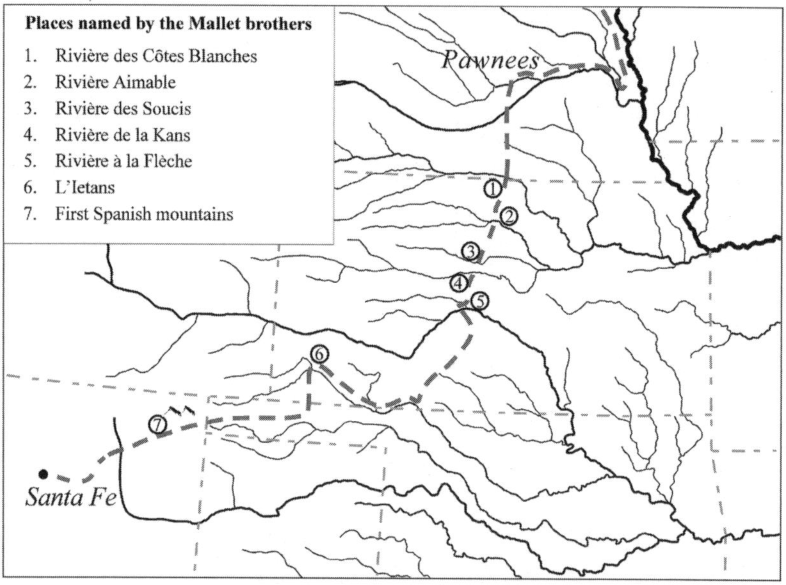

FIGURE 4.4 Landmarks along the route of the Mallet brothers, 1739. The place names are the only ones that occur in the brief abstract of the journal of their journey kept by the Mallets. All but the last appear to be translations of Pawnee place names (map by author).

Dog Trail, which ran along the divide between the Ninnescah and Chikaskia Rivers. Here they turned west and then south to the Cimarron River Trail. They followed this one upstream to Wagonbed Springs, south of present day Ulysses, Kansas. Here they obtained an Arikara guide who took them on to Santa Fe.[10] Their route across Kansas is shown in Figure 4.4.

—Chapuis and Feuilli, 1752

After the Mallet expedition, the Spanish response to French intruders was, if lenient, to prevent their return to Louisiana or, if not so lenient, to arrest them and confiscate their goods. This is what happened to two Frenchmen who arrived at Pecos on August 6, 1752. They were Jean Chapuis and Louis Feuilly, and they arrived at Pecos with a Skidi Pawnee woman for a guide and in the company of Jicarilla and Carlana Apaches.[11] They were carrying a passport and trading license signed by the French commandant of Illinois and had nine horses laden with trade goods.

Their adventure was an extraordinary one, as it began at the distant post of Michilimackinac in the Great Lakes country. In 1751, Chapuis obtained permission of the commandant of the French fort there to travel to Illinois. After his arrival at Fort des Chartres, he discussed the possibility of opening trade with New Mexico with the commandant, Benoit de St. Claire. St. Claire saw this as a grand opportunity and issued Chapuis a license, but neither passport nor license did him much good once he got to New Mexico.

From Fort des Chartres, Chapuis and Feuilli traveled to the Osages and Kansas. Then, after wintering at Fort Cavagnial on the Missouri River in what is now Leavenworth County, Kansas, the two set out with eight other Frenchmen who had agreed to join them. They first went northwest to obtain horses from the Skidi Pawnee. This places them in central Nebraska, and their route from there appears to have been down the Pawnee Trail.

In Nebraska or somewhere to the south, the other Frenchmen decided to abandon the venture, but Chapuis and Feuilli persevered in spite of harassment from Comanches and extortion of some of their trade goods. Somewhere on the frontier of New Mexico they encountered a fugitive Skidi woman who became their guide.

When they showed up at Pecos late in the summer of 1752, the mission priest, Fray Juan José Toledo, who spoke no French, reported the arrival of "Xanxapy" and "Luis Fuixy" to the Spanish governor in Santa Fe. The governor confiscated the French traders' goods, sold them at auction, and used the proceeds to pay for sending the hapless Frenchmen to the viceroy in Mexico City. From there they were shipped to prison in Spain.[12]

—Jean Baptiste Truteau, 1786

The sole record of the use of the Pawnee Trail by a man named Trudeau or Truteau was an inscription on the wall of a small cave near the Smoky Hill River crossing. In 1861, James R. Mead recorded it as reading, "TRUDO 1786."[13] The person in question is undoubtedly Jean Baptiste Truteau, known for his exploration of the Upper Missouri for the Missouri Company of St. Louis. His description of the Upper Missouri country was plagiarized by Perrin du Lac.

Three pieces of evidence suggest this identification of the man who made the inscription. First, although Truteau usually spelled his name with two t's, there are two instances of an autograph in which he spelled it "Trudeau."[14] He may have done this during the time when his patron was a distant relative, Zenon Trudeau, lieutenant governor of Illinois.

A second piece of information comes from his original description of the Upper Missouri. In it, a sentence was dropped from the Perrin du Lac

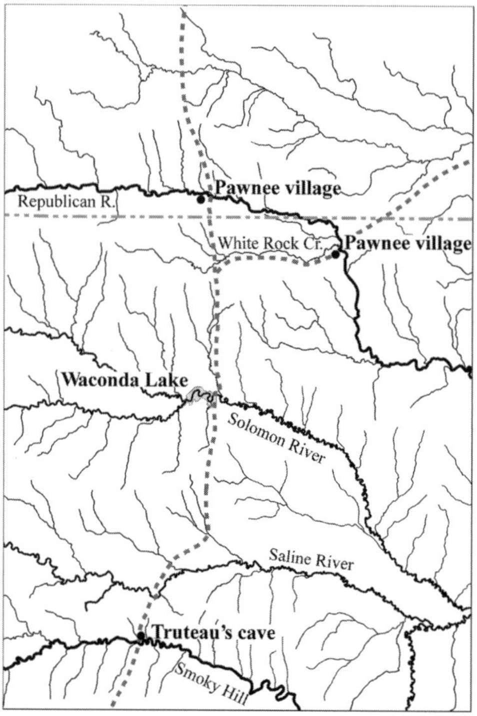

FIGURE 4.5 Relationship of Truteau's cave to the Pawnee Trail and villages. J. B. Truteau carved his name in a small cave near the Smoky Hill River. He is known to have lived among the Republican Pawnees in the 1780s (map by author).

version because it would have made the plagiarism obvious. It is a reference to having learned to make cache pits, for the temporary storage of goods, from Pawnees during a residence of several years among the Republican Pawnees. The latter band was first recorded in 1777,[15] and their villages on the Republican River provided ready access to the Pawnee Trail. It is likely that Truteau traveled with them on one or more of their hunts or visits to the Wichita, at which time he would have had opportunity to inscribe his name in the cave.

The third piece of evidence is an abbreviation in the Truteau manuscript. Instead of writing the full name then in use for the Apaches, namely "Padouca," Truteau abbreviated it to "Pado." The parallel between using "Trudo" as an abbreviation for Truteau or Trudeau and using "Pado" for Padouca helps to make the identity of the man obvious.

The relationship of the trail to the cave and the Republican Pawnee villages that Truteau may have visited is shown in Figure 4.5.

—Pedro Vial, 1793

Another Frenchman who traveled the Pawnee Trail was Pedro Vial. Born Pierre Vial, he was a French frontiersman who lived for a time among the Wichitas along the Red River. He eventually offered his services to the Spanish governors of Texas and New Mexico, who employed him as both an interpreter and a scout. In the period 1787 to 1803 he made a series of journeys of exploration for the Spanish, linking the Texas settlements with both Santa Fe and Natchitoches.

In 1792 he traveled from Santa Fe to St. Louis and returned the following year. On his outward trip from Santa Fe, he was captured by Kansa people in southwestern Kansas. They took him to one of their villages, but we have no record of the route for this portion of the journey. Freed from the Kansa village, he took a boat down the Kansas River to St. Louis.

Vial's general route for the return trip is fairly clear from the journal he kept. First he went up the Missouri River to a rendezvous spot near the mouth of the Little Nemaha River in southeastern Nebraska. This was an indirect route necessitated by then hostile relationships with the Kansa. Pawnee guides met Vial at the rendezvous and led him westward to the Republican Pawnee village near the mouth of White Rock Creek. Although his journal contains very few descriptions of the landscape that would make tracking his route easy, his mileage estimates and a few other clues make it possible to reconstruct the first leg of his journey accurately. Along it are three secure points: the rendezvous at the mouth of the Little Nemaha, the Republican Pawnee village at the mouth of White Rock Creek, and a spot on the Nebraska-Kansas border (between Rose Creek and the Little Blue River) where General Land Office surveyors recorded the presence of a native trail. Fitting these points to the Mallets' journal results in the route shown in Figure 4.6.

From the Pawnee village, Vial traveled southwest to the Pawnee Trail and followed it to the Arkansas River, as the following portion of his journal indicates.

> October
>
> 4—Before setting out, I regaled them [the Pawnees] with various items from those that I carried, and I set out from said village with seven of them, who accompanied me, and we stopped on the same river where they live. The course was to the southwest, and we traveled 3 [leagues].
>
> 5—I continued the march across the prairies, and followed the same course, traveling 6 [leagues].

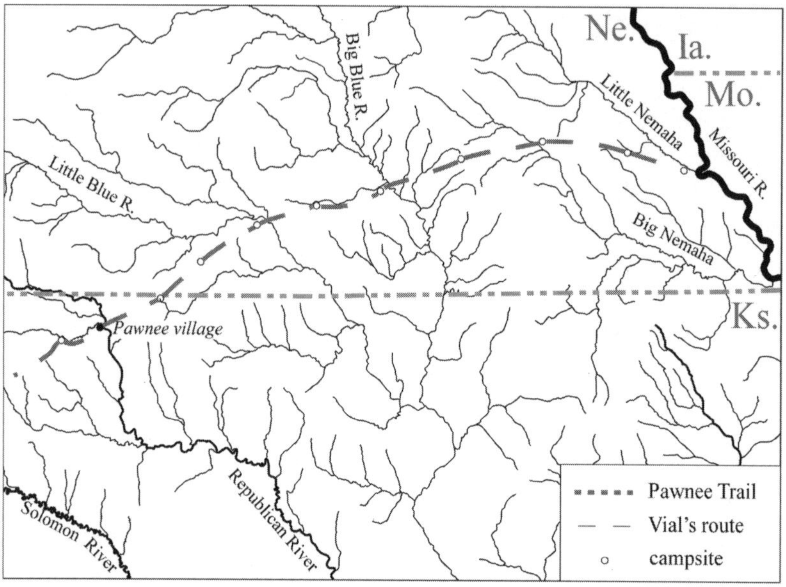

FIGURE 4.6 First leg of Pedro Vial's overland journey in 1793. The precise route that he followed has not been traced previously with any accuracy (map by author).

> 6—We continued on the same course, and stopped on a small stream [the Solomon River at the ford] 7 [leagues]
>
> 7—We set out at 5:30 in the morning, following the same course, and crossed several arroyos of the same river, traveling 7.
>
> 8—Across the prairie we marched on the same course. 6
>
> 9—The march was continued on the said course until a running spring [Spillman Creek]. There were traveled 7.
>
> 10—The course was to the west [the Pawnee trail runs west from Spillman Creek to the crossing of the Saline River], and we traveled until we reached a small stream that flows into the Kansas River. 7.
>
> 11—The course was to the southwest. We traveled 7.
>
> 12—On the same course across the prairie, we traveled 7.
>
> 13—The march was continued until we reached a small stream that flowed into the Río de Napestle [i.e., to the Pawnee Fork of the Arkansas River; "Napestle" is an Apache name that the Spanish used to designate the Arkansas].[16]

The portion of his route after leaving the Republican Pawnee village was first up White Rock Creek and along a trail described by Dr. J. Z. Scott in 1898: "A buffalo trail was seen in 1871. It was 20 to 30 feet wide, hollowed in the center. It passed from southeast of Mankato, to tableland at the south end of what is known as Switzer's Gap. On northeast in almost a straight line, it crossed the Persinger claims and ended at the head of Beaver Island in the Republican River."[17]

The route described by Scott places the trail on the south side of the prominent high hill marked "White Mound" on early maps, just southwest of the present-day town of Lovewell. If Vial had followed the creek as his journal reports, he would have been northwest of the hill at the end of the first day's travel from the village. In fact, there is a branch of the trail on the northwest side of the hill. It can still be seen in Section 24, according to Joe Stenson of Courtland. Thus, it is likely that Vial headed southwest from his first night's camp, just as the journal reports, and from there he followed the trail to the southwest where he would have encountered Limestone Creek and the Pawnee Trail after another half a day of travel.

The second portion of Vial's route, between Ford, Kansas, and the Canadian River in Texas, is pertinent to the Cardinal map discussed below. Since this portion of Vial's route has never been discussed in detail, it is necessary to review his journal and to relate it to the cultural landscape across which he traveled. Vial reported this leg of his trip as follows (with my interpretations in brackets):

> Oct. 15—On the same course, we crossed the Concha River [Mulberry Creek] and stopped to sleep at the *torcido* [i.e., the "twist" or "elbow"—the south bend of the Arkansas River] 5
>
> 16—We marched across good land on the said course, and slept at the Río Claro [Bluff Creek]. 7
>
> 17—We set out in the morning on the said course, [across] good land, and stopped on the Río Salado [Cimarron River], having traveled 7.
>
> 18—On the said course [we traveled] to the Río Arenoso [North Canadian], having traveled 6. [From there, Vial went upstream on the Canadian and then up Wolf Creek before cutting across to the Canadian River on October 27.][18]

My interpretation of this portion of the route is based on the distances Vial gives for his travel between streams. Southwestern Kansas does not have many of them, and when I initially tried to fit the details of the journal to a straight-line route, I got no matches. It was only when it occurred to me that he might have been following routes that were used in later times that the journal made sense and corresponded precisely to the distances between streams (Figure 4.7).

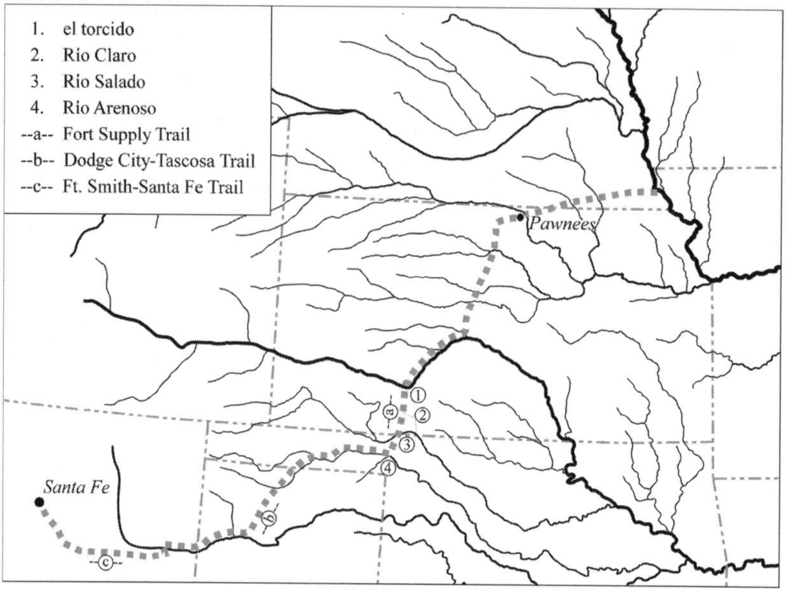

FIGURE 4.7 Relationship of the second leg of Vial's 1793 overland route to later trails. The numbered spots indicate the names that Vial used for various rivers. The sections of his route labeled "a," "b," and "c" were well-known wagon trails in the nineteenth century (map by author).

First Vial was on the Fort Supply Trail, then the Dodge City–Tascosa Trail, and finally on the Fort Smith–Santa Fe Trail. No other route matches the distances he gives in the journal. This is important to our understanding of the history of the region, as the histories of the later wagon roads make no mention of their origin as native trails.[19]

In 1797 Vial left New Mexico for Louisiana in the face of repression there against citizens of French origin. On a trading expedition to the Comanches, he exchanged a musket and his burros for some horses, and set out across the plains.[20] He lived east of the plains for the next six years, residing in 1799 in Portage des Sioux, north of St. Louis,[21] in 1801 at Florissant, and thereafter at a lead mine he exploited, La Côte des Cedres.[22]

He appears to have returned to Santa Fe in 1803, but there is no record of the route he followed. It probably involved the Pawnee Trail, because other evidence indicates that he stopped in one of the Pawnee villages. There he picked up another Frenchman who had been living among the Pawnees for at least eight years. That man was Joseph Chalvert, who figured prominently in later expeditions.[23] Together Vial and Chalvert escorted five Pawnee chiefs to Santa Fe. This happened to make both men available for the Spanish reaction to the Lewis and Clark expedition.

—Lewis and Clark, 1804–1806

Although the Lewis and Clark expedition of 1804 to 1806 did not come close to the Pawnee Trail, it did generate a good deal of traffic along portions of it. These movements were parts of the Spanish response to the Louisiana Purchase and the threat it represented to their colonial empire. They are succinctly reviewed by Cook.[24]

Spain had owned the former French colony of Louisiana since the 1763 Treaty of Paris that ended the Seven Years' War (the French and Indian War in North America), but in 1802 Napoleon wrested it back. After the failure of his invasion of Haiti, and in spite of promises to Spain, he sold it to the United States. At the time that this occurred, the borders of Louisiana were open to question.[25] Indeed, Spain had good grounds for considering the sale illegal.[26]

Nevertheless, once the purchase was consummated and preparations for the Lewis and Clark expedition were well underway, the American brigadier general James Wilkinson, who was an erstwhile agent of the Spanish government, recommended that Spain attempt to capture or repel the expedition.[27] The result was an order to the governor of New Mexico to send an expedition to the Plains to spy upon and, if possible, seize the American party. The same document recommended using the services of Pedro Vial in the effort.

The resulting expeditions are documented by Loomis and Nasatir, and by Cook, but only Cook ties them to the effort to impede the Lewis and Clark expedition. The first expedition left Taos in August of 1804 with fifty-two men. Pedro Vial was in command, and Joseph Chalvert (called José Jarvet by Vial when writing for his Spanish superiors) went along as an interpreter.

Following a route across the Sangre de Cristo Mountains, down the Purgatoire River to the Arkansas, and from there to the Platte,[28] Vial and his men reached the Pawnee villages on September 6. This was too late to intercept Lewis and Clark, who had already passed the mouth of the Niobrara River. Vial did gain information about them from Pawnees and Otoes and from some Frenchmen who were living in the Nebraska villages. He noted that the Americans were generous in their gifts to the leading men in each village and that they had been asking the chiefs to surrender any medals and like items that they had received from the Spanish.[29] Vial returned to Santa Fe with a Pawnee chief and eleven of his warriors. There the Pawnee chief received gifts from the Spanish governor to renew the alliance between his nation and Spain.

In 1805 Vial and Chalvert were commissioned to make a second expedition to the Pawnee country to intercept Lewis and Clark when they returned. This expedition left Santa Fe on October 14, 1805, with forty-eight soldiers, two carabineers, and six men from St. Louis. They were Laurent Durocher and Baptiste Lalande, three other Frenchmen, and James Purcell, an American. These men had arrived in New Mexico in at least two groups in 1804, and their presence will be discussed separately.

At Taos, the fighting force was doubled with the addition of another fifty men. It would prove inadequate. Taking the same route as previously, Vial led them across the Sangre de Cristo range and down the Purgatoire. At the junction of the Purgatoire with the Arkansas River, they were attacked by a band of about three hundred warriors. The attackers, unidentified at the time, may have been Skidis.[30] They succeeded in overrunning the main camp when most of the Spaniards were defending the horse herd. The Spanish lost two-thirds of the goods they had intended to take to the Pawnees and Otoes, and after a day of fighting, were low on ammunition. Under the circumstances, Vial had to return to Santa Fe with his mission a failure.

The urgency with which the governor of New Mexico viewed the circumstances is evident in the fact that he organized and outfitted another and larger expedition. This time, Vial and Chalvert were allotted three hundred men. It proved to be of no avail. Apparently the night attack on the last expedition had unnerved the men, because they mutinied shortly after leaving Taos, and Vial had to return once more to Santa Fe.

—Other Frenchmen, 1803–1807

In 1803 Joseph Chalvert had accompanied Pedro Vial and a delegation of Pawnees to Santa Fe. This was done in order to reaffirm peace between that nation and Spanish New Mexico. Chalvert, whose identity is something of a puzzle, had apparently lived among the Pawnees (or Wichitas) for at least eight years before arriving in Santa Fe. We know this because the 1806 Melgares expedition returned to Santa Fe with his ten-year-old son by a Pawnee woman.

Chalvert returned to the Pawnee country in 1804 in company with the expedition led by Pedro Vial. At this time, he made arrangements with an Illinois merchant named Morrison to guide Jeaunot Metoyer and Baptiste

Lalande to New Mexico. The deal involved trade goods for Chalvert that he could sell in New Mexico in return for his services.[31]

Apparently Chalvert was successful in this, as Lalande settled in Santa Fe. In 1805 he accompanied Pedro Vial, Chalvert, and Lorenzo Durocher on the unsuccessful attempt to journey once more to the Pawnee country. In 1807, still in the employ of the governor of New Mexico, Chalvert attempted to determine Zebulon Pike's true intentions. Pike extracted this information from him at saber point, but he was not successful in getting Morrison's original investment back from Chalvert, something he had been asked to do.[32]

The Lorenzo Durocher who was on the 1805 expedition from Santa Fe toward the Pawnee country was another frontiersman. He had left St. Louis for Santa Fe in 1804, possibly in the company of Jacques d'Eglise. Durocher was familiar with some of the Plains country from having been one of four men to share the Kansa trade monopoly in 1794. The commandant at St. Louis described him just prior to the trip as an older man "who knew how to go."[33]

His companion, Jacques d'Eglise, was another experienced hand. As early as 1790 he had a license to hunt on the Missouri River, and in 1791 he traveled to the Mandan villages on the Upper Missouri. He appears to have been the first Spanish subject to have done so. He made subsequent trips to the north each year from 1792 to 1795. His expedition to Santa Fe was less successful, for he was murdered there in 1806. His killers, Antonio Carabajal and Mariano Venavides, were executed in 1809.[34]

All of these men appear to have gone to New Mexico via one or another of the Pawnee villages, and most probably used the Pawnee Trail. The letter that DeLassus, commander at St. Louis, wrote to the governor of Louisiana states that Baptiste Laland and Jeaunot Metoyer were to meet Chalvert at a Pawnee village in 1804.[35]

The other Frenchmen and the American who accompanied Vial's unsuccessful 1805 expedition arrived in Santa Fe by a separate route. They were Dionisio Lacroix, Andrés Terrien, and James Purcell. Fur traders in the employ of Régis Loisel, they had gone up the Missouri River in 1804 to its headwaters. From there, they went to the headwaters of the South Platte to trap. There they were attacked by Kiowas and robbed of everything they had. Eventually they arrived in Santa Fe in the company of some Arapaho chiefs.

The governor sent all of these men with Vial on the 1805 expedition. Vial and Chalvert were to go to the Pawnees to try to apprehend Lewis and Clark, while the others were to go on to St. Louis to spy out the situation there: "On this occasion, Durocher and Lalande leave for their country, and the two other Frenchmen also go back, each with ideas of returning, and those who accomplish it will be able to give me interesting news."[36] With the failure of the expedition, all remained in New Mexico, where Zebulon Pike eventually encountered several of them.

—Facundo Melgares, 1806

The failure of two successive expeditions under Pedro Vial generated a final, gigantic effort. In 1806 Lieutenant Facundo Melgares was sent north with sixty soldiers to reinforce the Spanish garrison of New Mexico. He soon set out for the Plains with five hundred men (105 of whom were regular soldiers) and more than two thousand horses and mules. His orders were to intercept the Lewis and Clark expedition before it left Spanish territory. Unfortunately the diary and map of this expedition have been lost, and we have just the records of the Pike expedition as a primary source of information. Luckily, when Pike was arrested in New Mexico, he was entrusted to the care of Lieutenant Melgares for the long journey into Mexico, and as a result of the friendly interaction of the two men, Pike included an approximation of the route Melgares took in the map of this own expedition (Figure 4.8).

The map shows that Melgares headed east from Taos to the headwaters of the Canadian River. Melgares followed that river south and then east before crossing to the Red River, which he followed to a Taovayas village. Pike's map of this part of the expedition is incomplete; following the earlier Humboldt map, it conflates the upper Canadian (called the Río Rojo in New Mexico) with the Red River of Louisiana. The trek to the Red River was made in order to intercept the Dunbar expedition, but it was turned back by other Spanish forces.[37]

From the Taovayas village, Melgares headed north and then northwest on a less-known route to reach the Arkansas River near the mouth of Coon Creek. One portion of the trail he was following was recorded on surveyors' maps north of what is now Sun City, Kansas. From the Medicine Lodge River, the trail runs north along Turkey Creek and then turns to the northwest, toward a ford of the Arkansas River just outside present-day Kinsley. Melgares then took the Arkansas River Trail downstream to Great Bend, whence he followed the Pawnee Trail northward to a Pawnee village in Webster County, Nebraska.

After negotiating with the Pawnees, Melgares retraced his steps back to Great Bend. Cook argues that he aborted the attempt to arrest Lewis

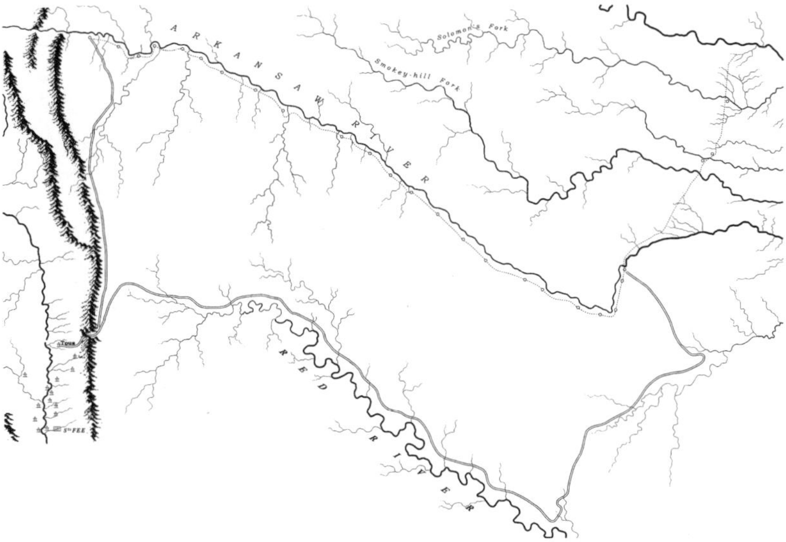

FIGURE 4.8 The Pike/Nau map showing the route of Facundo Melgares. Because Nau used the earlier Humboldt map as a base for his depiction of the Southwest, the Canadian River is conflated with the Red River, making it difficult to trace the middle portion of Melgares' route (from the 1810 report of the expedition).

and Clark because of resistance on the part of the Pawnees.[38] From Great Bend, Melgares followed the soon-to-be Santa Fe Trail into Colorado and then southwest to New Mexico. When Zebulon Pike eventually reached the Pawnee village, he found the Spanish flag flying above the chief's lodge. The Pawnees were most reluctant to replace the Spanish flag with the American flag that Pike gave them, having been far more impressed by Melgares and his men than by Pike and his little band.

—Zebulon Pike, 1806

Zebulon Pike led an expedition of exploration across the Plains in 1806, and his account of the adventure became a best-seller when published in 1810. It has been republished several times with scholarly annotations,[39] and attempts to trace his route are almost a cottage industry in the region he traversed. Yet while Pike is easily the most famous of the people to use the Pawnee Trail, it is difficult to find recognition of the native trail in the histories of his expedition.

Pike's party assembled in St. Louis in the summer of 1806. While he was there, he gathered information about the country he would be exploring

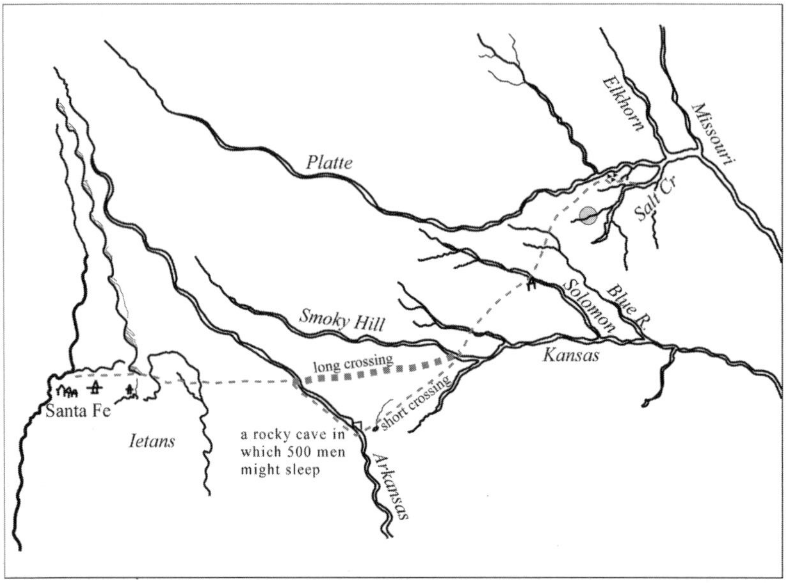

FIGURE 4.9 An interpretation of the Cardinal map. This map was drawn for Zebulon Pike by French traders in St. Louis before Pike set out across the plains. The details clearly are based on prior expeditions to Santa Fe (map by author).

from experienced hands, just as Lewis and Clark had done a few years earlier. One of the products of this effort is a map that is annotated in Pike's hand but which was apparently drawn with the guidance of a trio of Frenchmen whose names appear on it. They are Polite Cardinal, Jean Marie Cardinal, and Joseph Tibedeaux. For simplicity, I call it the Cardinal map.

The map is crudely drawn, with north to the left. Figure 4.9 is a cleaned-up version with legible labels.[40] It shows a trail, depicted as a dotted line that runs from Salt Creek in Nebraska to the south bank of the Platte River, near a native village depicted by three triangles. From there, it runs along the right bank of the Platte to the vicinity of the mouth of the Loup River, where it gradually swings south to cross both forks of the Blue River. Where it crosses the Republican River, a building is drawn that is similar to symbols used to depict Santa Fe and other settlements in New Mexico elsewhere on the map. This probably is a depiction of the Republican Pawnee village near the mouth of White Rock Creek.

From this village, the trail heads west for a little way and then swings to a more southerly direction to cross both the Solomon River and a stream labeled "Fork of S. Hill." Vial followed this same route in 1793. At the Smoky Hill, the trail splits, with one branch, labeled "Short Crossing," passing the west side of the Cheyenne Bottom to reach the "Arkansaw" at what is clearly Great Bend. This branch of the trail crosses the river at that point and follows the south or right bank to a meeting point with the other branch of the trail.

The latter, marked "Long Crossing," is marked as requiring eighteen days. No stream crossings are shown for this section of the trail, making any interpretation of it very difficult. Once it crosses the Arkansas and joins the other trail, however, its identity becomes clear. This portion of the route is the same as that taken by Pedro Vial in 1793: down the series of trails that became the Fort Supply, Dodge City–Tascosa, and Fort Smith–Sante Fe wagon roads in later years. Understanding the route clarifies the identities of the towns shown in New Mexico. In addition to Santa Fe, they are San Miguel del Vado and Pecos Pueblo, with their respective streams depicted.

There is one error in the map. In the reach between the Republican and Arkansas rivers, a major stream is missing. The sequence of stream shown is Republican, Solomon, Fork of the Smoky Hill, and Arkansas. The actual sequence is: Republican, Solomon, Saline, Smoky Hill, Arkansas. Thus, the "Fork of the S. Hill" of the map is a conflation of the Smoky Hill River and the Saline River, which is a "Fork of the S. Hill."

It should be pointed out, however, that even though some of the details of the Cardinal map match Vial's 1793 route, one does not. Vial set out over land from the mouth of the Little Nemaha River in extreme southeastern Nebraska, while this map depicts a route leaving from the lower end of the Platte. Thus this map depicts the route of at least one French expedition between St. Louis and Santa Fe that must have postdated Vial's but was prior to 1806. The depiction of two alternative routes across central Kansas may have come from yet another expedition or from information provided by natives.

The identity of the Short Crossing is made clear by the depiction of the Cheyenne Bottom and the general trend of the Arkansas River at Great Bend. Another clue to the general placement of the Short Crossing is a mark on the north bank of the Arkansas River upstream from the crossing. It is labeled "a rocky cave in which 500 men might sleep." This is a reference to Pawnee Rock, where a fallen rock slab once formed a huge shelter. I learned this from a man who related a family story about two men named Schultz who took shelter in the cave during a blizzard. Historic quarrying has destroyed this feature.

Pike, when he finally set out for the Pawnee country, ended up taking a different route to another Pawnee village on the Republican River. Traveling with Osage guides from an Osage village in western Missouri, he followed one of their trails along the divide between the Little Osage and Marmiton rivers into Bourbon County, Kansas. From there they forded branches of the Neosho and Verdegris rivers, and crossed the Flint Hills, then went up the Cottonwood River and across another divide to the Smoky Hill River.[41]

Eventually Pike arrived at the Pawnee village now known as the Hill site.[42] Here he browbeat the Pawnees into lowering the Spanish flag given to them by Melgares, and replacing it with an American flag. Judging from the tone of the interaction, the Pawnees probably shifted back to the Spanish banner as soon as Pike was out of sight. Just a few years ago, a Spanish flag was buried with an elderly Pawnee man, the property of his chiefly family that was kept a secret from outsiders because the family believed that "they were not supposed to have it."[43]

Many attempts have been made to trace Pike's route across the plains,[44] and it is only with a combination of Pike's journal, his daily maps of travel, the map drawn by Antoine Nau under Pike's direction, knowledge of the Pawnee Trail, and firsthand experience with the landscape that it can be followed precisely. Elliott Coues understood that he did not have all of this information and so considered his version of the route only a first approximation. "I understand that there was a certain 'Pawnee trail' once well known from this village to Great Bend on the Arkansas. If this be now determinable, it will represent Pike's route with a closer approximation to accuracy than I have been able to follow out."[45]

Pike's original route maps are difficult to interpret, and the map drawn for him by Antoine Nau (Figure 4.10) was done long after the fact, using a variety of other maps to fill in blanks, and with other errors along the route actually traveled. One of the most egregious of these errors lies just above the Great Bend of the Arkansas River. There Pike encountered the Cheyenne Bottom lowland while searching for the trail: "In the morning rode out in search of the south trace, and crossed the low prairie, which was nearly all covered with ponds."[46] The Nau map, however, shows this spot covered by a high ridge. This has to be an interpolation by Nau, and close inspection of the map shows that he used two shorthand symbols for the areas between streams. Between major streams, he drew chains of conical hills to represent the highest divides, and between other streams he drew plateau-like uplands. It is one of the latter forms that replace the Cheyenne Bottom, and the schematic nature of his depictions has led me to a new interpretation of the route.

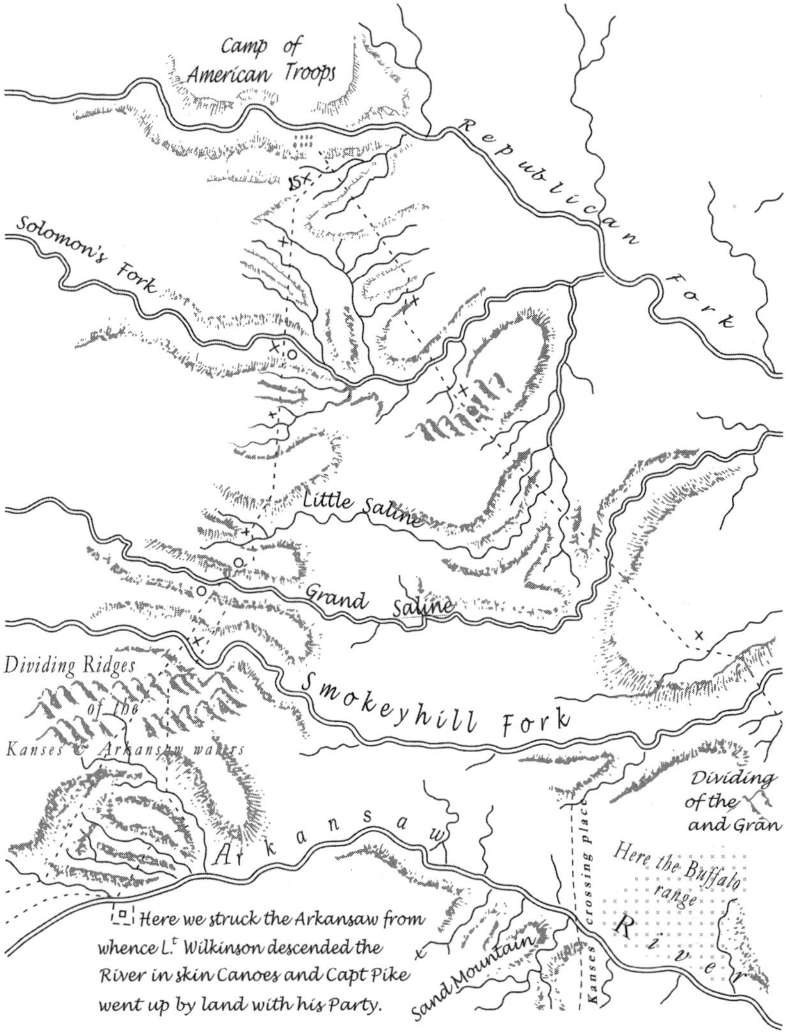

FIGURE 4.10 Pike's route across Kansas as mapped by Antoine Nau. The plateaus and lines of hills are conventions introduced by Nau and do not necessarily reflect the actual landscape (from the original report).

Rather than paying any attention to the uplands as Hart, Hulbert, and others did, I have focused on the depictions of stream crossings along the route actually traveled. Figure 4.11 compares the published Pike map to the Pawnee Trail and its vicinity. For ease of interpretation and explanation, it is divided into four sections, labeled "a" through "d." Section "a" covers the route from the Pawnee village on the Republican River to the crossing of the Solomon River at Waconda Lake. The Nau map traces the route from a crossing of White Rock Creek that is southeast from the village. At that point it runs west of south to cross three streams that Pike thought were tributary to the Solomon River. (Several such interpretations that he made are known to be gross errors). Because the Nau map shows the three streams crossed forming two major tributaries, with Pike traveling down the western one, several interpretations of the route have Pike coming down Oak Creek, which reaches the Solomon River right at the forks of the river, at the western end of Waconda Lake.[47] Such a route is not impossible, as the Pawnee sometimes used a ford upstream from Cawker City,[48] but an Oak Creek crossing does not fit with other details of the map. One counter argument is that, contra Hart and Hulbert,[49] Pike did not depict the forks of the Solomon. The North and South forks of the Solomon are nearly equal in size, but Pike depicts a single main stream and a much smaller stream to the south of it.

The next set of stream crossings fit perfectly the streams encountered south of the lake on the Pawnee Trail, and do not correspond well to the streams south of the spot where Hart and Hulbert place Pike's crossing. South of the Solomon River, the Nau map shows Pike crossing four small east-flowing streams (Figure 4.11b). These are Walnut Creek and three tributaries of Salt Creek. This is precisely the route of the Pawnee trail through the otherwise high and dry Blue Hills. This section of the trail also passes the single good spring in the area, which was recorded on the General Land Office survey map of the area. From the Salt Creek drainage, the trail swings toward the southwest to cross Spillman Creek just above its junction with Bacon Creek and then even more westerly to cross Wolf Creek.

Section "c" of Figure 4.11 shows a striking similarity between Pike's depiction of his own route as contrasted with that of Melgares and that of the Pawnee Trail. The Nau map shows Pike's route south from the Saline River as swinging a short distance to the southeast but then curving even more strongly to the west before reaching the Smoky Hill. This is where firsthand knowledge of the landscape comes in. Pike had lost the trail left by Melgares because the tracks of a large herd of bison had effectively erased it.[50] He reached the Saline River a bit east of where the Spaniards (whose camps are depicted on the Nau map) had crossed on the Pawnee Trail. Crossing instead at the site of the future Wilson Lake Dam, Pike was forced to travel around Hell Creek Canyon, which is essentially impassible when approached from the east. This explains the small detour shown on the Nau map, which Nau must have included at Pike's direction.

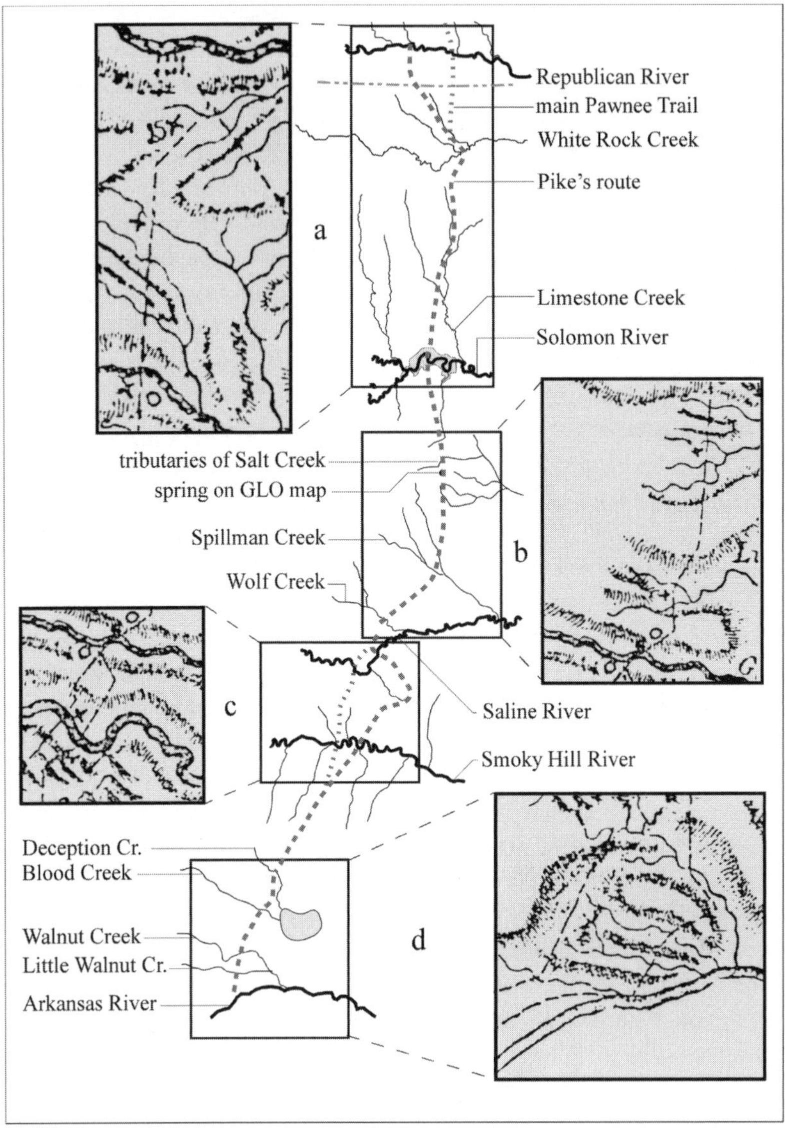

FIGURE 4.11 Pike's route and the Pawnee Trail. Shaded insets are sections of the Nau map, while the unshaded insets are from USGS topographic maps. The comparisons allow determination of the Pike route (map by author).

The last leg of Pike's trip south to the Arkansas River is the easiest to interpret. The Nau map shows him crossing four east-flowing streams, and there are only four creeks in the area: Deception, Blood, Walnut, and Little Walnut (figure 4.11, section "d"). From there Pike followed the Arkansas River west into the mountains of Colorado.

When Pike was eventually taken captive in New Mexico, Lieutenant Facundo Melgares took charge of the prisoner for the long trip to Mexico City. Pike obtained knowledge of the route Melgares took, but he never did learn that the objective of the Melgares expedition was Lewis and Clark, not Pike himself.[51] Apparently Melgares merely confirmed what Pike already believed about this.[52] That Melgares was capable of such misleading behavior is evident from his later interaction with David Meriwether, when he pretended not to know much about "Zebulondo" Pike (see below).

—Jacques Clamorgan, 1807

Pike was followed west by Jacques Clamorgan, a seventy-four-year-old pioneer of the St. Louis fur trade. In fact, Clamorgan, along with his partner, Manuel Lisa, was the dominant force in that trade. He had founded the Company of Explorers of the Upper Missouri (commonly abbreviated as the Missouri Company) in 1793.[53] The company, formed by an alliance of St. Louis traders in negotiations with Zenon Trudeau, governor of Spanish Illinois, had as its primary objectives the expansion of the St. Louis trade, defense of Spanish territory, and exploration of the Missouri country. Trudeau's superior, Baron Carondelet, spiced the pot with the offer of a prize of $2,000 to the first person to reach the Pacific Ocean via the Missouri River.[54]

As syndic of the Missouri Company, it was Clamorgan who had ultimate responsibility for the journeys of exploration and commerce made by Jean Baptiste Truteau, Jacques d'Eglise, James MacKay, and John Evans from 1793 to 1796. These were signal explorations of the region, and the information they garnered eventually passed to Lewis and Clark before they ascended the Missouri.

Clamorgan continued to be active in the Missouri River trade, reorganizing his company several times. By 1797 it was known as Clamorgan, Loisel and Company.[55] Gradually, however, British competition based in Canada and at Prairie du Chien began to cut into his profits. After the British acquired the allegiance of the Poncas and Omahas, these nations robbed Clamorgan's expeditions at every opportunity. The interference with the Spanish trade also served to limit the amount of trade goods reaching the enemy tribes upstream from the Poncas and Omahas. While Clamorgan had a supposed monopoly on the trade of all of the nations above the Kansas River with the single exception of the Pawnees in 1802 and 1803, he may have begun to look for other opportunities.

In 1804 Jacques d'Eglise left St. Louis for Santa Fe, and there is some reason to believe that he may have been in the employ of Clamorgan.[56] As reported above, d'Eglise remained in Santa Fe after the failure of the Vial expeditions against Lewis and Clark. Whether Clamorgan learned of this before his own expedition in 1807 is not clear, but by the time he arrived in Santa Fe, d'Eglise was dead.[57]

Clamorgan's party in 1807 consisted of himself, three Frenchmen, and a black slave. They had with them four mules laden with trade goods. From St. Louis, they are reported to have followed the Missouri River to the Platte, and to have ascended the Platte to the Pawnee villages.[58] From there, the account says only that they "cut across" to Santa Fe, but the primary route between those points in 1807 was the Pawnee Trail.

Clamorgan arrived in Santa Fe on December 12, 1807, but he and his party were soon sent to Chihuahua, as the Spanish country was closed to outside traders. Rather than being arrested as every other traveler since the time of the Mallet brothers had been, however, Jacques Clamorgan was allowed to sell his goods at a profit and to return home. He did so after a year, reaching Natchitoches via Texas in 1808. Surprisingly, accounts of this trip fail to attribute his friendly reception in Mexico to his earlier service to the Spanish crown.[59]

—Robert McKnight and James McLanahan, 1810

Two parties arrived in Santa Fe shortly after the publication of Pike's account of his expedition, and one or both of them may have used the Nau map to guide their travels. It, of course, would have taken them down the Pawnee Trail.

The first party, named for Robert McKnight, included also Samuel Chambers, James Baird, and Peter Baum.[60] Assuming that the Hidalgo revolution would succeed and so open Santa Fe to American trade, they traveled with goods they valued at $10,000 packed on six mules. When they arrived in Santa Fe on April 18, 1810, however, they were not only refused permission to trade, but their goods were impounded and they were imprisoned in Chihuahua. The charge against them was complicity in the Hidalgo revolution. Their property was used to pay for their keep in prison, at a rate of eighteen and a half cents per day.[61] They remained in prison for ten years, being freed only after the Iturbide revolution. In 1821 McKnight returned to the United States only to equip a second expedition with his brother, John. His brother returned to Missouri in company with the Jacob Fowler–Hugh Glenn party[62] but Robert McKnight returned to Mexico where he took citizenship. Baird and Chambers stayed in the United States and continued to be active in the Santa Fe and Chihuahua trade. Thomas James records that they left Santa Fe for Missouri in 1822, and over-wintered at the Arkansas River crossing. He says they eventually returned to Chihuahua on a subsequent expedition.[63]

The other party, under the leadership of James McLanahan, consisted of Reuben Smith, James Patterson, a guide named Manuel Blanco, and three black slaves.[64] Leaving St. Genevieve, a French village on the Mississippi below St. Louis, they were seventy-three days en route to Santa Fe. When they arrived there in February of 1810, they too were jailed and their goods confiscated. Unlike the McKnight party, however, they made no reference to the Hidalgo revolution, claiming instead that they were there to find a good place to settle. Perhaps because of this, they were jailed for only two years, and they returned to the United States in 1812.

—George Sibley, 1811

The Indian factor at Fort Osage since 1808, George Sibley made an expedition to establish a treaty between the South Band Pawnees and the Osages in 1811. He set out on May 11 with a party of fifteen people, including his servant, two interpreters, and eleven Osages.[65] Sibley's account of the trip describes both distances and directions for its various legs, but he is accurate in neither. Were not it for the fact that he visited some identifiable points, the route could not be interpreted at all.

On the first leg of the journey, he reported going "South 60° West, about 75 miles, along the Osage Summer hunting trace." From there, he went "North 70° West about 65 miles" to a Kansa village.[66] This took his party from western Missouri into southeastern Kansas and onto a native trail that followed the crest of the Flint Hills Trail to the Kansa village in the vicinity of present day Manhattan, Kansas. This is one of the well-documented spots along his itinerary.

From the Kansa village, Sibley went "North 40° West, about 120 miles" to the Pawnee village at Horse Creek, 25NC2.[67] The actual distance is about 170 miles, and the trail he would have followed is the one that later became part of the Oregon Trail, the same one that Dr. Wislizenus traveled in 1839.

From the Pawnee village, Sibley went to a summer hunting camp of the Little Osages. He gives the direction and distance as South 16° East, about 175 miles. Both direction and distance are off, and the direction may be a mistranscription for S16°W. Luckily, Sibley mentions using a ford of the Platte upstream from the one used on his approach to the Pawnees. He also mentions crossing the Republican River at a point about sixty miles from the Pawnee village. Judging from all of the available evidence, it was instead sixty miles from the crossing of the Platte, at Guide Rock on the Pawnee Trail.

Sibley next mentions moving from the Smoky Hill River to the Arkansas in a distance of about thirty-five miles. On the Pawnee Trail, the distance is around thirty-two miles, and the topography fits his description as well. "From where we crossed the Konsee to the Arkansas, it is about thirty-five miles and the country is much more level and less interesting."[68] This portion of his journey would have taken him in an arc around the west side of the Cheyenne Bottom, a country that is indeed low-lying and level. Clearly, he was on the Pawnee Trail. This portion of his route is shown on the Cardinal map, as mentioned above.

The day before he arrived at the Arkansas River at Great Bend, Sibley encountered a Kansa hunting camp on a small creek. This is likely to have been Walnut Creek, which the trail crosses several miles upstream from its mouth. The next day, apparently having traveled downstream on the Arkansas River Trail, Sibley found the hunting camp of the Little Osages. This appears to have been near the mouth of Salt Creek, at the spot marked "Kansa Crossing" on the published Pike map and the very same spot that the Miguel map of 1602 shows as the crossing spot of a trail that runs south to the Great Salt Flat in Oklahoma.

This, in fact, was Sibley's itinerary for the rest of his trip. He headed across the Arkansas and south, eventually visiting both the Great Salt Flats and the Rock Saline of the Cimarron River. From there he returned to Fort Osage, completing a trip of about a thousand miles in two months.

—David Meriwether, 1820

The story of one person's use of the Pawnee Trail is limited to a single account, an autobiography.[69] For that reason, and because the autobiography is filled with stories in which the author emerges as a hero, some doubt must be cast on it. On the other hand, the author was an extraordinary person whose career on the frontier began early and lasted long.

He was David Meriwether, born in Virginia in 1800 and raised since

1805 in Kentucky. When he was only fourteen, he was invited by John O'Fallon to accompany him up the Missouri River. O'Fallon was the sutler for the Yellowstone Expedition headed by Stephen Long and Henry Atkinson. During the expedition, Meriwether served as an assistant to O'Fallon and his partner Lewis Bissell, both as sutler and as an independent trader to the natives.

Meriwether reports accompanying an expedition to the Pawnees in about 1820. While in the Pawnee village, he participated in the ransom of a Spanish boy who was scheduled to be sacrificed to the Morning Star. Meriwether's account of this incident has him playing a larger role than is evident in other versions.[70]

Also absent from the other accounts is any mention of the boy's father, but Meriwether reports that he was also a captive among the Pawnees. This man reported having found some gold northeast of New Mexico, and this led Meriwether to propose to his employers that he accompany a Pawnee war party to New Mexico. They agreed, and Meriwether returned to the Pawnee village with a black servant named Alfred. There they joined a seventeen-man war party under the leadership of Big Elk, and began the long walk to New Mexico.

Meriwether's description of the route they used is unfortunately brief, saying only that, "We ascended the valley of the Arkansas for about a week when we forded the stream, which was very wide but shallow, and very soon came into sandy, arid country, where game appeared less numerous."[71]

The general description of the landscape is obviously accurate, but the lack of any landmarks other than the Arkansas River would make the route impossible to ascertain if it were not for the fact that Meriwether later returned to the Plains. Three decades later, Meriwether returned to New Mexico by the Santa Fe Trail. Near the Aubry crossing, he recognized the landscape and said that it lay only a short distance east of the route taken by the Pawnee war party.

Aubry's crossing is in eastern Hamilton County, Kansas, about four miles from its eastern border. A week or so of travel eastward, at the average rate of twenty miles per day, is Great Bend at the southern terminus of the Pawnee Trail. The clear correspondence between Meriwether's otherwise vague description and these two known locations offers substantial support to his story.

Having crossed the Arkansas, the Pawnee war party continued south on what was later called the Cimarron Cutoff of the Santa Fe Trail to the Canadian River. There they spotted tracks of men and horses, and because the Pawnees did not take what he considered sensible precautions, Meriwether and Alfred slept apart from them. At dawn, the Pawnee camp was attacked by Spaniards, and most of the men were killed.[72] Having become separated from the war party, Meriwether felt safe in approaching the Spaniards only to be arrested and taken in chains to Santa Fe. There he was questioned by Facundo Melgares, who by then was the governor of New Mexico. According to Meriwether, the interrogation included questions about the expedition of one Zebulondo Pike.[73] Meriwether had no way of knowing of Melgares' expedition to the Pawnees by about the same route he had followed with the Pawnees, nor did he have any inkling that it was Melgares who accompanied the captive Pike to Mexico.

Melgares released Meriwether only when he promised to leave New Mexico and never to return. He and Alfred rejoined the survivors of the Pawnee war party and headed north rather than returning by their original route. They did so in the hope of finding more game than they could farther out on the plains in winter. Even so, they eventually had to hole up in a rock-shelter near a tributary of the South Platte somewhere in Colorado. Here they waited out the worst weather, then descended the Platte to the Pawnee villages.

In a wonderful irony, Meriwether did eventually break his promise to Melgares never to return to New Mexico. First he returned to Kentucky where he entered politics. As a U.S. senator he was involved in discussions regarding the border with Mexico. After retiring from politics, he returned once to Washington to attend the inaugural of Franklin Pierce. While visiting with the new president, the subject of the border came up, and Meriwether's knowledge of it was impressive enough to cause Pierce to name him the first territorial governor of New Mexico. Meriwether accepted only after the president convinced him that he was going to American New Mexico, not Spanish New Mexico, and he therefore was technically being true to his promise.

—William and Paul Anderson, 1822

In the 1820s, the Santa Fe Trail came into existence, connecting the American frontier to the newly independent nation of Mexico. Where Spain had inhibited trade between New Mexico and the east, Mexico welcomed it. Much has been written about this trade,[74] but here we will concentrate on its effect on travel along the Pawnee Trail.

Immediately upon William Becknell's return from his first expedition to New Mexico with a profit big enough to wipe out all his previous debts,[75] the Missouri business community was abuzz with the news. In September of 1822, the *Missouri Intelligencer* of Franklin, Missouri, reported that a company of some fifty persons was on its way to Santa Fe. Among them was James Baird, formerly of the McKnight party, and the brothers William and Paul Anderson. Their route to Santa Fe is nowhere described, and the only clues to it are how long it took, some caches they created on the Arkansas River, and the fact that they returned to Council Bluffs rather than to St. Louis.

They left St. Louis on September 3 but did not reach New Mexico until February 2. This is 142 days, which, at the usual rate of travel for long expeditions of twenty miles per day, is time enough for them to have gone 2,840 miles. This is much farther than the distance from Franklin to Santa Fe and may indicate a roundabout route. An 1825 expedition from Council Bluffs to Taos took only fifty-six days, and adding three days for the trip from Taos to Santa Fe leaves eighty-three days unaccounted for. Since it is nearly as far from Council Bluffs to Santa Fe as it is from St. Louis, it should be clear that these men did not take the direct route.

On the other hand, they did run into a blizzard that killed their mules, and they had to finish the journey on foot. When this happened, they had to store their goods, and the pits they dug became a landmark for later travelers on the Santa Fe trail. Known simply as The Caches, this spot was a few miles west of present Dodge City, near several of the crossing points for the Cimarron Cutoff. Once the goods were safely hidden away, the trip from the caches to Santa Fe took only fifteen days.

Their luck did not change, however. A letter from Wilson McGunnegle, one of their companions, to the St. Louis *Missouri Republican* reported that he and the Andersons bought replacement animals in New Mexico and hired some local men to help them recover the goods. Back near the caches, they were attacked by Pawnees who killed one of the Spaniards and made off with all of their animals. This forced another "pedestrian tour of fifteen days." Only later in the spring were they able to recover the trade goods, and the gaping holes they left in the river bank reminded later travelers of the incident[76].

In Taos the Andersons dissolved the partnership with William Loughlin and Wilson McGunnegle. This was in September 1823, and the Andersons may have returned almost immediately. Thus Bartholomew Berthold wrote to Bernard Pratte and Company on November 14 that the firm of Tracy and Wahrendorff received beaver furs from McGunnegle and the Andersons.[77] Whether the Andersons actually returned at this time is not certain because in 1824 Jean Pierre Cabanné wrote to Pierre Chouteau that the Andersons and one Hubert had returned from Santa Fe with beaver.

What makes this letter intriguing is that Cabanné was at his "Establishment at the Bluffs" in eastern Nebraska, and Chouteau was in St. Louis. Thus, Hubert and the Andersons had gone from Santa Fe to Nebraska rather than to Missouri. This is some of the first clear documentation of the branch of the Santa Fe trade that came from the vicinity of Council Bluffs rather than Missouri. It also ties the Anderson brothers to the French Company, which was to dominate this part of the trade. The route it used was up the Platte to the Pawnees, then down the Pawnee Trail to the main Santa Fe Trail at Great Bend.

—The French Company, 1823–1825

Bernard Pratte and Company was part of the French fur trade fraternity on the Missouri River. David Weber's 1971 book *The Taos Trappers* details how Pratte and a host of his compatriots dominated the fur trade between Santa Fe and Council Bluffs during its brief lifespan. Pratte's man at Council Bluffs was Cabanné, but beginning in 1822 the Roubidoux clan that was to figure so prominently in the trade began arriving at the outpost. The first to arrive was Joseph Roubidoux, the oldest of six brothers, who was employed at the Oto post near Council Bluffs in 1822.[78] He was joined by his brothers François, Isidore, Antoine, Louis, and Michel, and soon there was a more or less continuous traffic of Roubidoux men passing along the Pawnee and Santa Fe trails.

It has been claimed that this began as early as 1822, but no substantial evidence exists for it until late 1823 or 1824. At the end of 1825, Louis Roubidoux claimed that he had been living in Taos for two years.[79] The 1824 expedition is better documented. In February 1824, Antoine Roubidoux obtained a permit to travel "in the direction of Santa Fe." An expedition later that year included François and Isidore Roubidoux, Antonio LaMarche, José Martin, Joseph Gervais, Astasio [Anastasio?] Lasalle, Charles Hotte, François Laroque, François Quenelle, Joseph Decary, Antoine Beacheam, and Manuel Alvarez. Since "Gervais" was one of the common spellings of Joseph Chalvert's name, one wonders whether this individual might not be Joseph Chalvert's oldest son, the one taken to New Mexico by Melgares.

Thereafter, the traffic was frenetic. On March 15, 1825, Joseph reported the return of Michel with thirty packs of beaver. Isidore and Antoine returned east and had obtained another permit to travel to Mexico on June 25, 1825, and other brothers returned in August. Still another party left Council Bluffs on September 30 of that year for Taos.[80] The intensity of the traffic seems to have faded after 1825, but it was in the context of the

French Company travels that two other expeditions were made between Santa Fe and Council Bluffs.

—The Mexican Expedition of 1824

The reaction of the Pawnee nation to the opening of the Santa Fe Trail appears to have been schizophrenic. On the one hand, it generated the fur-trade traffic that passed through their villages. There is absolutely no evidence that they offered any opposition to this. On the other hand, the main traffic passed along the route between Westport and Santa Fe, far to the south. This was Pawnee hunting land, but the Pawnees received no gifts from the travelers who hunted their game, and no one even asked their permission. For this reason, the name Pawnee came to be feared by all of the Santa Fe traders.

Those traders gradually had come to include Mexican entrepreneurs as well as people from the Missouri frontier,[81] and the Mexican traders based in Santa Fe and Chihuahua decided to resolve the Pawnee problem through a treaty with them, an idea that never seems to have occurred to the American traders based in Missouri. In 1824 Governor Bartolomé Baca wrote to the Indian agent for the United States, Benjamin O'Fallon, who was stationed at Council Bluffs. He indicated that two commissioners would leave Santa Fe in May and would need O'Fallon's help in dealing with the Pawnees.[82]

The expedition that eventually arrived there consisted of twenty-six men. Because a direct approach to the hostile Pawnees was impossible, they appear to have first traveled up the Santa Fe Trail to Westport and thence up the Missouri River to O'Fallon's headquarters at Council Bluffs. The Pawnee delegates appear to have traveled to Council Bluffs to make the treaty because in September O'Fallon authorized the payment of $39 to men named Charleville and Moreau for services rendered to the native deputation.[83] The Spanish delegation left Council Bluffs on September 11, 1824, and their return route probably was down the Pawnee Trail. The trail provided almost a beeline route back to the main branch of the Santa Fe Trail at Great Bend.

—James O. Pattie, 1825

In 1825, the much maligned James Ohio Pattie used part of the Pawnee Trail to go to Santa Fe. Pattie was a frontiersman whose name is remembered because of a book of his reminiscences that was published in 1830.

In that year, he showed up penniless in the office of an Ohio publisher, Timothy Flint. There his offer to sell the story of his travels in the West was accepted. Unfortunately for Pattie's reputation, he chose the wrong publisher.

Flint had previously published a novel about the West even though he had never been there. When Pattie's scribbled story turned out to be too scanty in terms of pages and high adventure for the audience that Flint envisioned, he embellished it with additions of his own invention. The most salacious involved the rescue of the naked daughter of the governor of New Mexico from hostile natives, an adventure that Flint cribbed from his own novel. It is only recently that Flint's own story has been separated from Flint's inventions so that Pattie's reputation could be restored.

In 1824 Pattie accompanied his father and several other men on an expedition up the Missouri with the intent of trading with the native nations there. They had no license for this trade, however, and at Council Bluffs O'Fallon denied them permission to go upriver. Luckily, however, Pattie's father had become acquainted with Sylvester Pratte of the French Company, and so he headed west to the Pawnee villages to join Pratte's men on one of their trips to Santa Fe. Trading there did not require a license from the U.S. government.

They visited the South Band villages on the Platte and may have gone to the Skiri village as well. (The book includes the story of a visit to a Pawnee village where they ransomed a boy scheduled for the Morning Star sacrifice, and it was the Skiri who performed the Morning Star ritual.) According to Pattie, the expedition that eventually headed south included 116 men with three hundred mules and a few horses.[84] Pattie says that his father was elected to head the caravan, but this seems unlikely given the prior experience of the men from the French Company. Perhaps this claim is one of Flint's inventions. In spite of the uncertainties about the accuracy of such information, Pattie's description of the trip is valuable because it is the only account of an expedition that followed a route similar to the "Long Crossing" of the Cardinal sketch map.

The caravan left the Pawnee villages in early August 1824. The first night out they camped on the banks of a creek, but the next evening, they were forced to have a dry camp. These events parallel those of the last Omaha bison hunt[85] and place them on a branch of the Pawnee Trail near Hastings, Nebraska. Later they camped beside Waconda Spring.[86] For the most part, however, the camping spots are not identifiable because Pattie does not give either distances traveled or directions. Furthermore, he (or Flint) seems to have used a copy of the Nau map of the Pike expedition as a reference, because after leaving Waconda Spring, he reports that they camped on one of the forks of the Osage. An error present in the Pike map would account for this otherwise improbable statement.

The next identifiable spot on their itinerary was at a spring that Pattie called Bellefontaine (perhaps a name in use by the men of the French Company). This campsite is identifiable because Pattie described it as running near the base of a column of stone eighty to ninety feet high that stood on level ground. There were other columns in the vicinity, but this one stood a bit apart from the rest. It is part of Castle Rock in Gove County, Kansas. I have visited the spot, and the course of the spring-fed rivulet, now dry, can still be discerned at the base of the rock pillar.

The Castle Rock campsite is adjacent to the Smoky Hill Trail of later years. Pedro de Villasur had traveled this route 104 years previously on his way to the disaster at the forks of the Loup and Platte rivers. From there, Pattie's expedition cut across the divide to the Arkansas River somewhere downstream from the Cimarron Crossing of the Santa Fe Trail.

On the Arkansas River they encountered Comanches and "Iotans." Since "Iotan" is an obvious derivative of "Ietan," a Wichita word for the Comanches, Pattie was confused about the identity of the people he met. He may have encountered several Comanche groups. After the meeting, Pattie's caravan crossed the river and traversed the dry sandy country to the south to reach the springs of the "Simaronee," the Cimarron River. At this point, and for the rest of the trip to Santa Fe, they were on the Cimarron Cutoff of the Santa Fe Trail.

This record, confused as it is, is the only one that describes this way of getting to Santa Fe. It may have been used on a regular basis by the expeditions of the French Company, since it is likely that its experienced voyageurs were guiding the Pattie expedition.

—Charles Augustus Murray, 1835

In 1835 Charles Augustus Murray, cadet son of a prominent Scottish family, toured the United States. Like so many other Europeans in this period, he was drawn to the Great Plains. While he was visiting Fort Leavenworth, he met some South Band Pawnees and joined them for a bison hunt. They guided him to the rest of their people, who had already set out on the annual summer hunt.

Traveling with his Scottish servant, John, a German named Vernuft, and an American boy, John Hardy, the Pawnees led him northwest from Fort Leavenworth, across the Big Nemaha and on to a ford of the Big Blue

River. When they reached the Republican River, probably near the mouth of White Rock Creek, they followed the river upstream until they met the South Band Pawnees.[87]

Once his party had joined the main Pawnee group, Murray no longer recorded his movements in any detail. The Pawnees appear to have hunted that year on the headwaters of the Kansas River system, but there are only two clues regarding the location of the hunt. Murray[88] describes seeing from a distance a fringe of timber lining the Arkansas River, suggesting that the southern extent of the hunt was the divide between the drainages of the Smoky Hill and Arkansas Rivers. The other clue is his description of a shaly height of land from which iron concretions the size of thirty-two-pound shot were eroding.[89] This probably was near the *Hañtso p'a,* or "Cannonball River" of the Kiowa.[90] The iron concretions are found in exposures of the Blue Hill Shale member of the Carlile Shale of north-central Kansas. "Even the most casual observer cannot fail to be impressed by the number and size of the concretions that stud the slopes of every large exposure of Blue Hill Shale."[91]

The Blue Hill shale outcrops widely, but concretions that fit the description of thirty-two-pound shot are not overly common within it. The concretions that best fit Murray's description occur in southern Osborne County and southwestern Mitchell County, where there is a zone of large, nearly spherical concretions.[92] That is, the shot-like concretions are to be found along the Pawnee Trail south of Waconda Lake. This placement fits the fact that Murray reports the concretions prior to reporting having seen the Arkansas River from a distance.

Murray recorded direct observations of the Pawnee Trail only after he was expelled from the company of the Pawnee. He had managed to insult the head chief, not just once, but on a continuing basis. Finally the chief put him and his companions in the charge of a guide and told them to leave. This happened on August 11, 1835.

Murray's party started out toward the northeast from the Pawnee hunting camp. As they rode, they twice encountered small parties of Pawnees who were not participating in the main hunt, an indication that they were following a main trail. At this time they were near the Smoky Hill River.

After crossing a high divide, the Pawnee guide pointed out the "Snake River" to Murray, a stream that they were about to cross. When they reached it, the water turned out to be salty, which helps to identify it as the Saline River. This stream turns notably salty only downstream from Paradise Creek, just above Wilson Lake and the Pawnee Trail. Then when traveling down a narrow, rocky canyon to the river, Murray reported seeing more rattlesnakes concentrated there than he believed could ever be found in one spot. This was in one of the little canyons that feed into the Saline River south of Wilson Lake, canyons that are marked by cairns of stones at their mouths.[93] This charming spot and its reptilian inhabitants may explain the Mallet brothers' name for the Saline River—the River of Worries.

At the river, their Pawnee guide abandoned them, leaving Murray and his companions to make their own way back to Fort Leavenworth. At first they had a great deal of difficulty with the hummocky ground in the immediate vicinity of Wilson Lake Dam, but eventually Murray had the good sense to find and follow the Pawnee Trail. This led to good fords of the streams they had to cross, and eventually it took them to a cross trail that they followed to the east. Murray was able to identify it as the route they had taken westward from Fort Leavenworth when he found a piece of a London paper that he had dropped on their outward trip.[94]

—Native Americans 1835–1868

The fur trade along the Santa Fe Trail rapidly ended when fashions in Europe changed, and beaver pelts were no longer in demand. After 1835, traffic along the Pawnee Trail seems to have been reduced primarily to Native Americans. Between 1825 and the 1870s, when the Pawnees abandoned their ancestral land in Nebraska for a reservation in Oklahoma, there was a gradual encroachment on their territory by Sioux and Cheyenne bands. The only oral traditions of Native American use of the trail that survive in the Waconda Lake area are by the Sioux and Cheyenne.

It seems also to have been used by the Kiowas. Mooney's analysis of the Kiowa winter count indicates use of the Pawnee Trail near Waconda Lake by this nation. In 1852, the Kiowas joined the Cheyennes in an attack on the Pawnee while the latter were on their summer bison hunt, a confrontation won by the Pawnee.[95] The Kiowa camp prior to this incident was on the Black River, a stream that flowed from the Black Hills. This was the name given by the Kiowas to the portion of the Blue Hills that lie between the Solomon (Hañtso p'a) and the Saline (Hotgyäsím p'a) rivers. The Black River, therefore, is either Salt Creek or Spillman Creek. From that camp, the Kiowas moved to join the Cheyennes who were on the Solomon River.

Later, during the native resistance to encroaching white settlers, the Pawnee Trail was used again. In the Cheyenne raid of 1868, two young girls were captured near what is now Beloit. They were Maggie Bell, age six, and Esther Bell, age eight, the daughters of Aaron Bell. The Cheyennes later abandoned the girls on the prairie near the Saline River. There the youngsters wandered for several days before being found six miles above the mouth of Spillman Creek. The man who found them took them to Fort Harker, whence word was sent to their parents. Whit McConnell[96] went with their father and other men to pick them up, taking a wagon as far as the Saline River.

In none of the accounts of this incident is the Pawnee Trail mentioned, yet it is likely that it was followed both by the Cheyennes and by the whites. The Pawnee Trail swings west after crossing Spillman Creek, so the girls ended up in a spot close to the trail. More evidence of use of the trail during the conflicts of the 1860s is cited in chapter 7. Until a railroad was built through Mitchell County, settlers there continued to use the trail, taking their wagons over it to Wilson, the nearest railhead. The wagon tracks still visible on the Debert farm south of the lake are the only trace of this activity left today.

—The Pawnees, 1874

The last recorded use of the trail is the saddest. In 1874 the Pawnees reluctantly gave up their Nebraska homeland to move to Indian Territory in what is now Oklahoma. They had been under increasing pressure from white settlers, and a combination of reservation policy and Sioux harassment had made their position untenable. So, late in 1874, they began to move south. The largest group of Pawnee migrants was accompanied by John Williamson, and he left an account of the trip that gives enough details to show that they were on the Pawnee Trail for the first portion of the trip. His account was never published, but Blaine[97] extracts the pertinent details.

They went south from Grand Island and reached the Republican River near Red Cloud, in the vicinity of the village visited by Pike. Then they descended to the Solomon, crossing that stream at a ford eight miles or so west of Cawker City. The next stream mentioned is Wolf Creek, north of what is now Wilson Lake. The crossing of the Saline River is not mentioned, but a stay near the town of Bunker Hill is related because a prominent warrior, Spotted Horse, died there. From this spot, the Pawnees went south to the Arkansas River at Great Bend. For this portion of the route, with the exception of the crossing of the Solomon west of Cawker City, the Pawnees seem to have been on the trail that bears their name.

South of Great Bend, however, they veered southwest instead of traveling southeast on Miguel's Trail toward the Great Salt Flat in Oklahoma.

The Pawnees had intended to travel a westerly route in the hope of finding some bison to hunt, and white horse thieves who stole a part of their herd also happened to go in that direction. The Pawnees had no problem tracking their stolen horses through the sand hills south of the Arkansas, and they eventually caught up with the thieves when they were attempting to drive the horses across a fast-flowing stream. The only significant stream in the region is Rattlesnake Creek, and at this point the Pawnees were approximately on the route that Melgares took northward in 1806.

The next named spot on their route was the Medicine Lodge River at Sun City. They camped in a protected spot on the south side of the river there and waited out a blizzard. The same protected spot, at the mouth of Elk Creek, was where the Mallet brothers crossed in 1739. Indeed, the Pawnees seem to have followed the same trail that the Mallets took southwest to the Cimarron, because the next spot mentioned in the account of the Pawnee Trail of Tears is the area around Camp Supply in Oklahoma. Following the Mallets' route would have taken them to what was to become the Camp Supply Trail running across the Cimarron River south of Ashland, Kansas.

—Summary

This review of the use of the Pawnee Trail in the period 1541 to 1874 shows its importance to the history of its region. In the span of nearly three centuries, almost every important European visitor to the region had some connection with the trail. Many of their stories are interconnected in various ways because this was the primary route of travel. Only after 1821, with the opening of the wagon road between Missouri and Santa Fe, did the Pawnee Trail start to become eclipsed. Even so, Euro-American use of the trail did not taper off until the collapse of the fur trade in 1835. The wagon ruts at the Walnut Creek crossing indicate that even later, during the early days of settlement, there was still occasional use of the trail.

5. Holy Ground

IN THIS CHAPTER, we will be examining a kind of geography for which our modern, mostly secular lives do not prepare us. It is a geography based on a very different cosmology than ours, and it is a geography in which features of the landscape have varying degrees of sacredness and morals to teach. This is not to say that we do not have our own sacred places, but for most American Christians, Muslims, and Jews, sacred sites lie across the ocean. Of course we do have sacred man-made structures that we visit, but that is not the same thing as living inside a sacred landscape. We also have some historic sites that have an aura of sacredness, battlegrounds mostly, where some of us do ponder moral lessons. But again, it's not quite the same thing. Neither are the wilderness tracts that we preserve with a quasi-religious respect.

—Native American Cosmology

To understand the geography, we need first to consider Native American cosmology. "Cosmologies" would be a better word, given the diversity of beliefs in Native North America, but there is some underlying uniformity within the diversity, and that will suffice for the level of explanation we need.

Picture this world as an island, surrounded by the primordial sea. It grew from a tiny bit of clay brought to the surface by a diving animal at the request of the creator. This is the earth-diver story, common to many Native American societies. Above this world is the sky world in which live the spirits of the sun, moon, stars, and planets. It is an orderly and predictable place, and humans need the help of the sky spirits to maintain a semblance of order in this much more messy world. Some native nations and parts of nations were founded when their ancestors descended from the sky. The Awatixa Hidatsas[1] and the Star That Came to Earth clan of the Osages[2] are examples. Humans can communicate with the sky world, especially at places where the earth reaches toward the sky or where the sky world is reflected in water. They can also send prayers via smoke (especially tobacco smoke), arrows shot high into the sky, and via the highest-flying birds such as hawks and eagles. The sky spirits in return may send down, or come down as, rain and meteorites.

The underworld houses a different set of spirits, but they are not essentially evil. They are opposed to the powers of the sky, however. This is why Hidatsa potters set their newly formed vessels to dry inside the lodge; pottery making has to do with the materials and sprits of the underworld, and if drying pots were set outside, the hawks would see and resent them and cause them to crack.[3] Some native nations, such as the Hopi, claim descent from ancestors who once lived in the underworld.[4]

Most of the spirits of the underworld are the spirits that animate the various species of animals. Such spirits are powerful, and they can take human lives. But they can also give humans the power to cure disease. The most powerful spirit of the underworld is usually termed a monster in English—a chimera with the parts of various kinds of animals. It has the horns of a hoofed animal and the tail of a serpent or alligator. Sometimes the emphasis is on the fact that this powerful spirit is an underwater as opposed to an underworld spirit.

Communication with the underworld often takes place in caves, in front of spectacular cliffs, or at springs or pools of water. Burrowing animals are especially important, as they spend time both in this world and in the underworld. Some native nations and clans were founded when their ancestors emerged from the underworld.

Water plays a special part in this cosmology. It is the one substance that communicates readily between the worlds. It falls from the sky as rain and rises as mist; it seeps into the ground and emerges at springs. And it has other important properties: it acts as a mirror and as a barrier to the passage of spirits. These last two ideas are related. A person's reflection is often interpreted as an image of the soul; that's why vampires can't see themselves in a mirror. And if the soul is reflected back, then water is a barrier to its free movement. Not surprisingly, then, places where a still pool of water can reflect the sky—especially the night sky filled with stars—are especially powerful spots.

Sacred Places

Sacred places and other places that are especially appropriate for communicating with the spirits of the sky or those of the underworld are scattered all across the Plains (and the rest of North America). Figure 5.1 shows just a representative sample of those on the Plains. They include mountains and hills, caves, other entrances to the underworld, springs, lakes, and meteorites and other rocks. Bear Butte, sacred to many nations, is the place where the Cheyenne culture hero Sweet Medicine received the four sacred arrows and their associated earth renewal ceremony.[5] Isolated and flat-topped hills seem to have been especially important (visualize Devils Tower). And places where rocks—especially red rocks—seem to jut toward the sky also were imbued with spiritual power. The rock formations in the Garden of the Gods in Colorado are one example.

Other rocks might also be powerful. This was often the case with large glacial erratics on the northern Plains—huge stones transported by the glaciers of the ice age many miles from their bedrock origins.[6] On the Plains, they are especially noteworthy, clearly out of place. A few of these stones have been marked by humans, with cup-shaped depressions or a combination of cups and linear grooves. The latter are intended to represent the spine and ribs of the buffalo, and are called ribstones. Groups traveling to hunt bison would make trips to ribstones to pray for success in the hunt.[7]

Meteorites were sought out and revered. The Alberta meteorite was revered as the most important of the ribstones, even though it had natural cups but no grooves. When it was taken away, the Cree and Blackfoot elders mourned its loss and predicted a dark future.

> "The old medicine men declared that its removal would bring great misfortune, and that war, disease, and dearth of buffalo would afflict the tribes of the Saskatchewan. This was not a prophecy made after the outbreak of smallpox which devastated the district when Captain Butler was there, for in a magazine published by the Wesleyan Society of Canada, there appears a letter from the missionary announcing the prediction of the medicine men a year before Captain Butler's visit, and concluding with an expression of thankfulness that their dismal prognostications had not been realized. A few months later, however, brought on all three evils upon the Indians. Never, probably since the first trader had traversed their land, had so many afflictions of war, famine, and plague fallen upon the Crees and the

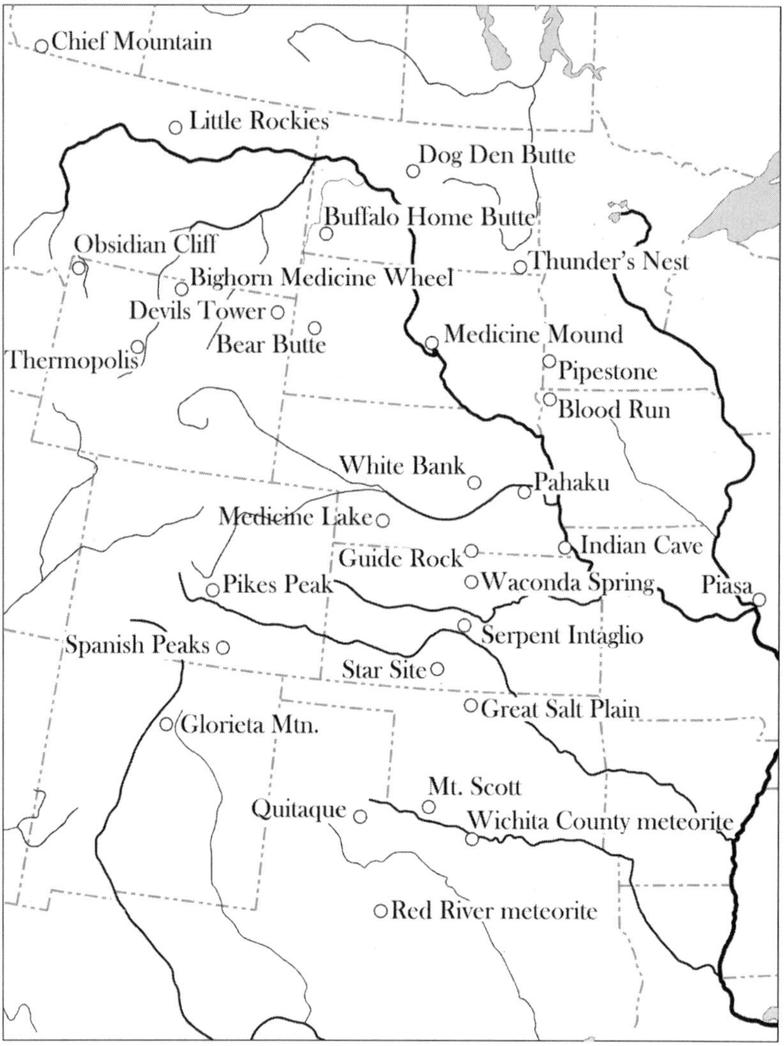

FIGURE 5.1 Selected Native American sacred sites on the Great Plains (map by author).

> Blackfeet as during the year succeeding the removal of their Manitou stone from the lone hill upon which the skies had cast it."[8]

We happen to have a clear description of a meteorite shrine in Texas that was discovered by a Pawnee war party. Meteorites were linked symbolically with buffalo; hence the meteorite is called a stone buffalo in this narrative. The same shrine is called the iron or stone man in another Pawnee account of the same events. "The people were on a buffalo hunt. It was wintertime and they had to journey far to the southwest, for they could not find any buffalo in their own country. When they had gone to where there were mountains, they could find no buffalo or game of any kind. Hunters went far into the country seeking game. One man went over some mountains and came to a small hill which was in a valley. The hill was round like an earthlodge. When he reached the top, he saw what seemed to be a holy place: a circle of buffalo skulls and in the center a stone buffalo."[9] On a return visit Pawnees found that some other people had placed offerings to the meteorite within the circle. They removed them and placed them at a distance, replacing them with their own offerings.

Ludlow Cave, in the North Cave Hills of South Dakota, is a premier example of an entrance to the underworld that provided access to the buffalo spirit.[10] And the size of a cave did not matter. A landowner near Quitaque, Texas, told me about a tiny cave on her property so small that only a single person could squat in it. It is midway up a sheer cliff, with a view of only the other side of the canyon. But someone had laboriously cut a set of hand- and toeholds in the cliff face in order to climb to it. Other entrances to the underworld were equally important. The narrows of Tule Canyon in the panhandle of Texas is the place where the ancestors of the Creeks emerged from the underworld.[11]

Manitou Springs, at the base of Pikes Peak, is an especially noteworthy set of sacred springs. The water that emerges from them is naturally carbonated; that is, the water already holds the essence of the sky world. Furthermore, the springs have built up travertine cones from the minerals in the water, so that the water emerges from the tops and sides of the cones, which reach toward the sky. And to top it all off, they are at the base of a high peak that generates convection currents that produce thunderstorms, sending the water back to earth.

Some lakes were sacred. For instance, the Naishan Dene (Kiowa Apache) report that they first obtained their Medicine Water or Four Quartz Crystal sacred bundle from a lake near the Black Hills. Medicine Water is their name for Bear Butte Lake.[12] Sacred bodies of water are often reported to be the homes of the underwater monster.

Pawnee Animal Lodges

For the Pawnees, the ability to cure disease was given to humans by animal spirits that resided in the underworld. In spite of the supernatural sanction that accompanied curing, Pawnee doctors were a class of people entirely separate from the priests whose job it was to care for sacred bundles and to lead their ceremonies. A person who felt the calling to become a doctor could either purchase the right to use the power and paraphernalia that had been granted to another person or could seek a new vision from an animal spirit. As a result, for each tradition of treatment, there was an origin myth that told a vision-seeking story.

For a recipient of a vision to become a successful doctor, however, he had to prove the potency of the power given to him by the animal spirit. This was done in two ways: by curing sick people and by participating in the Grand Doctors' Ceremony. The latter was an annual festival, held in the fall, in which the doctors demonstrated their supernatural powers through various (and often very impressive) sleight-of-hand tricks.

While this may sound to the modern ear like charlatanism, the effect was to generate belief amongst members of the Pawnee public in the potency of the powers granted to the doctors. Each doctor not only had been allowed the use of ceremonial regalia by the animal spirits and had been given songs to sing during the time that he treated his patients, he was seen to be able to do miraculous things. At minimum this brought into play what we now call the placebo effect—the tendency for patients to feel relief, if not to experience outright cures, simply because they believe that they have been given potent medicine. The story of how a truly successful doctor came to obtain his sacred power would be told and retold, becoming an origin myth for a sacred bundle and justification for the style of treatment he had originated.

While the families of Pawnee patients paid doctors for cures and attempted cures, being a doctor was not a full-time specialization. Doctors were not exempt from acting as warriors in defense of the village, or from acting as hunters or even horse raiders. Instead, it was a part-time specialization, like being an arrow maker or pipe maker.[13] Payment might take the form of a horse or other products that a man might be expected to produce for his household if he were not a doctor. Payment would also change hands, as mentioned above, if someone wanted to purchase the sacred knowledge and power obtained during a vision by a successful older doctor during a vision.

Early in the Historic period, the region around Waconda Lake was Pawnee territory, and the Pawnees recognized a set of sacred spots that were especially appropriate places for humans to communicate with the animal spirits of the underworld. The clearest description of these sites is in an

FIGURE 5.2 Earth-lodge-shaped feature at Thermopolis, Wyoming (photograph by author).

article by Douglas Parks and Waldo Wedel. The Pawnee term for these sites is *rahurahwa:ruksti:'u,* holy ground.[14]

Bob Blasing has investigated the animal lodges quite thoroughly, correcting some errors in the Parks and Wedel account.[15] For instance, Parks and Wedel reported that Pa:hu:ru' at Guide Rock, Nebraska, had been destroyed by highway construction. Blasing found it intact and was able to attribute the error to a picture that Parks and Wedel had been given of the site that had been reversed when it was printed from a glass negative. He also corrected the location of one shrine, determined the location of another, and visited all of them that he was able to identify, creating a list of attributes that these shrines share. Pa:hu:ru' includes a high hill with an excellent view of the surrounding land, a cliff or bluff, a source of water, an entrance to the underworld, an earth-lodge-shaped feature (Figure 5.2), a trail, and healthy vegetation, including a grove of trees. Actually, Blasing's original list specified hardwood timber, but this was when the known shrines were restricted to the area where such trees occur.

Parks and Wedel provided Blasing's starting point by combining the lists of animal lodges made by various ethnographers (George A. Dorsey, Melvin Gilmore, George Bird Grinnell, Alexander Lesser, and James R. Murie). They had made overlapping lists of these homes of the animal spirits, or animal lodges as anthropologists now call them. Parks and Wedel provide both a master list of fourteen animal lodges and a map of the locations of those they identified, but a close reading of the sources indicates that the list is incomplete and the map misleading. For instance, in the story of the creation of the first Pawnee medicine lodge, associated with Pa:haku, an animal lodge on the Platte River, the young man who is given the requisite knowledge is first invited into an animal lodge on the Missouri River—a lodge not on the list. As for the misleading nature of the map, Parks and Wedel note that only one animal lodge lies outside the area of the Platte and Loup river valleys where Pawnee villages are found, and that the exception (Waconda Spring) was sacred to many nations other than the Pawnees. The problem is that Blasing and I have identified other Pawnee animal lodges, some securely and some tentatively, and many are outside the area where the Pawnee villages lay, and some even are outside the extensive Pawnee hunting territory. My own hypothesis is that four of the most distant may have been the corners of what the Pawnees conceived of as their terrestrial universe—a concept shared by many nations.

One of these places is the lodge that Dorsey identified as the Great Cave of the Bears without recording its Pawnee name.[16] This place also shows up, again without its name being specified, in Murie's account of Pawnee ceremonies. It is the animal lodge that is associated with the ceremony of the bear doctors: "The hill was high and projected out toward the west, and right under it the hill was level. There were hills around this place covered with cedar trees." The bear spirit lodge was "right under one cedar tree, the entrance being on the west side of the plateau."[17] This appears to be a description of Bear Butte, in South Dakota.

Blasing has also identified quite clearly one of the most important of the Pawnee animal lodges. It is the one called Paksuktu' or Head with Soft Down Feathers. It is Pikes Peak in Colorado, and, as Blasing has shown, this animal lodge also incorporated the Garden of the Gods, known to the Pawnees as the Garden of Evening Star, the place where human beings were created.[18]

Still another animal lodge distant from the Pawnee villages is the one recorded by Alexander Lesser as "asatatkitaruts," On Top of Hill Fresh Dung of Horses but No Horses. I believe that this is Quitaque Peaks in Texas, the name of which is derived from the Comanche Kwita Kowah, which refers to horse manure. The peaks are erosional remnants adjacent to the great Llano Estacado mesa, and Brad Cole, one of my students, reported that there are rock formations on top of the largest peak that look like horse manure. The landowner, Jim Doucette, showed me a series of springs near its base.

Thus we have Bear Butte in the north, Pikes Peak in the west, and Quitaque to the south, all quite distant from the Pawnee homeland. Anyone familiar with Native American cosmology would automatically ask about the identity of the animal lodge far to the east. Here we have no direct information, only surmise. The myth that tells the story of Pa:haku on the Platte, however, begins with the underwater monster telling a young man to travel to the Missouri River.[19] This is not terribly far to the east, certainly not as far as the other distant lodges from the Pawnee homeland, but there is a site associated with the underwater monster that is quite distant and on a large river. It is the spot marked by the "Piasa bird," a huge painting of the underwater monster on a cliff above the Mississippi River in Illinois. We also have a reference to annual visits by the Pawnees to the Illinois early in the eighteenth century.[20] The Piasa is my candidate for the easternmost Pawnee animal lodge.

Not only do the Pawnee animal lodges have a much wider distribution than originally understood by modern scholars, there is not as clear a difference between the Pawnee variety and those of other nations than Parks and Wedel imply. They emphasize that most Pawnee animal lodges, and the ceremonies associated with them, involve the spirits of all of the animal species, while other nations revered similar spots on the landscape that were home to only a single animal species. Parks and Wedel do note that three Pawnee animal lodges—Elk Home, Fresh Dung of Horses, and Great Cave of the Bears—were species specific, but they list these three under the heading "other lodges."[21] Still other such lodges are mentioned in the information collected by Murie. One is a lodge of the buffalo spirit below the water of a lake in the south; others include a bullfrog-only lodge and a butterfly-only lodge.[22] Thus, of the Pawnee animal lodges for which we have mention, six were homes to the spirits of individual species, seven are clearly associated with multiple animal spirits, and we have no clear information for the rest. At the same time, not all other nations had equivalent places that were the homes of only single species. For instance, Dog Den Butte and Singer Butte in North Dakota, sacred to the Hidatsas, were the homes of multiple animal spirits.[23]

The Pawnee animal lodges are thus an expression of a much wider pattern of animal spirit shrines scattered all across the Plains, unique in some ways but not so strongly as Parks and Wedel imply. What is more, many of the Pawnee animal lodges were revered by other nations. Pikes Peak was sacred to many nations; so was Bear Butte. Hence Waconda Spring does not stand out from the other Pawnee shrines in this regard, and Parks and Wedel mention that the Lakotas revered Pa:haku, and that individuals from many nations made pilgrimages to it.[24] For most of the rest of the Pawnee animal lodges we simply do not have information regarding whether they were known to and revered by other Native American societies.

There is another aspect of Pawnee animal lodges that has not yet been addressed in the scholarly literature. It is the symbolism that connects them both to meteorites and to the down feathers of eagles. This symbolism is explicitly connected with Waconda Spring. "In the White Beaver ceremony of the Chawi, in the portion of the ritual in which breath is blown into the drums, a meteorite is taken from the bundle and placed in a container of soft feathers."[25]

The animal lodges are intimately connected with the Grand Pawnee ritual called the Doctors' Ceremony. In that ritual, the men who dress as buffalo doctors wear soft down feathers on their heads.[26] The origin myth for the Doctors' Lodge says that the man who visited the animal lodge at Waconda Spring saw it covered with soft down feathers from a flock of birds: "It seems that the flock while flying over the mound were dropping their soft down feathers to the animals in the lodge, for the man who was on the mound saw that it was covered with soft down feathers."[27]

The connection between meteorites and downy eagle feathers is clear in the following Pawnee account:

> A war party started out into the enemy's country. One man was selected to go ahead to see what was before them. He strayed off and was traveling in the night when he saw a meteor shoot out from the heavens. He could see it plainly, for the meteor made a bright light. He saw it shooting downward. It seemed to shoot slantwise when it struck the earth. The ground shook. The man stopped, and when he looked it was dark again. He went to where the meteor dropped; when he came close to the place he stopped, lay down, and went to sleep. In the morning he got up and walked around looking for the meteor, but could not find it. In the afternoon, he saw eagles flying around in a circle; some of them flew downward toward a stream. He walked on and, when near the place where the meteor had fallen, he saw many eagles sitting down near the stream. He stopped. Some of the eagles flew up; others flew down. Late in the evening the eagles all flew away. The man then went to the place and there he saw many feathers scattered around. In the center was a pile of soft down feathers in a circle. The soft feathers were so placed as to make the picture of a man's face. The man removed the soft down feathers and began to dig in the sand, and there he found the meteor. He dug it up and found it to be the size of a man's fist. It was heavy and still warm.[28]

The animal lodge at Pikes Peak is called Paksuktu'—Head with Soft Down Feathers. It cannot be mere coincidence that the *Catalogue of Meteorites* lists a meteorite at Colorado Springs, another at Waconda, and a third at Penokee (which is discussed later).[29] Unfortunately, the context in which they were found was not recorded. In addition, the Stone Buffalo or Iron Man meteorite shrine discussed above was described as being shaped like a lodge, and according to a Wichita tale it was the home of some spirits.[30]

—Kicawi:caku, or Waconda Spring

The animal lodge that the Pawnees called Kicawi:caku and that we call Waconda Spring now lies under the waters of Waconda Lake. Before its was drowned by the lake, it was an impressive place: "Waconda Springs. Three springs of mineralized water occur in the Solomon River valley in Mitchell county about 2 1/2 miles southeast of Cawker City. The largest one, known as Great Spirit spring, is the only one usually visited. It is situated at the northern edge of the river plain and by precipitation of the less soluble compounds which the waters carry in solution has built up a mound 42 feet high with a diameter at the base of 300 feet and at the top 150 feet. The top is nearly flat, with a craterlike depression in the center 35 feet deep and about 54 feet across. This depression is filled with water, but overflow is rare, due to escape of the water through openings on the flanks of the mound."[31]

Bailey adds, "The mound is situated within 200 feet of a limestone bluff, which rises perhaps twenty feet above the level of the spring."[32] The minerals gave the water a distinctly salty taste and led to the development in historic times of a myth that the spring had some sort of direct connection with the ocean. The idea was probably reinforced by the fact that the water sometimes overflowed the hilltop, as though influenced by the tides. This historical myth is discussed more fully in the next chapter.

Another physical feature of the site is visible in an aerial photograph taken in 1965 (Figure 5.3). The photograph faces northwest, putting the hotel that was built there directly behind the spring pool. The path from the hotel to the spring is visible directly above the pool. What is of particular interest is another, fainter path that connects the pool to the eastern edge of the mound. It appears to run due east from the pool, but if it connected the pool to some sort of access or egress on the east side of the mound, that is not clear in the photograph. Two other possible trails run SSW from the pool, but they are obscured by light-colored material, probably mineral

FIGURE 5.3 Aerial view of Waconda Spring (courtesy U.S. Bureau of Reclamation, Nebraska-Kansas Office).

deposits from the occasional overflow of the spring that was reported to run off in the direction of the river. It is possible that one or more of these apparent trails is aboriginal in age.

This is the exterior of the animal lodge. For the interior, we have a description of how various animal spirits arranged themselves in pairs on the north and south sides of the circular lodge. Beginning on the west side of the lodge and proceeding to the east were a series of pairs of animals—beavers, otters, owls, wolves, dogs, bison, eagles, bears, hawks, and jackrabbits—one of each species on the north and the other on the south. At the east end, near the entrance to the lodge, were a jackrabbit on the north and a raven on the south, and a muskrat on the north and a mudpuppy (salamander) on the south. In addition, there were two errand men (an honorable role in a Pawnee ceremony): a muskrat on the north and a magpie on the south.[33]

The story indicates that the white beaver took the lead role at Waconda Spring,[34] and his position opposite the (eastern) entryway is the position of highest honor. There is some obvious color symbolism at work, but not all of the details are given. When colors are indicated, for the animals on the west side of the lodge, the northern animals are black and the southern animals are white, but in the eastern half of the lodge, the pattern is reversed. Raven and mudpuppy, two very dark animals are on the south side, paired with lighter-colored animals on the north. The same pattern holds for the errand men, who in a Pawnee ceremony would have been stationed near the door, that is, at the eastern end of the lodge.

George Bird Grinnell obtained the following account from Pawnee informants: "This is a mound, shaped like a dirt lodge. At the top of the mound, in the middle, is a round hole, in which, down below, can be seen water. At certain times, the people gather there, and throw into this hole their offerings to Tirawa, blankets and robes, blue beads, tobacco, eagle feathers and moccasins. Sometimes, when they are gathered there, the water rises to the top of the hole, and flows out, running down the side of the mound into the river. Then the mothers take their little children and sprinkle the water over them, and pray to Tirawa to bless them. The water running out of the hole often carries with it the offerings, and the ground is covered with the old rotten things that have been throw in."[35]

Another detail recorded for Waconda Spring is the use of the water, mixed with earth, to make a face clay paint.[36] This use has some interesting symbolic parallels. The Pawnee also used urine from hermaphroditic bison mixed with clay to make bluish face paint used by warriors.[37] As we will see shortly, the Potawatomis dipped their arrows in the water of Waconda Spring to give them special potency. Far to the northwest, the Clackamas also dipped their arrows in water found in cavities of the Willamette meteorite and mixed the same water with clay to make war paint.[38] Here are more connections between animal lodges, meteorites, and bison. This time it is in connection with warfare, and the plains nations made their war shields with the hide of the bison bull.

Other nations also revered Waconda Spring. According to Patrick, every nation in the region visited the spring for religious reasons. Dowd, a descendant of the family that ran the resort at Waconda Spring in later years, lists twenty-nine nations and says that the spring was a "neutral area."[39] Gentleman lists Pawnees, Arikaras, Wichitas, Comanches, Cheyennes, Sioux, Osages, Kaws [Kansa], Kiowas, and Arapahos. Patrick also discusses the Potwatomis, and cites an Ernest Kisner (who was born near the springs in 1873) as remembering two nations visiting the springs. "One came from around Marysville and the other from somewhere in Nebraska. They would stop at the spring on their way home from buffalo hunting farther west. They would stay a week or more, tanning hides and holding ceremonies. The camp was south of the river. He says they stopped coming in the 1880s when whites began to exploit the spring."[40] One of the nations

FIGURE 5.4 Postcard image of Omaha Indians at Waconda Spring, 1878 (courtesy U.S. Bureau of Reclamation, Nebraska-Kansas Office).

mentioned in this source may be the Omahas, whose presence at Waconda Spring is recorded on a postcard image (Figure 5.4).

Patrick reported that the Potawatomis regularly visited the spring on their way to hunt bison and dipped their arrow points in the water. He also said that they used mud from the spring for war paint for their faces, making their appearance "frightful in the extreme."[41]

Isaac McCoy says the Kansa people called the spring *Ne-Wohkon daga,* meaning "spirit water." *Ne* is water, *Wahkan* is "holy," and *daga* is McCoy's version of *tonka,* "great;" hence the name meant Great Spirit water or spring.[42] Furthermore, the Kansa name for the Solomon River is *Nepaholla,* "water on a hill." This is essentially a translation into Kansa of the Pawnee name for the spring.

Albert Gatschet wrote the following:

> A sacred well of uncommon interest is situated in the western portion of Kansas, about a quarter of a mile from Solomon River, which runs in a southeasterly direction, and joins the Kansas or Kaw River at Abilene, Kansas. This curious water-receptacle is situated on top of a hill, and has a nearly circular form with about thirty feet diameter. All the hunting tribes of the prairie regard it with a religious interest mixed with awe; the Páni called it, or call it still, Kitch-Wálushti, the Omahas Ní-wáxube, both names

> signifying "sacred water." The miraculous quality of this pool, which chiefly astonishes the Indian mind, consists in a *slow rising* of the water, whenever a large number of people stand around the brink. The water of the pool is perfectly limpid and considered to be bottomless; it harbors an aquatic monster which engulfs all the objects thrown into it, and never sends them up again. Indians offered to it beads, arrows, kerchiefs, earrings, even blankets, and all this sinks down immediately. Before putting clay or paint on their faces, the Indians impregnated these substances with the water of the well. They never drink of this water, but to allay their thirst go to the neighboring Solomon River. Before buffalo-hunting became a thing of the past, large parties of natives often gathered around this pond-source, and the following narrative circulated among them as a truthful report of what really occurred: "Two Pánis once returned with their horses. Having dismounted near the 'sacred water,' one of the men stepped upon a turtle of the large species frequently found in the vicinity, about three feet long. The man's feet stuck to the back of the turtle; he could not disengage himself from its treacherous shell, and when the turtle ran with his charge into the pool, the Indian was soon beyond possible rescue. His stupefied companion had seen the occurrence, and went home to tell the tale." The story also occurs in the traditions of the Dakota tribes, as Mr. Dorsey affirms me.[43]

The Cheyennes relate a similar story about the sacred lake at Bear Butte and a young man who became stuck to the underwater monster who lived beneath the surface.[44]

Patrick reported that many relics had been "fished" from the pool, including bows and arrows, a bent rifle or two, arrowheads, colored stones, medals and beads (one medal bearing the stamp, "The Fur Company of 1844"), and the figures of a white man and native making friends over a pipe of peace, articles thrown in to propitiate the Great Spirit.[45]

—Man-made Sacred Shrines

In addition to the natural features described above, human-made features mark some sacred places. These include the modified boulders mentioned above, along with boulder outline figures, mounds, petroglyph sites, and intaglios—figures carved into the earth.

Here is a description of one such site, apparently composed of nothing but bison skulls. In 1839, when he and his companions reached the forks of the Platte River, Friedrich Wislizenus climbed to a high point on the bluff on the south side of the river. "Arriving at the top I found considerable 'strong medicine.' Thirty buffalo skulls, adorned with all kinds of gewgaws, lay before me in a magic circle, as cunningly arranged as 'Caspar' in the 'Freischütz' could have done it."[46]

Of course, this shrine—a circle of bison skulls with associated offerings—sounds very much like the "stone buffalo" meteorite shrine described above. It is certainly possible that Wislizenus simply did not recognize that a rock in the center of the circle was a meteorite. There were very few people in the Euro-American tradition who could have made such an identification in 1839; the recognition that meteorites occasionally fall from the sky had only been proposed in the United States in 1807.[47] Whether or not there was a sacred object in the center of this circle, however, is not pertinent to another fact: this kind of shrine would decay away, leaving no evidence that it was a sacred place.

Earthen and rock-filled mounds occur near Waconda Lake. The Range Mound (14ML307), apparently of Archaic age, was mentioned previously. Other mounds occupy the bluffs on the south side of the river below the dam. We visited one in 1991 that seemed especially prominent. When we got there the reason was obvious. A farmer had bulldozed the stones, pushing them to the edge of his field, forming a pyramid-shaped pile in the process. Today such sites are protected, but the act was legal at the time.

Other kinds of sacred places, called ground figures, are images created by modifying the face of the earth. They can be made by removing stones from a desert pavement to expose lighter ground beneath, by arranging boulders into figures, by creating earthen effigy mounds, or by removing sod to carve the figure into the ground, producing what is called an intaglio. The Great Plains does not have desert pavements, and effigy mounds are concentrated in the upper Mississippi valley (with a notable outlier at the Great Serpent Mound in Ohio). Most boulder outline figures are in the northern Plains,[48] but there is one at Penokee, Kansas, that is a figure of a giant human (14GH308).

The meteorite found at Penokee has already been mentioned. Another was taken from a hill in South Dakota by C. P. Chouteau, a leading fur trader in 1857. As best can be determined, he removed it from a boulder outline effigy of a snake on *Paha wakan,* "sacred hill," a possible animal lodge about eighteen miles from Fort Pierre.[49]

Intaglios are rare everywhere, but three sites have been reported in Kansas, two of which are described below. The first to be reported is the figure of a serpent on the end of a ridge in Rice County.[50] Like the Great Serpent Mound in Ohio, the serpent appears to hold a circular object in its open mouth. The second site found is the Sage site at Waconda Lake, described below. The third is a complex site near Lake Afton in south-central Kansas that includes sod walls and ditches in addition to apparent intaglios.[51] Intaglios are the most fragile of the ground figures, as a single plowing can destroy all trace of them. There are a few hints in the ethnohistoric literature that suggest they may have been fairly common.[52]

—The Sage Site

In 1990 our survey at Waconda Lake came upon an unusual depression on a ridge top along the south shore of the lake, approximately two miles south and a bit west of Waconda Spring. It was irregular in outline and was distinguished by the growth of low grasses inside it as compared with taller grasses outside. I might not have noticed it if I had not been familiar with the Serpent Intaglio in Rice County that was brought to the attention of the archaeological community by the late Clark Mallam. That feature consists of the figure of a serpent some forty-eight meters (158 feet) long. Lying on a high ridge, it is marked by a shallow depression and a difference in vegetation: only short grasses grow inside the depression in contrast to the mixed grasses that surround it. Even so, it is a subtle feature today, not an obvious one. The same is true of the Sage site, which is surrounded by recent man-made terraces. I had walked through the depression and had continued part of the way down the ridge before the similarity to the Serpent Intaglio occurred to me.

Mallam's investigations showed that the open jaws of the Rice County serpent were aligned with features called council circles in two adjacent Great Bend Aspect village sites. Furthermore, a test trench he excavated across the neck of the serpent uncovered two small flakes of Alibates chert. That stone type, from the panhandle of Texas, is rare to absent in most sites in the region, but is fairly common in Great Bend sites there. Thus his investigation identified the serpent as the work of the people who created the Great Bend Aspect sites—the protohistoric Wichitas.

The figure at the Sage site is much more difficult to trace than is the serpent in Lyons County (Figure 5.5). Initially we doubted that it was actually an archaeological site. In order to investigate it, we mapped both the outline of the depression and of the growth of short grasses. These yielded somewhat different outlines, neither of which were especially convincing. But personnel from the Mitchell County Soil Conservation Office concluded that the land surrounding the figure had never been plowed because the vegetative cover was native prairie. This made the presence of a prehistoric figure feasible. The lines of trees and bushes along the

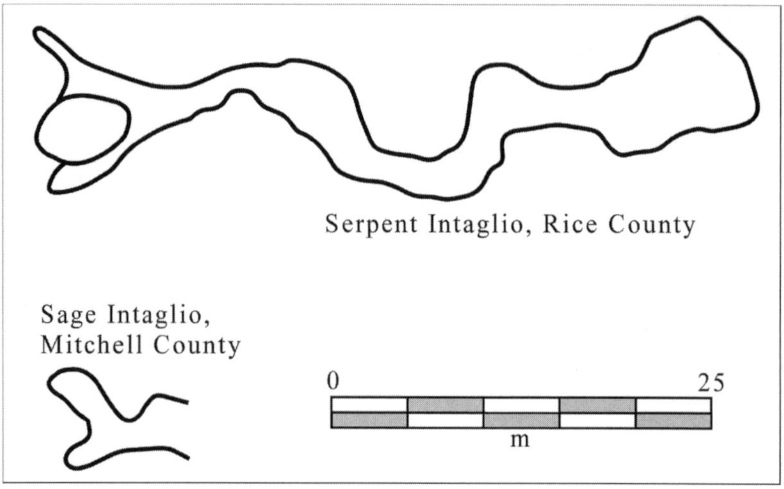

FIGURE 5.5 Comparison of the intaglios at Waconda Lake and in Rice County (maps drawn by Leślie McQuade under direction of author).

man-made terraces turned out to have been planted by the Fish and Game people as food for wildlife some time after Glen Elder Dam was built, that is after the 1960s. These trees were planted in slight terraces that approximate following the contour lines of the ridge.

The Soil Conservation Service Office had some aerial photographs of the region taken in the 1950s, that is, prior to the filling of Waconda Lake. Examination of these revealed that the main depression was present at that time but that the terraces were not. This demonstrated that the main depression was not a product of the terracing of the hillside. The aerials also showed a farm track that ran from the farmstead at the base of the ridge directly past or across the western end of the depression. Subsequently, the oldest aerial photograph of the region, taken in 1938, was obtained from the National Archives. It too shows the depression as a light spot, but unfortunately the quality of the photograph is not good, and the outline of the figure cannot be discerned clearly. Thus the aerial photos indicate that the figure predates the terracing of the ridge and provide a minimum age of fifrty-five years for it.

In order to investigate the figure further in an attempt to determine whether it was of cultural origin, we asked Dr. David May to perform a geomorphological evaluation. His investigations were conducted in 1990. The results[53] are paraphrased here in order to incorporate some information not available to him.

In order to investigate the nature and age of the depression, he used a bucket auger to sample the soil at 10 cm depth intervals from three core holes. Hole 1 was placed in the center of the depression, Hole 2 on the uphill lip, and Hole 3 downhill from the depression. These locations were chosen to determine whether any soil had been removed from the depression and placed uphill from it, as Mallam concluded had been done at the Serpent Intaglio. Hole 3 provided a control sample to determine what the undisturbed soil profile looked like. Samples were collected to a depth of one meter or until large fragments of weathered bedrock prevented deeper coring. Hole 1 was cored to a depth of 55 cm, Hole 2 to 90 cm, and Hole 3 to a depth of one meter.

Some of the results of physical and chemical analysis of the samples from the cores are presented in Tables 5.1 and 5. 2. A number of considerations indicate that the site is not a natural feature. If it were an erosional gully, one would expect it to be oriented more or less to the slope of the land, but it lies more or less at a right angle to it. Furthermore, the depth to bedrock within the depression is 60 cm, compared to the 90 cm immediately uphill from it. This, along with the lack of evidence for subsurface dissolution of the bedrock, eliminates a sinkhole as a possible cause.

Evidence from the analysis of the cored soil indicates instead that the depression is of cultural origin. First, the low percentages of organic matter from Hole 1 inside the depression indicate that the topsoil has been removed from it. If the depression were natural, runoff that collected in it

TABLE 5.1. Organic matter and calcium carbonate distributions at the Sage site

	% Organic Matter			*% Calcium Carbonate*		
Depth (cm)	*Hole 1*	*Hole 2*	*Hole 3*	*Hole 1*	*Hole 2*	*Hole 3*
0–10	0.1	2.4	3.1	5.0	30.0	5.5
10–20	0.1	1.2	1.1	9.0	29.0	4.5
20–30	0.1	0.3	0.5	45.5	33.0	0.0
30–40	0.1	<0.1	0.5	62.2	38.5	10.0
40–50	0.1	0.1	<0.1	79.0	39.0	9.0
50–60	0.1	<0.1	<0.1	76.5	52.0	5.0
60–70	–	<0.1	<0.1	–	62.0	4.5
70–80	–	<0.1	<0.1	–	71.5	15.0
80–90	–	<0.1	<0.1	–	41.0	37.0
90–100	–	–	<0.1	–	–	65.5

TABLE 5.2. Clay, sand, and soluble salt distributions at the Sage site

	% Clay			*% Sand*			*Soluble Salts (mmhos/cm)*		
Depth(cm)	*H 1*	*H 2*	*H 3*	*H 1*	*H 2*	*H 3*	*H 1*	*H 2*	*H 3*
0–10	31	32	23	6	15	7	2.8	2.8	0.0
10–20	36	36	29	5	9	7	12.8	0.0	0.0
20–30	58	44	30	7	7	6	12.8	0.0	0.0
30–40	77	48	33	11	7	6	11.5	0.0	0.0
40–50	100	50	35	0	8	6	3.0	0.0	0.0
50–60	81	59	35	1	11	4	2.4	0.0	0.0
60–70	–	59	32	–	18	5	–	0.0	0.0
70–80	–	65	38	–	17	6	–	0.0	0.0
80–90	–	32	36	–	11	6	–	3.7	0.0
90–1m	–	–	45	–	–	32	–	–	0.0

would have kept the soil in it more moist than the surrounding area, and this should have generated higher, not lower, percentages of organic material.

The soil taken from the depression seems to have been deposited on the uphill lip where Hole 2 was placed. The concentration of calcium carbonate in the upper 10 cm of this core was 30 percent. This level of calcium carbonate is not found until a depth of 80 cm in the control sample (about 20 cm above bedrock) and until a depth of 30 cm in the depression. Its presence at the top of the Hole 2 profile suggests that soil from fairly deep in the depression was placed on top of the upper lip. Combined with the current depth of the depression, approximately 40 cm of soil may have been removed from the figure to create this effect. Indeed, there is reason to think that these data indicate use of the intaglio over a lengthy period of time.

To understand why this is so, it is necessary to consider the process by which a recognizable figure could be excavated from the hillside. What was probably done was first to outline the figure desired with stakes or other markers. After this was done, all that would be necessary would be to remove the sod and to place it grass side up outside the excavation. Note that this process would not bring calcareous subsoil to the surface beside the depression. To remove the sod in blocks would require the removal of only about the top 15 to 20 cm of soil, which would not originally be rich in calcium carbonate.

In order to get the subsoil from the depression to the surface of the lip would require either inverting the soil as it was dug from the excavation or to have repeated the removal of blocks of sod in order to renew the figure. Inverting the soil as someone digging with a shovel might do, however, would have ruined the outline of the figure and produced an amorphous blob. Thus to bring calcareous soil from fairly deep in the depression to the surface of the uphill lip probably involved the renewal of the figure after its initial construction. Once grasses had re-established themselves in the depression, the figure may have been renewed by once again removing blocks of sod, and eventually this process would have brought up subsoil and deposited it on the surface along the upper edge of the depression.

A very rough estimate of the age of the depression can be obtained from a consideration of the physical and chemical properties of the three core holes (Table 5.2). The clay, organic matter, and soluble salt contents of soils all change with time. Of the three properties, the clay content of soil horizons changes most slowly. In this case, the clay contents of the various levels of Hole 3 provide a baseline to which the clay translocation and soil development within the depression (Hole 1) and on its lip (Hole 2) can be compared.

The clay content of Hole 3 increases gradually from 23 percent in the near surface layer to 35 percent at a depth of 50 cm. At lower depths, it fluctuates slightly before increasing to 45 percent at 90–100 cm. In contrast, the sand content (which is immobile in a soil horizon) fluctuates between 4 and 7 percent in the upper 90 cm of the core. This indicates that the soil formed in homogenous parent material, in this case weathered limestone that contains some sand. In contrast, the clay appears to have been translocated from the upper 40 cm of the soil (the A horizon) downward to the zone between 40 and 90 cm (the B horizon). Specifically what the control sample shows is that in this environment we can expect to find a 12 percent difference in the clay content of the A and B horizons.

Significantly, the clay content of Hole 1 in the depression is much greater than that of either Hole 2 or Hole 3. Thus, the depression appears to have received runoff containing suspended clay particles for many years. Within this core, clay appears to have been eluviated (removed) from the upper 20 cm and deposited at lower depths. Unfortunately, varying sand contents indicate variations in the parent bedrock material, making determination of the extent to which this happened uncertain. Nevertheless, based on some studies of the rate of clay translocation in soils in Iowa, May concluded that the depression is older than one hundred years, perhaps much older.

This conclusion is buttressed by the data from Hole 2 on the upper lip of the depression. The sand content of the upper half of this core is fairly uniform, but the clay content is not. It increases gradually from 32 percent in the top 10 cm to 59 percent at 60 cm. The apparently greater clay translocation here compared to the control sample may be the result of the better downward drainage through the soil, resulting from its location on the high lip of the depression.

The fact that the clay content of Hole 2 increases with depth is indicative of considerable age. The piles of material placed on the upper edge of the depression would originally have had a profile different from Hole 3. If it were a single spoil pile, the last material excavated from the depression would end up on the top of the pile, creating an inverse of the original soil profile. If sod were removed from the depression and placed uphill from it, and if this process were repeated after an interval of many years, the profile of the pile of sod would be more complex but still should have more clay near the top (that came from the original B horizon) than at greater depth. The gradually increasing amount of clay with depth in Hole 2 indicates that a great deal of clay translocation has occurred since the depression was excavated. Thus the spoil pile, like the depression, is older than one hundred years, and it is likely to be several hundred years old.

Other data from the test cores indicate a second kind of cultural activity at the depression, one that is probably unrelated to the original excavation. They are the very high levels of soluble salts from every depth within the depression and from the surface layer of Hole 2. The salt content of the depression is six times more than that required to classify a soil as a desert soil and three times more than that needed to classify a soil as a saline soil. In contrast, soluble salts were not detected in any level of Hole 3.

These data suggest that the depression was used as a spot where salt was provided to livestock. The old farm track that ran across the western end of the depression may be related to this activity. The repeated and recent disturbance of the surface of the depression by this use would explain both the high salt content and the low organic matter content of Hole 1. The organic-matter contents of natural soils in humid and subhumid environments increase very rapidly to equilibrium amounts of 2 to 5 percent in as little as fifty to one hundred years after disturbance of the soil or deposition of new parent material.[54] Similarly, the soluble salts, such as sodium, calcium, and magnesium cations, and chloride, sulfate, and bicarbonate anions, are usually leached from soils in humid and subhumid environments (Donahue et al 1983), as is the case in Hole 3. Thus there is every reason to believe that the salts are a recent addition to the soil profile and more recent than the depression itself.

In 1991, Rob Carlson of Wichita volunteered to fly me over the site in a small plane so that an aerial view could be obtained. The figure shows up quite well in the photographs because the grasses inside it, which had been mowed two weeks previously, had yellowed. As a result, the figure stood out clearly on the ridge top, but the nature of the animal represented remained elusive. Examination of the pictures taken, however, revealed a bluish spot just downslope from the figure that had not been noticed during ground investigations.

When Bob Blasing and I returned to the site in the spring of 1992, we investigated the source of the bluish spot. It turned out to be a large, roughly circular community of sage (*Artemisia ludoviciana* Nuttal). A search of the rest of the ridge and cursory examination of the ridges on either side revealed no other such communities. We considered whether the sage might have been introduced by humans in the context of ritual activities, as sage (called *Kiwaut* by the Pawnee) was commonly used to purify participants in sacred activities. Gilmore says that "it was always proper to begin any ceremonial by using *Artemisia* in order to drive away any evil influences."[55]

In October of 1992, Blasing arranged for comparative magnetometer and resistivity surveys of both the figure at Waconda Lake and the Serpent Intaglio. Dr. John Weymouth of the University of Nebraska provided both the equipment and the technical expertise, while students from Wichita State University provided volunteer labor.

In order to perform the resistivity and magnetometry surveys, it was necessary to establish a one-meter grid over both sites. The grids were used to remap the surface depressions and the vegetation patterns so that all of the data from the sites could be compared directly. Mapping the depressions proved fairly difficult, as the depressions are shallow in spots, and the figurine at the Sage site appears to have suffered from various disturbances. At the Serpent, it was especially difficult to determine the outline of the egg-shaped object in its jaws. The tail section was also very shallow so that it was difficult to trace its outline.

During the mapping of the Serpent, it was noted that sage plants were thinly scattered over the site. One of the students, however, found a much denser patch uphill from the intaglio but did not report it until after we had returned from the field. I later returned to the site to confirm the presence of this patch of sage, but it does not stand out from the background distribution as clearly as the patch at the Sage site.

The data from both the magnetometer and resistivity surveys were filtered by Weymouth to remove noise. This was especially necessary for the resistivity data from the Sage site, which were subject to a steep gradient down the ridge, apparently generated by the underlying bedrock. Both data sets recorded the presence of the intaglio at the Sage site, and both indicated a basic similarity between it and the Serpent Intaglio.[56] In addition, the resistivity results indicated the presence of a possible feature near the center of the patch of sage at the Sage site. Unfortunately the similar patch of sage at the Serpent was not reported until after the fieldwork had been completed.

What both data sets for both sites indicate is that the figures appear to have been created by the removal of the sod and accompanying topsoil, which was stacked in piles adjacent to the excavations. The increased thickness of the topsoil, which contains relatively abundant iron, produces a signal in both magnetometers and resistivity meters.

In both instances, the surface depression did not match the magnetometry and resistivity data precisely. There is a spot near the head of the serpent where an apparently recent surface disturbance has distorted the apparent outline, which is clearer in the resistivity and magnetometry data. These data also indicated that the tail of the serpent had been misinterpreted when it was studied originally by Mallam. The tail area is quite shallow and difficult to see, and Mallam, apparently using the Great Serpent Mound in Ohio as a model, had mapped it as ending in a broad oval as though the tail were coiled. The magnetometry and resistivity data, when combined, show the tail not as coiled but as continuing through one more meander.

The relationship between the surface depression and the remote sensing data at the Sage site is also not one-to-one. In fact the mapping of the depression was very difficult. The magnetometry and resistivity maps both correspond well to the apparent head of the figure, but the west end is impossible to trace in both. This is the area where a farm trail can be seen on old aerial photographs, and several pieces of metal detected by the magnetometer probably are associated with it.

What kind of animal was intended to be represented by the figure at the Sage site is still unclear. The head does bear some resemblance to the head of the Serpent Intaglio, but there is no raised oval in the mouth area. Our original interpretation was that it represented some sort of a quadruped with a broad tail, but no definite conclusions can be drawn. One possibility is that it was a beaver, as the only ceremony known to have been held by the Pawnee at Waconda Spring was the White Beaver Ritual.[57]

6. Creating the Post Rock Landscape

—Crowding the Land

Warfare was an occasional part of life in this part of the world for at least two thousand years. During Solomon River phase times, raiding seems to have been a part of life all across the central Plains. Scalping marks and club wounds on skulls, decapitation, and trophies made from skulls are found.[1] And in the succeeding Oneota expansion, warfare seems to have been more prominent. Warfare continued into the Historic period. When Juan de Oñate visited Kansas in 1601, he found Apaches (whom he called Escanjaques) at war with the Wichitas living in the vicinity of Arkansas City (whom he called Quivirans).

The Apaches had arrived in the Plains from Canada some time in prehistory, as judged by linguistic evidence. They were followed by incessant waves of immigration during the historic period, each one generating new enmities as newcomers encroached on the hunting territories of those already present. The new arrivals squeezed the Wichitas and their Pawnee relatives, until the native-versus-native warfare climaxed in a terrific battle in 1854 that pitted the western newcomers against even more recently arrived eastern groups.

In the 1630s, Dhegiha Sioux-speaking refugees, including the Osage and Kansa people who were to dominate eastern Kansas, arrived from the Ohio River valley. The archaeological record shows that they took the eastern hunting lands of some of the Wichita bands,[2] and by the early eighteenth century, they had driven the Wichitas south into Oklahoma and Texas.[3]

When first contacted by Europeans, Osage villages lay in west-central Missouri, but a splinter group later established itself on the Arkansas River in what was to become northern Oklahoma and southern Kansas. In addition to the Wichitas, the Osages once fought regularly against Comanches, Kiowas, and Pawnees.

At about the same time that the Osage and Kansa people entered the eastern Plains, ancestral Pawnees arrived in central Nebraska. While they may be descended in part from the much earlier Central Plains Mosaic peoples who lived there, a gap in the archaeological record exists in this region that has yet to be filled.[4] An old but still viable hypothesis is that prior to 1650 or so, the populations that were to become Pawnees were living in South Dakota. Judging from the record at Waconda Lake, part of the accommodation between the Pawnees and the Wichitas, with whom they were usually on friendly terms, was an adjustment of hunting territories, with the Wichitas ceding the land around Waconda Lake.

The Omahas, part of the Dhegihan migration along with the Osage and Kansa people, retained memory of a great peace treaty established in the late seventeenth century.[5] The Omahas became the neighbors of the Pawnees, with a hunting territory that extended across eastern Nebraska to the Platte River in the south and to Shell Creek in the west.[6] Later the Otoes also came to share this territory, with a village just south of the Platte (cf. Figure 4.9). In later years the Omahas and Pawnees occasionally used one another's hunting territories when bison were scarce in their own, and after the Pawnees moved to Oklahoma, the Omahas continued to hunt in the former Pawnee territory in Kansas.

The Western Nations

In the early eighteenth century, Comanches swept down from the north and drove most of the Apache bands from the Plains. (A few survived in Texas to become the Lipans, and another band that allied itself with the Kiowas and Arapahos survived in the northern Plains to become the Kiowa Apaches.) Previously the Comanches had lived in southern Wyoming, but they now pushed south, to take advantage of the growing wild horse herds and of opportunities to raid isolated settlements in Spanish New Mexico. Sometime around 1750, the Comanches formed an alliance with the Wichitas, who supplied them with French trade goods, and in 1786 they made peace with the Spanish as well.[7] By the end of the century, the high plains of Texas and New Mexico belonged to the Comanche nation.

The Comanches were followed south by Kiowas who drifted east and south from a homeland north of Yellowstone Park to the Black Hills before being pushed south by Sioux attacks and pulled south by the lure of wild horse herds. While they were in the north, they were allied with the Crow nation, and after they moved south, some Kiowa families maintained a long-distance friendship with some of the Crows.[8] With the Kiowas was a band of Apache speakers who participated in the Kiowa tribal rituals but who sometimes allied themselves with other nearby nations.[9] Once they reached the southern plains, the Kiowas and Kiowa-Apaches fought against the Comanches for control of what had been the northern reaches of Comanche territory, but in 1806 they made a lasting peace and became so closely allied that one band was known as *nimikaiwa*, "Comanche-Kiowa."[10]

In the south, the Kiowas also fought the Osages, and the first entry in the famous Kiowa calendar (for 1833) records an Osage raid against a Kiowa camp in what is now Oklahoma. The Osage warriors cut off the heads of the Kiowa dead and placed them in the camp kettles.[11]

Even before that fight, more northerners had arrived. The bands that became the Southern Cheyennes and Southern Arapahos came south from South Dakota and Wyoming in the first quarter of the nineteenth century. The Cheyennes had come ultimately from western Minnesota, pushed west by groups that had acquired firearms.[12] Truth be told, we don't know where the Arapahos came from; there is one oft-repeated tradition that they also came from Minnesota, but it is likely that many of their ancestors were on the Plains well before the Cheyennes arrived. The Southern Cheyennes and Southern Arapahos established themselves in eastern Colorado, intruding on lands used by the Pawnees, Comanches, Kiowas, Apaches, and Utes.

Needless to say, warfare followed, but in 1840 the Cheyennes and Arapahos made a lasting peace with the Comanches and Kiowas,[13] with the Arkansas River as the boundary between their respective territories. War against the Utes to the west and the Pawnees to the east continued throughout the historic period.

Next to arrive were the Brule and Oglala Sioux, whose homeland at the beginning of the historic period was also in Minnesota. They were part of the great movement west of the Lakota Sioux who came to dominate most of the Dakotas. Eventually two bands began to move south. A group of Brule Sioux first ventured into what then was Pawnee country in response to an invitation to Bent's Fort in 1828. On their return trip they fought Pawnees in a battle on the Republican River. They came south again in 1830 to join Cheyennes in the massive attack on the Pawnees.[14] Then in 1835 the construction of Fort William (the predecessor of Fort Laramie) drew both Brules and Oglalas to the North Platte.[15] Eventually they occupied a territory centered on the spot where Fort MacPherson was later built, just below the forks of the Platte in southwestern Nebraska.[16]

The Brules and Oglalas had continual clashes with the Pawnees thereafter. In the 1840s, John Young Nelson witnessed the horrendous mutilation of over one hundred Pawnee dead by a successful Brule war party: "The most ghastly part of the business was the mutilation of the corpses. They were treated to every indignity conceivable, and with an extraordinary ingenuity of purpose. I was never particularly squeamish, but my 'first fight' nearly settled me from a stomachic point of view."[17] This fight occurred on the headwaters of the Little Blue River, apparently along a section of the Pawnee Trail.

Other than the old friendships between Kiowas and Crows and between the Lakotas and the Cheyennes and sometimes the Arapahos, the history of the intertribal relationships among the western groups included fierce warfare. The 1833 Osage attack on a Kiowa camp has already been mentioned. Crows frequently fought against the Lakotas, Cheyennes, and Arapahos, while the Cheyennes and Arapahos had fought against the Comanches, Kiowas, and Kiowa-Apaches.

That began to change in 1834, when the United States intervened in the hostilities between the Kiowas, Comanches, and Wichitas, on the one hand, and the Osages on the other. A military expedition (accompanied by the artist George Catlin) traveled west to visit Comanches and Wichitas in the Wichita Mountains. The following year the peace was brokered, and the Osages became allies and trading partners of the Comanches, Kiowas, and Wichitas.

Then, in 1840, the Cheyennes and Arapahos made peace with the Kiowas and Comanches, and hence, by extension, with the Osages. The peace gave the northern groups access to the large mustang herds of the southern plains, and the southern nations access to the better bison hunting in the north. The treaty might not have held were it not for the fact that it turned out to be so timely. In 1836 Texas became independent of Mexico, and the new republic refused to recognize any native claims to land. Fighting broke out in 1840 with the massacre of Comanche negotiators at the Council House Fight. It accelerated when the Texas Rangers adopted the Colt Paterson revolver, giving them a firepower advantage over Comanche forces almost regardless of their numbers. By the 1850s, the fighting had moved to the Red River country, pushing the Comanches north.

At the same time that the Comanches were pressed north, the Cheyennes and Arapahos were pushed east, not by other people, but by Mother

Nature. Evidence derived from tree ring studies[18] shows that the years 1845 to 1856 were marked by a severe drought. Although the drought-affected area extended at times as far north as the Assiniboine country and as far east as the reservations in eastern Kansas,[19] it was centered on eastern Colorado, the normal hunting territory of the Southern Cheyennes and Southern Arapahos. The drought appears to have been more severe than that of the 1930s, and the result had to have been an enormous reduction in the grazing available to bison herds. Bison adjust to drought by moving long distances to find better fodder, and that response would have meant disaster for the southern Cheyennes and Arapahos unless they shifted their hunting to the east, right into the teeth of the Pawnees and emigrant nations described below. The rights to the crowded buffalo hunting grounds had become very serious business.

By 1840, then, the various fairly recent arrivals to the western plains—Comanches, Kiowas, Kiowa-Apaches, Cheyennes, Arapahos, Oglalas, and Brules—had formed a loose alliance among themselves and with the Osages. They were being pressed from the south by Texans and from the west by drought. Their fiercest enemies were the Pawnees of south-central Nebraska and the people who had been forced onto reservations in eastern Kansas by the United States.

The Eastern Nations

Beginning immediately after the American Revolution, the new republic began pressing Native American groups westward. What began in disorganization evolved in the first quarter of the nineteenth century into an organized policy to remove eastern nations to an Indian Territory west of the Missouri River. Beginning in 1825, a series of treaties freed land in eastern Kansas and Oklahoma for reservations that were to be the new homes for native nations from all over the east.

Treaties with the Osage and Kansa nations appeared to clear title to large areas for this purpose, but from the beginning there were problems. The lands described in both treaties included areas beyond those normally used by the Osages and Kansas (the extent of which can be determined by the reports of various parties that encountered their hunting camps).[20] None of them indicate that either nation hunted west of what became Dodge City. Yet the Osage treaty of 1825 described the western boundary of their ceded land as a "line to be drawn between the head sources of the Kansas River, Southwardly through the Rock Saline."[21] The Kansas treaty also assumed that the Kansa owned land all the way to the headwaters of the Kansas River.[22] In fact, the western end of both tracts included country that was the traditional bison hunting territory of the South Bands of the Pawnee[23] and that was being contested by the Southern Cheyennes and Southern Arapahos.

While the geographical errors in treaties with eastern nations were sure to generate problems, the initial treaties between the United States and western nations made no reference to the treaties already made with eastern groups. As Schultz puts it, "Government officials had never given much consideration to the problems of peaceful relations between the intruder and the intruded in Indian territory."[24] Furthermore, the new reservations were not always surveyed prior to settlement. Fighting occurred between newly emigrated the Iowas and the Sacs and Foxes prior to survey of the line between their reservations.[25]

Even if there had been no problems in defining tribal and reservation boundaries (figure 6.1), the placement of thousands of "emigrant Indians" on the edge of the plains was bound to generate controversies over hunting rights. Beginning with the Shawnees in 1825, eastern Kansas became home to many nations, including Delawares, Sacs, and Foxes, Potawatomis, Iowas, and so on. In 1839 Isaac McCoy, who was prominent in the push to create the Indian Territory, estimated that there were 73,200 emigrant Indians there, in addition to 26,660 previous residents.[26]

The large numbers of newcomers had two effects: they changed the military dynamic, and they made conflict with the western nations inevitable. On his early tours of the territory, Isaac McCoy found the Shawnees huddled in villages on the Missouri border because they feared the Pawnees and Comanches farther west.[27] As more and more emigrant nations poured into Kansas in the 1830s, however, their combined population made them a potent military force.

At the same time, the large populations forced hunting parties beyond the western limits of their reservations. All of the emigrant groups depended partly on hunting and fishing for their subsistence, but eastern Kansas could not provide them with what they needed. Fishing in Kansas was not nearly as productive as the areas from which some of the groups had come, and large numbers of hunters meant declining game populations. Farley reports that the game had been hunted out on the Delaware reservation as early as 1840.[28] There had been bison in eastern Kansas, but soon the hunters were forced to go farther west, into the hunting territories of Pawnees, Cheyennes, Arapahos, Sioux, and Kiowas.

Some of the emigrant nations evolved an adaptation that not only included bison hunting west of their reservations but also fur trapping in

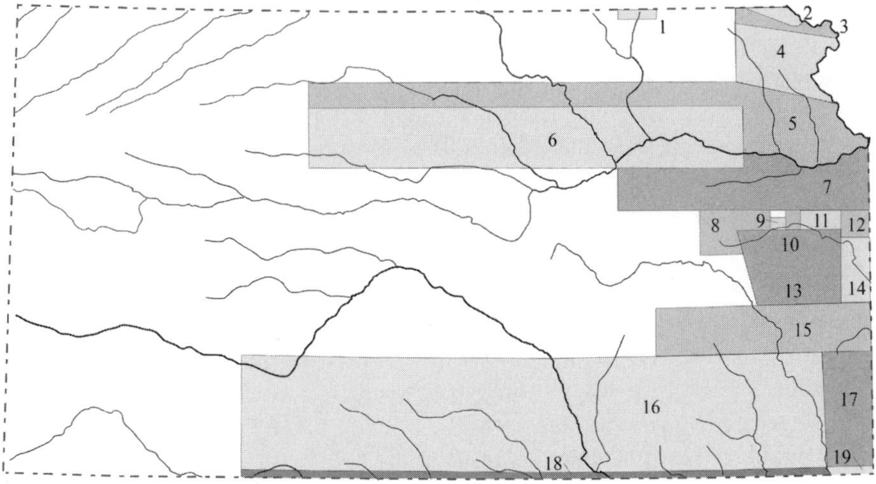

FIGURE 6.1 Reservations in Kansas in 1846 (map by author).
1. Oto and Missouri; 2. Iowa land; 3. Sac & Fox of Missouri; 4. Kickapoo; 5. Delaware and Wyandot; 6. Kansa; 7. Shawnee; 8. Sauk & Fox of Mississippi; 9. Chippewa; 10. Ottawa; 11. Peoria/Kaskaskia; 12. Wea/Piankeshaw; 13. Pottawatomi; 14. Miami; 15. New York Indians; 16. Cherokee neutral; 17. Osage; 18. Cherokee; 19. Quapaw

the Rocky Mountains.[29] At least some of the newcomers had a long history of involvement in the fur trade in their eastern homelands, and the fur trade in the southern Rockies had opened up just prior to the creation of their new reservations.[30] The native trappers traded their furs for a variety of goods, including rifles and shot, at the trading posts on and near their reservations. That trade provided them with weaponry far superior to that of their western foes, weaponry that turned the tide in the great battle of 1854.

The western hunting and trapping expeditions ignited conflicts. For instance, in the fall of 1831 two Delawares and their wives were hunting buffalo west of their reservation when they were attacked by Pawnees, who killed three of them. One woman escaped and survived on roots and berries for several weeks. A second party was wiped out by Pawnees in the same year. The Delaware response was a war party that burned a Pawnee village when its inhabitants were away on a buffalo hunt.[31]

Peace negotiations in 1833 sponsored by the federal government did not stop the bloodshed. The 1833 treaty between the United States and the Pawnees provided for cession of all Pawnee claims south of the Platte River. That ground was supposed to become a commons on which all of the nations could hunt.[32] The same treaty stipulated, however, that the

Pawnees were to remain at their agricultural villages year-round to protect the government-financed teachers and farmers along with the stock and mills provided by the government.[33] Such a provision ignored the fact that the Pawnee adaptation required lengthy bison hunts in the summer and winter that kept them from their villages for months at a time.

So the conflicts continued. In 1835 a Delaware hunting party killed twelve Pawnee horse raiders, but they let one member of the surrounded party go free to report home what had happened. During the same time frame, the Delawares also fought the Sioux along the Platte and in South Dakota, and the Comanches south of the Red River.[34]

The easterners also adopted the Plains tradition of horse raiding. One of the earliest large battles between newcomers and resident nations was the result of one such raid. In 1836 a Sac and Fox raiding party found a Comanche camp from which most of the able-bodied men were absent on a hunting expedition. They overran the camp and then retreated toward their reservation with the loot that included a number of Comanche ponies. When they reached the Neosho River, however, their way was blocked by an enormous flood that covered not only the bottomland but some of the higher ground as well. Thinking they were safe, they camped on Indian Hill near a ford of the river between the later locations of Strawn and Hartford. There Comanche warriors caught up with them and fighting began. Thirteen of the Sac and Fox men tried to escape by swimming their horses across the stream, but only three survived. Apparently none of the rest of the Sac and Fox party survived the fighting on the west bank of the stream.[35]

In 1848 the Indian agent for the Potawatomis reported a battle between a joint hunting party of Kansas, Potawatomis, Sacs, and Kickapoos versus some Pawnees. Several Pawnees were killed, and in retaliation Pawnees stole over forty head of horses from the Potawatomi reservation. Nevertheless, the fighting had begun with a misunderstanding, and in 1852 the Potawatomis made a peace with the Pawnees that proved valuable in the years leading up to the battle of 1854.[36]

Prologue to the Battle of 1854

The story begins prior to 1820, somewhere on the high plains, probably in Colorado. An enterprising trader from New Mexico had traveled north with a mixed bag of goods, including an old set of armor. It included a helmet with a neck flap, and a leather shirt and matching leggings that were covered with overlapping iron plates. An Arapaho warrior traded for it, and he in turn sold it to a Cheyenne.[37] Eventually the armor passed to a Cheyenne chief named Medicine Water.

In 1844 when Medicine Water and his band of Cheyennes were camped with some Brule Sioux friends on a tributary of the Arikaree Fork of the Republican River, they were attacked by a party of people they called *Savanaho.* The name, derived from "Shawnee," was applied first to the Shawnee who came to Kansas in 1825. When other eastern nations arrived, the meaning of *Savanaho* was extended to include them because they too were partly acculturated to Euro-American ways and, to Cheyenne eyes, looked pretty much the same. The equivalent Kiowa word was *Sakibo,* from "Sac." The party of Savanaho in question was actually Delawares.

At the onset of the battle, Medicine Water gave his Spanish armor to his nephew, Alights on the Cloud, who bravely acted as a decoy, riding along the Delaware front, drawing their fire. Then, before the Delawares could reload, the combined Cheyenne and Brule force attacked and killed all seventeen of the enemy. His act of courage sealed Alights on the Cloud's reputation, and soon the Cheyennes considered him a chief.[38]

In 1852 the Southern Cheyennes called on Sioux, Arapaho, Kiowa, and Kiowa-Apache allies to join in a strike against the Pawnees. On the warpath, the allies came upon a recently deserted Pawnee hunting camp, where they found the body of a Kiowa warrior who had been tied to a stake before being scalped and mutilated. In a battle the next day, Alights on the Cloud was killed by the Pawnees, in spite of the armor that had served him so well in the fight against the Delawares. A lucky Pawnee shot resulted in an arrow that went though his eye into his brain. Both the Kiowas and the Cheyennes were left thirsty for revenge.

Another Cheyenne, Little Robe, had lost a son in the same battle. In 1853 he carried the war pipe to various Cheyenne camps and to the Brules, Arapahos, Comanches, Kiowas, and Kiowa-Apaches. All ten of the Cheyenne bands responded and joined forces with warriors from the other nations and with a few Crows who had been visiting among the Kiowas. When the Cheyenne and allied warriors found a Pawnee hunting camp, two Cheyenne scouts crept up to spy on the activities. After observing the Pawnees for a while, "they discovered other Indians standing in the shadows, off to one side. They recognized them as Savanaho, for they wore white-man hats with feathers tied to them, and they were carrying the long rifles that the Savanaho used."[39] These Savanahos were Potawatomis.

The next morning, the Cheyennes and their friends attacked the camp. Initially they were successful, but then the Potawatomis, who had camped separately from the Pawnees, came to the aid of their allies:

> They were fine shots, these Savanaho, and their bullets immediately cut down both horses and men. When the People's [Cheyenne's] warriors saw that, they turned and ran, their allies riding off with them. The Savanaho rode after them, chasing them a long way, keeping right after them. Then the courage of the People's warriors returned. Suddenly they and their friends wheeled their horses. Then they came charging back. The charge was no good, however, for soon horses were dropping on all sides, their riders falling to the ground as well, struck down by the Potawatomi rifle balls. The Savanaho rode up to where these dead Cheyennes were lying. They jumped off their horses and, in clear sight of the watching Cheyennes, cut open the dead men's breasts. Then they tore the hearts from the bodies and stuffed them in their bullet pouches. After that they thrust their hands down into the dead men's chests, smearing the Cheyenne blood across their faces. The People's warriors and their friends watched all this with growing fear, for it was said that the Savanaho used their enemies' hearts for making the strong medicine they rubbed on their bullets, so that they never missed a shot when they fired at their enemies.
>
> Now, when the People's warriors saw the Savanaho cutting open their men, they turned and ran away.[40]

Clearly, "shock and awe" is not a recent invention.

At the battle's end, the Cheyenne had lost eighteen warriors, the Kiowas and Kiowa-Apaches two each, while the Arapahos had lost one. One of the Kiowa dead was the brother of chief Stumbling Bear.[41] In raids later that summer, Cheyenne parties burned a Pawnee village and killed four in another fight, but their thirst for vengeance had not been quenched, and the Kiowas and Kiowa-Apaches had not yet taken revenge. The stage was set for the great battle of 1854.

The Battle of 1854

We have multiple accounts of the battle of 1854 derived from statements of the participants. Combatants on both sides reported details to their Indian agents, who in turn provided summaries to the Office of Indian Affairs. In addition one Sac told his version of the battle to George Bent.[42] Other accounts from the western nations include one Kiowa and several Cheyenne sources. The Kiowa account is reported by James Mooney in his classic *Calendar History of the Kiowa Indians.* It is a history of the Kiowas based on a mnemonic history that had been created by a man named Little Bear. Originally, the calendar history had been painted on bison hide, but the version Mooney obtained had been drawn on paper with colored pencils. It contained pictures meant to help recall two important events that occurred each year, one in the winter and one in the summer. The pictures were used to prompt memories of the important events of each year, with the historian and members of his audience responsible for recalling the details. Mooney's informants did not necessarily agree on all of the details.[43]

Information from several Cheyenne informants has been summarized by Father Peter Powell in *People of the Sacred Mountain,* his massive history of the Cheyenne. Although Powell consulted the classic ethnographies of the Cheyennes, his account is drawn ultimately from Cheyenne informants: Porcupine Bull, a Southern Cheyenne who corresponded with the anthropologist George Bird Grinnell, and George Bent (the Cheyenne son of the trader William Bent), who corresponded with the historian George Hyde. Other Cheyennes contributed details about some of the participants. In fact, Powell's book reads like the remembering that a calendar history was supposed to generate, with various voices, now relegated to footnotes, amplifying the fateful events of each year.[44]

I have combined the various sources in an attempt to provide a single clear narrative of the battle of 1854, as seen by the participants. It begins in the winter of 1853–54, when Stumbling Bear and other Kiowa and Comanche chiefs carried the war pipe to camps of their allies in the Arkansas River and Canadian River valleys. We have a Cheyenne account of their visit to the Wu'tapiu, one of the Southern Cheyenne bands. There the Kiowas and Comanches entered the camp as mourners for their dead relatives and as petitioners asking for the aid of Wu'tapiu warriors when they sought revenge against the Pawnees.[45]

About seventeen of the Wu'tapiu warriors agreed, including Bear Feather, the band chief, and Old Whirlwind, his son-in-law (Cheyenne men traditionally lived with their wives' kin). The Kiowa and Comanche men then went on to visit camps of the Arapahos, Kiowa-Apaches, Lakotas, and Osages. According to Cheyenne memory, the resulting war party that formed in the summer of 1854 included all of the Kiowa and Kiowa-Apache warriors, most of the northern Comanches, Bear Feather's band of Wu'tapiu warriors, and a few Arapahos and Osages. The few Crow warriors mentioned by the Kiowas appear to have escaped the notice of the Cheyennes, but they say a few Lakotas were also involved.[46]

All accounts agree that the western allies gathered opposite the mouth of the Pawnee Fork of the Arkansas River. The Kiowa account says that there were "several hundred" warriors in the party; the Cheyennes do not say how many in all, but do specify that only sixteen or seventeen of their own people were included. The Sac and Fox estimated fifteen hundred warriors against their own party, but perhaps it just seemed like fifteen hundred. At any rate, the numbers on the emigrant Indian side were much smaller, around one hundred men, mostly Sac and Fox but including some Potawatomis.[47]

According to the Kiowa account, they left the camp opposite the mouth of Pawnee Fork going northeast. This places them on the old Arkansas River Trail that ran along the south bank of the Arkansas west of Great Bend (Figure 4.9). The Kiowas told Mooney that they crossed the Arkansas River (probably near the mouth of Walnut Creek) and reached a spot that he interpreted as being on either the Smoky Hill or Solomon River, "about midway between the present Fort Harker and Fort Hays." The stream that the Kiowas named Gúigyä P'a was interpreted by Mooney to be the Smoky Hill, but the name means "Pawnee River" and probably meant the Republican River, on which Pawnee villages had once stood. It is likely that the war party was traveling toward the Gúigyä P'a when they encountered the eastern warriors. Their most likely route of travel was north on the Pawnee Trail. Unfortunately they described the location of the fight only in general terms—about halfway between Fort Harker and Fort Hays.[48]

There one morning a party of Kiowa Apache warriors under chief Plenty of Camps came upon the Sacs, Foxes, and Potawatomis who were on a buffalo-hunting expedition. The latter party included no women and children because the emigrant Indians had heard rumors of the great war party and had left their families safely behind.

The initial clash is described in the Cheyenne account as a running fight. In it, the easterners killed Plenty of Camps, and his disheartened men retreated to the main body of the great war party. When the others were informed of the skirmish, their first response was to dress for the coming battle, as Plains warriors relied on the spiritual powers that resided in their headdresses, shields, and war shirts for protection in battle. When they finally caught up to their enemies, it was about midday.

The one part of the Cheyenne account says that the easterners made a stand on a high ridge, while the Sac and Fox agent reported that they had taken shelter in a ravine or low spot and were surrounded for a time. The Cheyenne warrior, Old Whirlwind, said, "The *Savanaho* were fighting on foot in a little hollow—a place like a buffalo wallow." Perhaps the two positions occurred in sequence. At any rate, the allied warriors charged one of these positions repeatedly, but were unable to penetrate their enemy's position.[49]

The fight was decidedly one-sided in favor of the Sacs and Foxes. They had good rifles obtained in trade at their reservations, while the westerners, with the exception of the Osages, had very few guns.[50] The Sacs and Foxes were excellent shots, and by firing their weapons in relays, they were able to keep their more numerous enemies far enough away that their arrows and lances were useless. Only the few Osages that had rifles were able to do any damage to the Sacs and Foxes. As Agent John W. Whitfield put it: "The prairie Indians were armed with the bow and arrow, while the others had fine rifles. One is a formidable weapon at close quarters, but worthless at more than about fifty yards. The rifle told almost every shot. It is easily accounted for why one hundred whipped fifteen hundred. The former had a weapon to fight with; the latter none at the distance they were fighting."[51]

The battle is said to have lasted for about three hours before the western warriors pulled back for good. The Kiowa counted twelve of their own dead, among them Tseñ-kóñyä, "Black-horse," one of their war chiefs. None of the Cheyenne or Arapaho warriors was killed, but the Cheyennes grumbled that the Arapahos had hung back from the actual fighting. The Kiowa Apaches had done worse, losing a second war chief, named Bob-tailed Horse. Several Comanche warriors and a few Osage men were also dead. The Kiowas estimated the total number of dead on their side as twenty. Agent Whitfield learned that the number of wounded was about one hundred.[52]

In contrast the Sacs and Foxes and their Potawatomi friends had lost only six men. All of them had been killed by rifle bullets, and they correctly assumed that the Osages were responsible for the deaths.

Mooney referred to "this great war party, which went after wool and came back shorn." At the time he did not know just how apt his metaphor was. The fighting was so intense that the Cheyenne warrior Old Whirlwind lost most of his war bonnet. "Time after time he rode straight into the enemy fire, until all the feathers in his war bonnet had been shot away. Then only the sacred stuffed hawk, tied to the brow of the war bonnet, remained untouched." Shorn indeed.[53]

There are a few discrepancies in the various accounts of the battle. We have already noted the varied descriptions of the terrain on which the fighting occurred. Mooney reported that the Kiowa chief Stumbling Bear said that the expedition was supposed to attack the Pawnees in order to avenge the death of his brother the year before, but that other Kiowas said that the intent was to exterminate the emigrant nations. The Cheyennes reported that the Kiowas told them that they would attack any enemies they might meet, whether Pawnees or emigrant easterners. The point is moot; revenge against both groups was required, given the losses suffered in 1853.

The Aftermath

In Plains warfare, the death of a relative in battle required a revenge raid, and these began before the year was out. The Sac and Fox agent reported the revenge that one warrior took for the death of his brother. Blaming the Osages for all of the Sac and Fox deaths, the man "left here by himself, went within four hundred yards of an Osage encampment, met two Osage men, shot one down and went up and scalped him; could have killed the other, but wished him to live to carry the news of what he had done to the Osage camp; waited until he had done so; heard the cries and lamentations of those in the camp for their dead kinsman, mounted his horse and returned with his scalp."[54]

The Cheyennes and Kiowas also sought revenge for their various losses over the previous few years. In the winter of 1854–55, a Cheyenne war party intercepted a party of Pawnee horse raiders on the Saline River and killed several, and in the summer of 1855 two other Cheyenne war parties had success against the Pawnees, killing twelve of them. In 1856, they killed another five, and in 1857 still another.[55]

In the winter of 1854–55, Kiowas attacked an unidentified group described as living north of the Osages, where they killed a man. They killed another the following winter. Then, in the summer of 1857, some of them participated in an expedition against the Sacs and Foxes. The party consisted primarily of Comanches led by chief Mäwi. According to the brief account given to Mooney, they engaged the Sacs and Foxes northeast of the site of the 1854 battle and managed to kill several of them.[56]

We have an account of another raid from a settler named Ellen Goodnow. In a letter to her husband who was on a trip to the East Coast, she reported having to flee to Manhattan from their cabin in Shannon, a little settlement on Wildcat Creek, because of a Cheyenne attack on Delawares in which white settlers had been caught up.[57]

Finally, James R. Mead ran across the site of a recent fight in northern Lincoln County in 1859. He described it thus: "On the next small creek were evidences of war. Scattered about were broken pots, kettles, pans, and camp equipage; some of them with bullet holes through them. Probably a small hunting party of Delawares had been surprised and driven out by the Cheyennes, who were jealous of this, their country. What they did not choose to carry away they had destroyed."[58] He found more remains on Wolf Creek—the skeletons of two men: "Stuck fast in the bones were about thirty iron arrow points. Our verdict was, thieving Pawnees, overtaken by Cheyennes, evidently a large party, as each warrior shoots an arrow into a fallen enemy and those they cannot pull out remain, except the shaft, which is pulled off."[59] Mead's guess as to the identity of the attackers is supported by another account, also in Lincoln County, in which Cheyenne warriors left sixteen arrows in one body and fourteen in another.[60]

—Natives versus Settlers

In the years after the Civil War, the flood of white settlement washed west with incredible speed—up to one hundred miles a year. It had been stalled by the war and the conflicts leading up to it, but Commissioner of Indian Affairs George Manypenny had seen it coming as early as 1854: "Already the white population is occupying the lands between and adjacent to the Indian reservations and even going west of and beyond them; and in no distant day all of the country immediately to the west of the reserves which is worth occupying will have been taken up."[61]

The inhabitants of most of the reservations were forced south by government in the 1850s and 1860s, legalizing the taking of reservation lands and resources that had begun earlier.[62] This movement brought settlers into the area contested by the native nations, and some of them became eyewitnesses to the conflicts. For instance, in 1862, two Sioux warriors pursued a Pawnee into the cabin of Ashbury Clark in what was to become Jewell County. Clark gave up the refugee with the stipulation that he not be killed in the cabin, so the Sioux took him outside and chopped him to pieces.[63]

Attacks on settlers soon followed. In fact there were attacks on the surveyors who preceded the settlers. At first the attacks took the form of warnings; later they were in deadly earnest. For instance, on October 28, 1858, a Pawnee chief warned surveyors in Republic County to leave. The next day, six of his mounted men charged abreast and knocked one of the surveyors to the ground. A few days later the same survey party was scolded by Pawnees when their campfire got out of control and started a prairie fire.[64] The Pawnees were hunting in the area and said that the fire would drive the bison away. By 1866, warnings were a thing of the past. In that year, E. Roche, an enlisted man in the Second U.S. Cavalry, was killed by natives while on escort duty with Elisha Diefenbach, who was surveying the township lines in what is now Osborne County. Then, in 1868, Sioux warriors attacked surveyors on Prairie Dog Creek with the intent to kill them all.[65]

The same pattern can be seen in the attacks on Euro-American settlers. Early in the 1860s, intimidation often served to get settlers to leave claims that were well in front of the line of settlement, but by the end of the decade, large-scale raids with multiple casualties were the rule.

The first small waves of settlers along White Rock Creek, from 1862 to 1865, were scared off by what they saw as intimidation by Indians. In fact some of the events appear to have been more or less friendly visits by natives traveling through who hoped to get a meal and some coffee. In Native American societies, hospitality was a given; from the point of view of isolated settlers, and especially in the eyes of women who happened to be alone at the time, the visits were terrifying.

In Lincoln County the first settlement was in 1864, and in May of that year the Moffit brothers and some companions were killed by Cheyennes. Three other young men were luckier. Jack Peate and two companions went up the Pawnee Trail from the Saline River to Limestone Creek where they were captured and later released by Cheyennes under Roman Nose. So was E. T. Carr, who was stripped naked and robbed of his outfit while hunting on what was later named Carr Creek.[66]

By 1867 and 1868, friendly visits were rare and deadly raids were the rule. Cheyenne Dog Soldiers (a warrior society within the Cheyennes that eventually established itself as a separate band and took the lead in the defense of their territory against Euro-Americans) and their Sioux allies raided homesteads on the Saline, Solomon, and Republican rivers, and attacked people on the Sante Fe Trail and the Kansas Pacific Railroad. In 1867 John Higgins was killed while hunting buffalo near the headwaters of Oak Creek in what became northeastern Osborne County. The raids reached well into the then-settled area east of Beloit.[67]

Much of the hostile activity was on or near the Pawnee Trail. In 1868 Cheyennes or Sioux (or both) killed two hunters and "land-lookers" near the forks of the Solomon. The next attacks were on workers on the Kansas Pacific Railroad at the Bunker Hill station just south of the Saline River. Then the raiders moved back north along the trail, attacking settlers on Spillman Creek. In 1870 another attack killed three men near the mouth of Limestone Creek.[68]

The most famous events of the period were the raids that resulted in the capture of two adult women and two little girls. The little girls were the daughters of Aaron and Nancy Bell. In August 1868 the Bell family had traveled a few miles from their claim in what is now Beloit to the land being improved by Bell's brother-in-law, David Bogardus, to help in the construction of a new log cabin. There a band of some forty Cheyennes and Arapahos attacked the settlers. They killed the two men and mortally wounded Mrs. Bell. Mrs. Bogardus managed to elude capture, along with her nine-month-old son and the infant daughter of the Bells.

The story of the captured girls has been told and retold, perhaps with embellishments over the years. The most detailed account is the one assembled by Alan Houghton, but it has some inconsistencies:

> After the renegade band left the Bogardus place they stopped on a high mound a few miles to the south. The white girls were bound, wrist and body to the rolls of clothing, sacks of corn and settlers' stolen tools carried by their ponies. The Indians headed southwestward to the Saline river. The Indians took from Esther a small doll that she had clung to through all the excitement; it seemed to hold their fascination and it was never returned. But the Indians were not unkind to their two young white captives.
>
> The first night, Aug. 12, the two girls slept on coyote skins in a hastily erected tepee. For dinner that evening the Indians had fed them water and buffalo meat covered with sugar stolen from some settler's cabin, a great luxury by the savage's standards. Next morning, Aug. 13, the group was up early and kept to a fast pace. After an early-afternoon powwow, the braves left the two girls with the squaws to reconnoiter; their scouts returned late the night before had reported soldiers from Fort Harker, near present-day Ellsworth. The Indians returned to the band that afternoon highly excited. They had spotted the soldiers only 10 or 12 miles to the southeast. They immediately freed the girls there, some 30 miles south of the Bogardus cabin, abandoning them on the open prairie with no food or water.
>
> The young wanderers found their way to the banks of the Saline River and they spent that night, Aug. 13, in an abandoned dugout they discovered. Next day, Aug. 14, they wandered along the river, hungry and lost with only water from the stream and perhaps a few berries along the bank to assuage their thirst and hunger. That night they slept on open prairie beneath a tree. On the 15th the two girls continued their trek northwestward, using the sun as a guide. They mistakenly assumed the Saline was the Solomon and thought that they would eventually reach home if they followed it far enough upstream.
>
> It was this afternoon that they were discovered by two settlers, Mark (or Mart) Hendrickson, and a Mr. Erhart, who were scouting. Mistaking the approaching horsemen for Indians, the girls hid along the river bank,

> beside a large tree. The riders also mistook the girls for hostiles. Esther, sticking her head above the bank, was nearly shot before the men noticed that she wore a red bandanna around her head. They were found, according to Adams in his "Homestead Guide," about six miles above the mouth of Spillman Creek on the Saline. Mrs. Hennes [daughter of Esther Bell], who later visited the site, places it some 10 miles east of present day Lincoln on the Saline.[69]

Clearly, some of the information in Houghton's account ultimately came from one of the captured girls, but other details are clearly invented or are otherwise in error. We can start with a simple misprint: the location where the girls were found has to be west, not east of Lincoln. The mouth of Spillman Creek is about four miles west of the town, and a spot of discovery six miles west of it fits with the distance of ten miles, but not the direction Houghton reported.

If the girls were headed upstream when they were found, then clearly they did not understand that they had been taken southwest from the point where they had been captured. The direction that their captors followed, then, is a conclusion drawn from knowledge of where they were taken and where they were rescued. It is not information provided by the girls. One of them might have remembered the high mound south of Beloit, the lost doll, the food they were given, and sleeping on a coyote skin, but the other details are clearly an invention. How could the girls have learned that scouts had reported a column of soldiers leaving Fort Harker—actually Fort Zarah, according to the military records[70]—on the night of August 12? And how did they figure out that the men had seen soldiers "only 10 or 12 miles to the southeast"? Did the scouts speak English so that their young captives could understand the situation? And were they kind enough to convert their own units of distance into miles? Unlikely.

If we return to the few known points, however, the route can be reconstructed. The raiders started from the vicinity of Beloit and headed south to high ground. There is a high north-south trending ridge that forms a prominent point a few miles south of Beloit, east of Laban Creek. From there they could have traveled west to the Pawnee Trail by following the divide at the heads of the creeks that flow into the Solomon River, a distance of fourteen miles or so. If they followed the trail south, they would have been in the general vicinity of Spillman Creek when they let the girls go. This is the point where the trail swings west to the crossing of the Saline River at present-day Wilson Lake. From there the two girls would have traveled south about five miles to the Saline River on which they were eventually found.

In October 1868, another raid led by the Cheyenne war leader, Tall Bull, resulted in the capture of two women, Mrs. George Weichell and Mrs. Suzannah Alderdice, from Lincoln County. Mrs. Weichell was rescued at the battle of Summit Springs in 1869, but both Mrs. Alderdice and Tall Bull were killed during the fight. The Pawnee scouts under the leadership of Frank North played an important part in the fight, and his younger brother, Luther, left an eyewitness account of the battle and the rescue of Mrs. Weichell.[71]

Response to the raids included the formation of volunteer units. Kansas governor Samuel J. Crawford formed a company of volunteers at Salina and led them to the area in which the raids occurred. He resigned his civilian office in order to take command of the volunteers, and he made sure that the settlers were well armed.[72]

Part of the army's response to the raids was the creation of blockhouses on the Saline, Solomon, and Republican rivers. "Troops stationed on the Little Arkansas [Fort Sedgwick] and detachments from Ft. Riley and Ft. Harker were at once transferred to the Saline and Solomon region. Sheridan then ordered Gen. Sully to erect block houses on the Saline, Solomon and Republican. These forts were garrisoned with infantry while the region lying between the posts was patrolled by cavalry."[73] The troops who came to the Solomon valley included Company G of the Seventh Cavalry, under the command of Lieutenant DeRudio. As soon as they went into their first camp, which was near the mouth of Asher Creek, two warriors boldly went up to the picketed horses and stole the fine animal ridden by the lieutenant. The blockhouse is described as having been built in the fall of 1868, two miles south of Cawker City, which would place it in the vicinity of the forks of the Solomon River. It was manned by Company G of the Seventh Cavalry under Lieutenant DeRudio. The blockhouse was not occupied long, and in 1869 a Dr. Rose took possession of the abandoned structure only to by killed by natives when he was traveling toward Glen Elder.[74]

Once again the army established a temporary post, this time west of Waconda Spring. Initially, it was manned by a battery of the Fourth United States Artillery, commanded by Captain H. C. Hasbrouck. In April 1870 that unit was replaced by Company G of the Seventh Cavalry, still under the command of Lieutenant DeRudio. In May 1870 the cavalrymen rode to the rescue of settlers at the mouth of Limestone Creek who were being attacked by a band of Arapahos and Cheyennes. The latter post appears to have been on the site of Cawker City. Elder George Bascom reported finding a battalion of infantry there, "encamped on the bend of the river, about halfway down to the forks, in the site of Cawker City" in the summer of 1870.[75]

That raid had started on Oak Creek.

> On May 9, a party of Cheyennes and Arapahoes came down Oak Creek, and near the county line came across a party composed of Lew J. Best, Hatcher, R. G. F. Kshinka and John A Seger, from the settlement of Cawker City, who were looking up valuable tracts for settlers, and "rounded them up" in a buffalo wallow for several hours. The party of four were well armed, and by lying close to the ground and keeping up a continual firing at any advancing Indians, kept them at bay for several hours. Lew J. Best was wounded by a stray bullet in that part of his anatomy most exposed lying prone upon the ground. The Indians, finding the party difficult to capture, abandoned them, and passed east to the Limestone, and down the creek until they came upon the little settlement at Glen Elder, where they killed Solomon Meiser, John Geer [*sic,* Gear], and Mr. Kenyon. The bodies of these men were found in the river, a few yards below where the mill now stands. Mr. Geer was killed by a stroke in the forehead with a tomahawk, and was lying on a sand bar where the road crosses the stream, Kenyon was shot with a revolver, and Meiser was pierced with several arrows, which were still sticking in his body.
>
> The settlers fled in different directions, but nearly all found shelter at a stockade erected on the farm of George W. Stinson. Among those who sought shelter at that time were Hon. D. C. Everson, John Neve, Milton Spencer, Scott Guffey and many others. The troops came down from Spirit Springs, and the Indians fled, one party going north, and the other southwest.[76]

Pawnees inadvertently got caught up in this fighting. A party of forty of them came down the trail in 1869 and stopped at the homestead of a Mr. Skinner where, according to the settlers' point of view, they compelled Mrs. Skinner to cook for them. They were followed down Table Rock Creek to Mulberry Creek by an armed posse. Some of the Pawnees came up to the settlers, waving pieces of paper that turned out to be documents showing that they were members of the Pawnee scouts. The most recent duty of the scouts had been to protect the workers along the Kansas Pacific Railroad from attacks by Sioux and Cheyennes, and Pawnee scouts had participated in the Battle of Summit Springs that led to the rescue of Mrs. Weichell. In spite of this, the settlers opened fire on these Pawnee men and then chased the rest of the party into a cave where all but a few were killed. The next day one of the survivors was tricked into approaching another pair of settlers who shot him as well. Then, in a gruesome end to a nasty affair, soldiers were sent to cut off the heads from some of the bodies.[77] They were sent to Washington, D.C., for scientific study (James Riding In, personal communication).

After the flood of Euro-American settlement, which became overwhelming after 1870, the attacks ended. The last one, with no casualties, was on July 3, 1870.[78] Native Americans continued to come into the region around Waconda Spring for a few years, however. The Omahas came through on bison hunts, and a photograph of one of their camps ended up on a postcard (Figure 5.4). Their presence along Prairie Dog Creek in 1871 caused a minor scare, and Howard Ruede saw them on the South Fork of the Solomon in 1877.[79] He reported that on March 22, some six hundred of the party had already headed back to Nebraska, while a few remained to work for some Euro-American hunters. The party he saw was on its way home from the Omahas' last winter hunt.

Francis La Flesche told Melvin Gilmore about that journey, saying that the great hunting party gradually broke into smaller groups, traveling slowly and separately in order to hunt and trap, heading slowly toward their reservation in Nebraska. Since they did not have to be back home until planting season, they were in no hurry. He also said that the Omahas first worked their way eastward along various streams in northern Kansas to minimize travel in Nebraska where they were likely to encounter more severe winter weather.[80]

Those who remained in the camp on the South Solomon that Ruede saw (or at least the women in the party) were curing bison hides by their traditional techniques, for which they earned some of the hides. In one letter he says they worked for halves, but in another he said that "It costs one robe to have 2 finished by the Indians, and they are the only ones who know how to do it. The local value of a dressed winter hide was ten dollars."[81]

The Omaha camp was in the vicinity of present-day Bloomington, which places it about sixteen miles downstream from the point where the Omahas reached the river on the outward leg of their journey in December 1876. Then they came down a more westerly trail, reaching the North Fork of the Solomon at the town of Cedar and the South Fork at Woodston. They were forced to go all the way to White Woman Creek in Wichita County before they found a herd of bison. It was their last tribal hunt, and the future ethnologist Francis La Flesche was one of the scouts. Ruede also mentions a camp of about eighty Potawatomis in August of 1877. They were from the reservation in Jackson County and were one of the few emigrant nations who successfully resisted the pressure to vacate Kansas.[82]

The last "Indian scare" in the Waconda Region occurred in 1878. In that year, Dull Knife led the desperate run of a band of Northern Cheyennes back toward their traditional homeland.[83] Ruede reported the incident from his point of view:

> Tuesday, Oct. 8, and Wednesday, the 9th, were the dates of the memorable Indian scare, and many people left their homes and fled to Osborne. We did not go. A man informed me he had been told by one who had come from Russell that day, that there were 6,000 Indians between here and Russell. But I didn't believe it. Bill Garman and Fogel went to the Saline to see the red men, which they did not succeed in doing.
>
> The most probable clue to the cause of the excitement was obtained from a gentleman we met at the Covert post office, who had ridden from Hays City since Sunday morning. He states that, in view of the known fact of the Indians having crossed the Kansas Pacific Railroad some distance west of Hays City, it was thought advisable by some of the citizens of that town to appraise the settlers on the Saline adjacent to that place of the *possible* danger of a raid. The warning was taken as an alarm, which has spread with growing exaggeration down the valley.[84]

—Hunting out the Bison

Bison populations in North America seem to have reached a peak in the early historic period. In prehistory there had been times when there were few bison on the southern Plains, and the same seems to have been true in the central Plains as well.[85] The population growth may have been a response to the Little Ice Age, a climatic episode that brought lower temperatures to the Plains between A.D. 1400 and 1850. This meant increased effective moisture and hence better forage for the animals.

An eyewitness reported impressive bison herds in the Solomon River valley as late as 1869: "To the northwest, toward the head of the Limestone, for about 12 or 15 miles, west across that valley to Oak Creek, about the same distance away to the southwest to the forks of the Solomon past where Cawker City now is located, about 25 miles south to the Solomon River and southeast toward where Beloit is now situated, say 15 or 20 miles, and away across the Solomon as far as the field glasses would carry the vision, toward the Blue Hills, there was a moving, black mass of buffalo, all traveling slowly northwest at a rate of one or two miles an hour. The northeast side of the line was about one mile from us; all other sides, beginning and ending, were undefined."[86]

Soon after their population reached a maximum, a variety of factors conspired to reduce the bison to near extinction. The first of these was the adoption of the horse by the natives of the Plains. Horses became available after the Pueblo Revolt of 1680, and by the middle of the eighteenth century, nations as far north as Canada had taken to horses. This meant that they could hunt bison more easily and transport more meat to their homes. Long-distance bison hunting started before the arrival of the horse (see chapter 2), but horses made the hunts far more productive.

The second factor was an increase in the human population. In spite of the fact that epidemic Old World diseases devastated local populations, people poured into the Plains to take up bison hunting. Seen from the perspective of Waconda Lake, we have Comanches, Kiowas, Osages, Kansas, Cheyennes, Arapahos, and Sioux coming on the scene. They were followed by the emigrant nations who were moved to reservations in the eastern part of the state. All of them hunted bison.

Even before the advent of the horse, the strongest factor of all began to play a role, even though it was small at first. This was the connection of bison hunting in the Plains to the world economy. In the seventeenth century, after the founding of the Spanish province of Nuevo Mexico, bison hides, robes, and dried meat had a small market. Spanish governors sent out trading parties as early as 1630 to trade with the Apaches for these products, and soon these products were included in the annual mule trains that were driven to Mexico Viejo. Later French Louisiana and Spanish Texas opened up other markets.[87]

Then came the wave of Euro-American settlement that swept westward across Kansas after 1850. Human populations shot up, and local bison herds were exterminated quickly. The large herds were to be found only west of the line of settlement. Next the advent of the railroads made large-scale shipment of hides to market cheap and easy. Finally, extermination of the bison became quasi-official government policy—a certain way to force the native populations onto reservations and to begin farming. With a flurry of industrial-scale hunting in the 1870s, the bison were gone and a way of life came to an end.

In the account of the Ise family, who homesteaded in eastern Osborne County, only a single bison was reported locally in 1874.[88] Howard Ruede briefly mentions local men who hunted bison to the west. This was a winter occupation open to homesteaders and a potentially profitable one. He estimated that a three-month hunt had brought five to six hundred dollars apiece to some men in his neighborhood, at a time when a quarter of land with a few improvements could be purchased for seven hundred dollars.

—Establishing the Grid

The modern cultural landscape began to form when the land was surveyed. The system used in the surveys came into use as part of the provisions of the Land Ordinance of 1785, which made available for settlement lands west of the thirteen original colonies. It set out the rectangular survey system that governs land records today over most of the United States, creating townships six miles on a side, divided into one-mile-square sections.[89]

After the Louisiana Purchase and subsequent treaties with Native American nations, the amount of land available for settlement was enormous. Therefore, in 1812, Congress created the General Land Office (GLO) and charged it with surveying, managing, and disposing of public lands under the provisions of a series of laws including the Preemption and Homestead acts.

The system used started with a set of north-south and east-west base lines called meridians and standard parallels. Once these had been surveyed by the best teams available, the borders of townships were surveyed and marked. Finally, after the borders had been laid out, the section lines inside each township were surveyed. The whole process could take several years, and the teams that surveyed the meridians were usually different from those that did the work on the township and section lines. These survey teams differed in their expertise and in the quality of the work that they did.

The survey teams were instructed to keep notebooks in which they recorded information that might be critical to the settlers who would follow them. Some of the information they were supposed to record included:

> Intersections by line of water objects. All rivers, creeks and smaller streams of water which the line crosses. . . .
>
> Timber—the several kinds of timber and undergrowth, in the order in which they predominate.
>
> Springs of water—whether fresh, saline, or mineral, with the course of the stream flowing from them.
>
> Improvements. Towns and villages; Indian towns and wigwams; houses or cabins; fields, or other improvements; sugar tree groves, sugar camps, mill seats, forges or factories.
>
> Roads and trails, with their directions, whence and whither.

> Natural curiosities, interesting fossils, petrifications, organic remains, &c.; also all ancient works of art, such as mounds, fortifications, embankments, ditches, or objects of like nature.[90]

Unfortunately many of the surveyors were lax in following these instructions, and a road or trail may show up on a meridian line but not on township lines, and might be recorded on some section lines but not on others. In some cases a road shows up in the section-line notes but not in those of the earlier surveys because it came into existence after the initial surveys had been done.

The various survey teams turned in their notebooks at a regional office before getting paid for their work. It was then the job of a man in the office to create a map of each township from the survey notes. These maps are accurate along the various survey lines, but it was up to the mapmaker to guess where road intersections and stream courses lay inside the various one-mile-square sections. Even important features, such as springs, that could not be seen from the survey lines might not be shown on the maps.

The notes, and a summary description of each township, were available for potential settlers to peruse in the land office. But out in the countryside, only the corners and half-section corners were marked. Where timber was available, a wooden post was erected in an earthen mound and adjacent trees were blazed to make the marker easier to find. In areas where wood was scarce, stone markers were used. But many homesteaders had a hard time finding the original corners of their claim and had to stake them out partly by guesswork.

Figure 6.2 combines information from four GLO maps to show what the landscape looked like at the beginning of the homesteading era. The township lines were surveyed in 1866 by Elisha Diefenbach, and the section lines were filled in by E. C. Manning and D. E. Ballard the same year. They recorded a variety of natural resources such as the trees along the steams and all of the creeks and springs, along with a very few cultural features. They recorded not a single road, trail, or ford, but they did note the work of a handful of hardy squatters. In the 144 square miles in the four townships, the surveyors saw a total of three planted fields, the largest of which covered about three acres. They saw cabins beside two of the fields; the third may have been accompanied by a dugout. They did not record the names of the men who were living there, probably because they did not meet them. It is unlikely that any of the three stayed in this part of the Solomon valley through the Cheyenne and Sioux raids that began the next year.

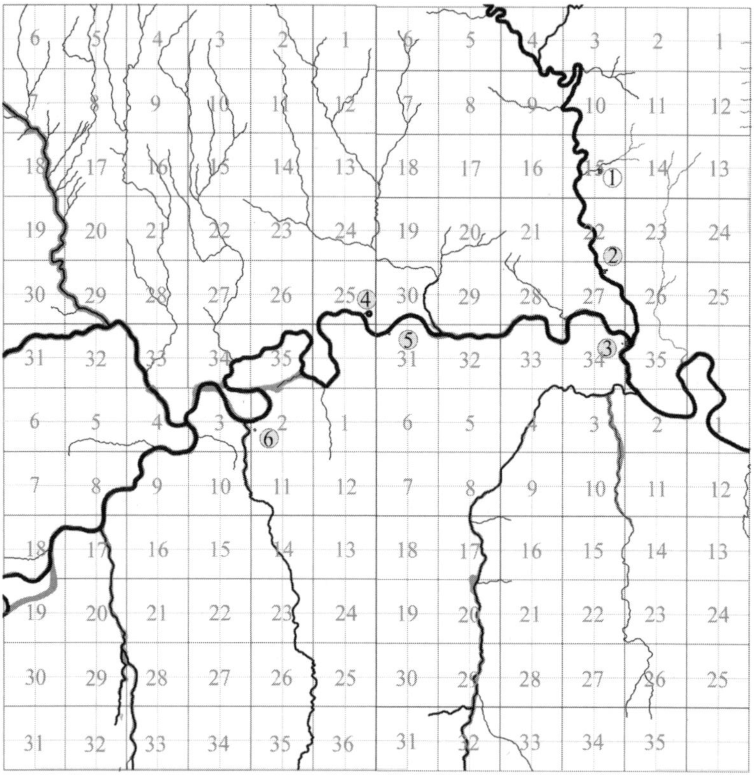

FIGURE 6.2 GLO maps of Townships 6 and 7 South, Ranges 9 and 10 West, surveyed by Manning and Ballard in 1866 (redrawn by author).
1. Cornfield of about two acres; 2. One-acre cornfield and cabin; 3. Three-acre cornfield and cabin; 4. Waconda Spring; 5. Saltwater spring; 6. Freshwater spring

The surveyors did better with the natural features. In addition to recording the widths, depths, and nature of the bottoms of the rivers and creeks, the species of tree, and undergrowth that grew along some of them, they noted the potential of the limestone that lined the valley, saying, "There is some very good limestone in the township [6 South, 10 West] that could be used for building purposes." They paid even more attention to Waconda Spring: "In the SE 1/4 of Sec. 25 is a remarkable Salt Spring known among the Indians and hunters that frequent that region as the Wac-an-da or Great Spirit spring. The spring of itself is a natural curiosity, it being located on the summit of a cone-shaped limestone rock. The rock is circular, about 120 feet in diameter at the base, and about 30 feet high. Upon the summit of this rests the spring, the basin being circular and about 80 feet in diameter. Its outlet is a trough apparently formed by the action of the water upon the rock. The water in the spring is about 20 feet deep and exceeding strong with salt; indeed the flesh of a buffalo that by some means had found its way into the spring, was found to be perfectly cured as it could have been by the application of any known process of curing meat."[91]

Even after the land had been surveyed and homesteaded, section line roads developed only gradually. At first the settlers walked, rode horses, or took their wagons on the straightest feasible routes to their destinations. The result was a landscape in which the prairie was crisscrossed by trails of varying visibility, on which the novice traveler was apt to lose his way. Then, as the various quarter sections were claimed and the homesteaders began to plan for breaking out the sod over large areas, they tried to discourage travel across rather than around their land. Howard Ruede described the process in Osborne County in 1877: "The prairie here is covered with trails running in all directions. It does not take many trips over such a trail to make a pretty good road, and when the track gets muddy, travellers turn out to one side, making a whole lot of ruts and putting the sod in very bad shape for breaking. To turn travel onto section lines is a hard matter too, for in spite of the board set up in the trail bearing the word, 'Closed,' some people always follow what they believe is the shortest road to wherever they are going. Stretching a wire with dangling rags across the road only makes matters worse, for the travelers drive around the end of the 'fence' and cut back to the old road at various angles. A furrow or two is sometimes drawn across the trail, as a warning to keep off and follow the section line."[92]

Often the section-line roads required improvements, especially at stream crossings and gullies, before they could see regular use. Ruede and his companions worked on the section-line road that was along the southern boundary of their respective claims in order to meet their poll tax obligations. The official sent out to supervise the work, however, told them not to work too hard.[93]

Sometimes the development of roads generated conflict within the emerging rural communities. Rosie Ise related a fierce conflict over replacing a section-line road with a half-section-line road. The section line in question fell along the course of Kill Creek so that it crossed the streambed repeatedly. This made it very difficult for some settlers to get to town whenever it rained. They signed a petition asking for the development of a half-section-line road west of the creek, but the people whose land would be bisected by the new road (and who eventually would have to build an extra mile of fencing) objected. The result was a series of lawsuits, the last of which was won by the opponents of the half-section road.[94] In spite of that outcome, the road had already been built, and people continued to use it. It is still in use today.

—Homesteading

We are fortunate to have, for the area near Waconda Lake, two extraordinary historical resources for the homesteading era. One is a set of letters written by Howard Ruede, who homesteaded in Osborne County in 1877. Ruede was an intelligent man and a close observer of his environment, and his letters provide insights to the day-to-day experiences of the people who came to settle this region. Specifically, he came as a bachelor with few monetary resources. Another account, by John Ise, is based on his mother's recollections. She came to the country as a married woman and was considerably better off at the beginning than Ruede, although far from rich.[95]

Homesteading in this region began in the late 1860s, with most of the land filled in a decade later. The new residents were drawn both from eastern states and from Europe. Germans, from Pennsylvania and other states, Germany, and Russia, were the largest identifiable ethnic group that came to the region, but Czechs, Danes, and Swedes also formed communities there. There were a few African Americans in the mix, but if there were any settlers of Native American descent, they kept the fact to themselves.

Settlement of the Midwest began under the provisions of the Preemption Act of 1841.[96] This law required the prospective settler to establish a home and then pay $1.25 or $2.50 an acre depending on whether land was within ten miles of a land-grant railroad. The claimant could buy up to a quarter section (160 acres). The basic cost was thus $200 to $400. The Homestead Act of 1862 reduced the financial requirements considerably. Under this law, a settler could claim either 160 or 80 acres depending on the distance to a land-grant railroad. The person had to stake a claim, pay a ten-dollar fee and four-dollar commission, take possession within six months, and live on and cultivate the land for five years.[97] The law allowed men over twenty-one years of age or any head of a family to homestead. After the five years of "proving up the claim" he or she then paid a four-dollar filing fee to take full possession. Alternatively a well-to-do person could pay $200 for title after only six months of residence. After 1872 the political clout of the veterans of the Union Army came into play, and the time provisions of the Homestead Act were loosened for veterans of the Union Army.[98] Ruede initially intended to take advantage of this recent law, but then he realized that he could avoid paying taxes on the land by waiting before establishing full title.

Henry and Rosie Ise homesteaded a quarter section of land a few miles northwest of Downs in 1873. Henry had filed the claim the previous year and built a cabin before marrying Rosie and bringing her west from her home in Holton, Kansas. Compared to many of their neighbors, they were relatively well off, owning seven cows at the time of their marriage.[99]

Howard Ruede and two other young men, Levin Brunner and a man referred to only as Jim, came to homestead in Osborne County from Bethlehem, Pennsylvania, in March 1877. They took adjacent claims on Kill Creek, about twelve miles southwest of the town of Osborne, and set about simultaneously proving up their claims while supporting themselves as best they could. They quickly used up the money they had brought from home, and Howard took pride in their self-reliance. He wrote to his mother to say, "A man in rags is as much respected as if he was dressed in broadcloth, provided he shows himself a man."[100]

The single constant factor involved in homesteading was hard work for men, women, and children alike. Howard Ruede's description of building his first dugout is a case in point. He and his two friends laid out a ten-by-fourteen-foot dugout on his claim, and went to work digging in order to make it six feet deep at the back end. Two of them began digging on Wednesday, March 28, with all three pitching in until the digging was done on Saturday. They dug in shifts—a necessity since they had only a single shovel. Then, with the help of neighbors, they cut sod and laid the walls in a single day. The walls were twenty inches thick at the base, with the individual sod bricks two to four inches thick, twelve inches wide, and twenty inches long. A man could carry four of them in a wheelbarrow from where they had been cut to the site of the soddy. To support the roof, they bought a burr oak tree for a dollar, trimmed off the branches, and hauled the trunk to the dugout in a borrowed wagon. Then they began roofing, which involved laying rafters covered with straw and then sod. Then Ruede headed to town to buy hinges while the others built a door and a bed. Not too long after their soddy was finished, a heavy rain caused it to collapse; they had not laid the walls vertically enough.[101]

Breaking the sod to begin farming was equally difficult, even with draft animals. Ruede noted that he expected the breaking of his first eight acres to take five days, if all went well.[102] Then there was the cutting of firewood, planting, cultivating, harvesting, and processing of crops to do. This, along with constructing the other buildings necessary for a functioning homestead. Digging a well took still more effort, as many of their first tries failed to find water.

Many people did this sort of work without access to all of the necessary tools, at least at the beginning. Ruede and his friends first bought a shovel and an axe in order to create their first soddy. These were their first possessions in the new country other than their clothing and a tin cup for drinking water. They borrowed a pick to help in digging the heavy clay soil, and one day Ruede walked for miles to return one pick and borrow another. Even a shovel constituted capital goods, however. After the purchase, Ruede was hired to do some digging by another homesteader, for which he was paid a dollar a day plus board.[103]

Poor food, and not enough of it, was another issue. By the time Ruede arrived on the Solomon in 1877, all of the big game in the Kill Creek valley had been hunted out. He wrote to his family in Pennsylvania, "In regard to hunting and fishing, there is nothing of the latter; of the former there is a good deal in the rabbit line." But the rabbit supply tended to be seasonal. Harvest activities often started up rabbits, and the men became expert at killing them with thrown objects—whatever was at hand. But purposeful rabbit hunts at other times of the year were often unsuccessful. Ruede reported one hunt that brought no rabbits to the dinner table but did yield one chicken hawk, and in one Sunday letter he reported eating rabbit again—his first meat since Tuesday.[104]

At other times there was meat but of dubious quality or kind. "Apr 17: Bill of fare—mush and broiled ham. The meat flies have got at it, and it must be used up soon." Later he reported having brushed thousands of fly eggs off of the meat he used for his dinner. When a neighbor treated him to a dinner in which the main course was raccoon, Ruede made absolutely no complaint.[105] Neighbors of the Ise family, however, looked down on their postmaster who was reputed to eat skunk.

The homesteaders drank a coffee substitute made from browned rye seeds. It supplied no caffeine but was an excuse for a hot drink. In spring, dandelion leaves, lamb's-quarter, and sorrel were picked for greens. Sorrel (which has a tart taste) was used for pies when no fruit was available. Soon after building his first soddy, Ruede transplanted some gooseberries to have a source of fruit. Rosie Ise and her children picked wild plums and made plum butter that occasionally fermented in the keg, with spectacular results for their cellar and for the livestock that got into one batch. Many of the homesteaders set out fruit trees as soon as they were able.[106]

Another persistent fact of life for many was poverty. Ruede had $75 when he left Pennsylvania, but most of it went to pay for transportation and food on the way to Kansas. By April 16, he had $2 in hand and $1.50 owed him. The next week he tallied the household possessions that he shared with his two buddies: "Apr 22: possessions for 3: 2 buckets, 1 crock, 1 earthen dish, 3 pie plates, 3 china plates, 3 pr knives and forks, 3 spoons, 3 cups and saucers, 1 cracked china cup for salt, 1 tin cup, 1 axe, 1 shovel."[107]

One source of cash was bison hunting. Ruede reported that some of his neighbors would head west to the remaining bison range for three months in the winter. For their work, the cost of their provisions, and the dangers they faced, they could expect to net five to six hundred dollars each when bison robes were bringing ten dollars each. This profit came after paying Omaha women a third of the robes for tanning them.[108]

Because many of the homesteaders were cash poor and without all of the tools they needed to make a living, a barter economy developed. At various times over the course of a year, Ruede recorded the following:

working at sawmill for a pick and some lumber
work for a neighbor in exchange for breaking sod
being given dinner for a morning of shelling corn
cutting wood in exchange for breaking sod: 3 cords for an acre
cutting wood in exchange for potatoes planted
cutting and stripping sorghum cane for half the molasses
working for $12 a month, cash or kind
a man working for a gallon of molasses per day.[109]

At the end of November of his first year, Ruede totaled his purchases over the previous seven and a half months. They came to $60.04, of which he paid $11.25 in kind. Other homesteaders would have had a higher proportion of in-kind purchases, but Ruede had a part-time job in the newspaper office that paid him in cash. Of his sixty dollars in purchases, $14.71 was for food, including eight bags of grain.[110]

In addition to the bartering, there were some modern elements in the economy. There were transient threshing teams that came through at harvest time, just as they do today. On one occasional, Ruede and his two friends negotiated with a widow to farm for her. She was to provide the seed, teams, and implements while the boys were to get half of the crops.[111] This is not very different from many present-day deals worked out in rural Kansas, but both this kind of deal and the migrant threshing teams might be thought of as holdovers from the earlier homesteading economy.

The truly modern elements of the farming economy in Mitchell and Osborne counties developed after the arrival of a railroad in 1879. This led to the founding of the town of Downs, with a variety of businesses including a lumberyard, making it possible for people to build frame houses and other buildings. It also allowed for relatively inexpensive shipment costs for exports. As a result, one bumper crop did not lead to a reduction in crop prices because there were crop failures in England. The presence of a railroad also allowed some of the area residents to eke out a bad year in 1881 by collecting bison bones to ship east for making fertilizer.[112]

The rural communities that developed during the homesteading era are often romanticized. Indeed they had many fine qualities. Hospitality was a given, including both a place to sleep and food for a hungry traveler. People loaned various kinds of equipment to one another and were usually happy to see any visitor. They ran errands for one another when they went to town, and in the winter, when the workload was less, there were impromptu parties that featured games and singing.[113]

In addition, divisions that became important later were subdued. Ruede was impressed by the fact that people from various religious denominations shared services:

> The people here don't go to church—they "go to meeting." Services are held in private houses. The various denominations are not exclusive, and everyone is welcome to the services whether he is of the particular faith of the preacher or not. A Roman Catholic and a Hardshell Baptist, or a Methodist are on just as friendly terms as though both had precisely the same creed and observed the same forms in their worship. A visiting preacher, no matter of what denomination, is always sure of an audience in proportion to the size of the house in which he has been invited to hold the service, and often the room is full and others unable to get into the house stand by the doors and windows to catch what they can of the sermon.
>
> At whatever house the services are held all the people present are expected to stay for dinner, which follows the sermon.[114]

Even the Ise family, which was not especially religious, occasionally hosted a meeting.

On the other hand, these men outnumbered women in the beginning. John Rees, writing from Asherville in Mitchell County to the Junction City *Union* said, "A word to the ladies: If you want to get married, come out here as we have a host of bachelors; but be sure to bring plenty of means with you, for that is the excuse 'can't support a wife till I raise a crop.'"[115] As Ruede put it, "Old bachelors are at a discount up on the creek, and I don't believe you could sell one for a quarter because nobody would bid."[116] Many of the men were quite rough, and it was hard to tell the gentlemen from the rough customers when both were dressed in rags and might have gone months without shaving and weeks without bathing. In addition, at any given moment, many of them were transients and perhaps criminals. One of Rosie Ise's neighbors was raped, and at various times when she was home alone, Rosie shot at one intruder and ran off another merely by pointing her revolver at him.[117]

The most widely hated criminals, but very common, were the horse thieves. Horses were expensive capital goods, and every homestead needed a team for transportation and plowing. Some people got by with an ox team, but oxen made for very slow traveling. Since the theft of a team could cripple a homestead operation, it is no wonder that horse thieves, when they were caught, usually paid with their lives. Two were lynched in Jewell County in 1871.[118]

Minor but persistent discouragements for the homesteaders included snakes, mosquitoes, fleas, and bedbugs. Soddies were especially prone to bedbugs that took refuge in the walls, and Ruede learned that plastering the walls was a good means of reducing the population. Visiting neighbors and other travelers, however, would replace the population eradicated by a conscientious housewife. Fleas were another nuisance. The Ise family was not bothered by them because they had a cellar under their floor, so that the fleas did not have a ready refuge from Rosie's killing hand. One of their neighbors who was not so lucky kept a toad under the floor of her cabin to eat the fleas and to serve as a pet to her children.[119]

Mosquitoes were a problem in wet years and in any farmyard that was not paved around the well. Ruede reported, "The easiest way, and one much used here, to get rid of mosquitoes in the evening is to make a 'smoke fire' before the door and let the smoke blow into the house." The solution, however, caused eye irritation, and people had to make a choice between forms of discomfort.[120]

Episodic discouragements included droughts, floods, blizzards, tornadoes, prairie fires, grasshopper plagues, rabid animals, and illnesses of both people and livestock. People tried to protect themselves from prairie fires by plowing firebreaks around their land, around their homes, and around their haystacks. But sometimes a fire was driven by wind so strong that the firebreaks were inadequate, and a homesteader might lose everything. Some people gave up and went back east, especially in the grasshopper year of 1874 and again during the droughts of 1880 and 1881. Others

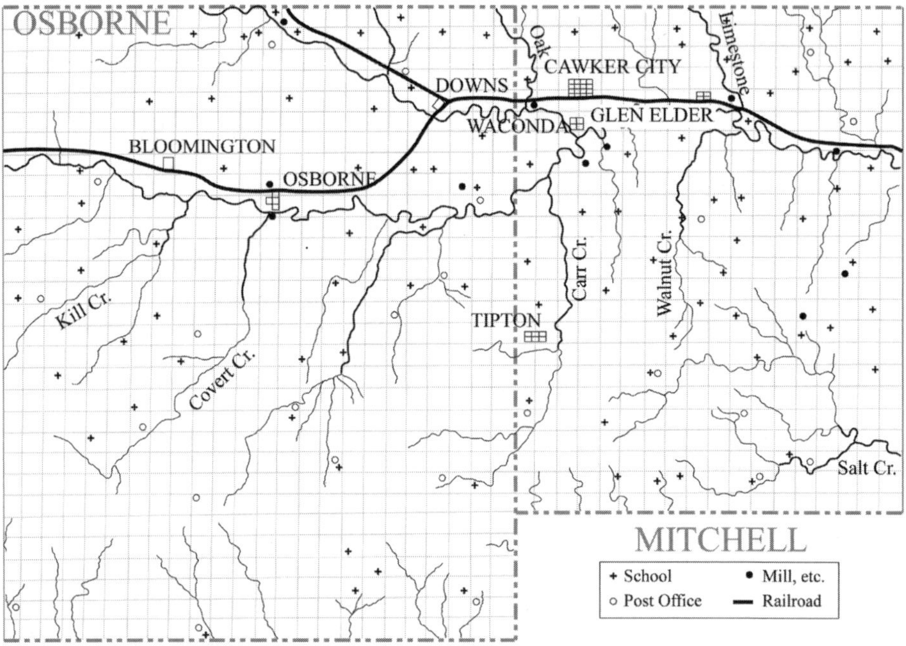

FIGURE 6.3 Map showing selected improvements made by homesteaders as of 1880 (redrawn by author using maps published by the Kansas State Board of Agriculture).

stayed on, more or less in spite of themselves: "When we have rain and crops, we don't want to go, and when there ain't no crops, we're too poor to go; so I reckon we'll just stay here till we starve to death."[121]

People did stay, and homesteads grew into farmsteads over the decades. The dugouts and soddies were replaced by stone or frame houses. Barns and other outbuildings were added, while the stables made of poles and straw were replaced. Some outbuildings were torn down; others were moved and adapted to new uses. In particular, a privy was a most welcome addition to the farmyard. Some of the growth that occurred in the decade since the flood of immigration in 1870 is recorded in maps published by the State Board of Agriculture in 1880. Figure 6.3 extracts the cultural features recorded on the maps for parts of Mitchell and Osborne counties. Towns, railroads, dozens of schoolhouses, mills, and the like crowd the landscape. The era of homesteading was over, and farming and commerce reigned.

Later maps were published as parts of county atlases by a variety of publishers. These maps show roads and the locations of residences, as well as springs and other natural features. I have taken maps from two atlases to create Figure 6.4, which shows the area around Waconda Lake as it was in 1900. In 1900 the average farm included 132.5 acres, and 44 percent were still the original 160 acres that had been homesteaded. Many had been subdivided, so that 47 percent of the farms were less than 160 acres. Only 9 percent were larger, with the largest ones containing a full section of land. Still the large farms accounted for only 21 percent of the land outside the towns. The growth of large farms still lay far in the future.

Our archaeological survey of the federal land around Waconda Lake found many traces of the homesteads and farmsteads occupied between 1870 and 1960 along with a variety of other features of the rural landscape. We found the remains of two wooden bridges across small stream courses. Both were on section-line roads. We also found the remains of a railroad trestle at the old crossing of Oak Creek. In addition, we came across seventeen historic trash tips. These are a common find in rural areas and usually are located at the edges of fields, at the heads of ravines, or in old structure depressions such as dugouts. Farms created a variety of trash that required

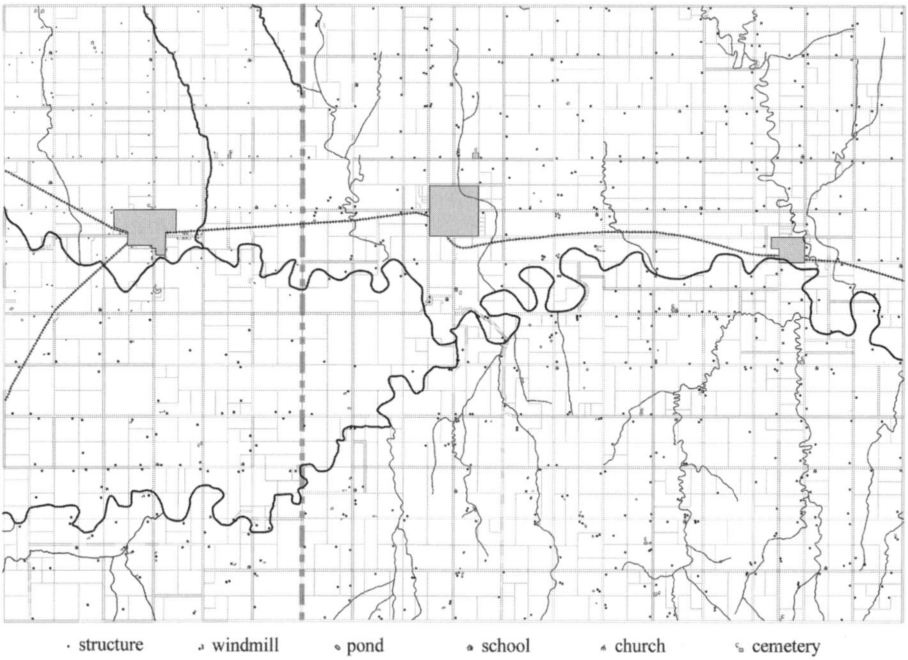

FIGURE 6.4 Cultural landscape in 1900 (redrawn by author from maps in various county atlases).

disposal, and any convenient spot that was relatively out of sight might be used.

We found a total of twenty locations of former homesteads and farmsteads. Since all standing structures were bulldozed after the government bought the land (because they would eventually become dangers to visitors), most of them were not readily visible. In two cases, we found only a single feature—a well or a cistern. In other cases, patterns of vegetation gave away the locations. We were alerted to the presence of one site by a growth of asparagus and to another by an iris bed. Eventually, we used aerial photographs, including a set taken in 1938, to determine locations of farmsteads and went looking for those we had missed.

When we found farmsteads with more than one foundation, we located all that was visible and mapped the remains. Sometimes we could distinguish the functions of many of the structures, such as house, well, barn, privy, and so on. The crews got to be quite efficient at this, and we thought we were getting a pretty good handle on how the farmsteads were laid out. Then we received the paperwork from the University of Nebraska project of the 1960s. Included were a set of contour maps made at the time the land was purchased that showed the locations of all of the buildings standing at the time of purchase of the various farms. To our dismay, we found that in no case had we come close to recording the locations of all of the buildings. Traces of many of the outbuildings had been completely eradicated, and our efforts to reconstruct what the farmsteads had looked like were shown to be seriously deficient. Since that effort had seemed the only reasonable thing to do with the remains—farmsteads occupied for more than a decade are notorious for having poor archaeological context—we are left with no coherent material record of the farmsteads. In the 1960s, documentation of standing structures and oral histories, which might have given us a decent permanent record, were not part of the research repertoire.

—Creating the Post Rock Landscape

On the south side of Waconda Lake, the flat-topped hills are underlain by the Greenhorn formation. This is a series of beds of alternating limestone and shale formed on the bottom of the sea during the Cretaceous era. The topmost bed is a solid limestone that, for reasons that will become obvious, is called the Fencepost Limestone bed. The flat-lying bed, less that a foot thick, is overlain by fairly thin soils, and along the sides of ravines and stream valleys it is exposed in minor escarpments.

The story of how this rock formation shaped the cultural landscape of north-central Kansas is told in an unusual book, *Land of the Post Rock*, by Grace Muilenburg and Ada Swineford.[122] Muilenburg, who worked for the Kansas Geological Survey, recognized the unique contribution that the Fencepost Limestone had made to the regional geography, and wrote a pamphlet about it that was distributed by the Survey. Later, with the help of Ada Swineford, she expanded the pamphlet into a unique book that combines geography, history, geology, and architecture to provide a coherent explanation of a unique cultural landscape.

The region around Waconda Lake is made unique by tens of thousands of miles of fencing held up by massive limestone posts. An estimate made in 1950 said thirty to forty thousand miles of stone-post fencing still stood in Kansas.[123] Elsewhere in Kansas, wooden posts and hedgerows were used at first and frequently have been replaced in more recent times by steel posts. But in this one region homesteaders and farmers made the decision to use stone posts, and many of the resulting fence lines still stand. Muilenburg and Swineford explain why and when the settlers made this decision and how they created the posts.

After the Civil War, when the bison herds were mostly gone from this part of Kansas, cattlemen drove herds of Texas longhorns onto what had become free range. Thus, in 1869, an expedition scouting for a railroad route up the Solomon valley encountered and killed a stray Texas steer and had steak for breakfast on a cold, rainy day.[124] By 1871 and 1872, Texas cattle were being herded along the Solomon River, where there was plenty of grass and easy access to water to fatten them before shipping them east.[125] But this was also the time that the land was being claimed by homesteaders who intended to farm rather than to herd, and the two did not mix well. Cattle were as happy to feed on corn as on grass, and the settler's crops were at risk. Incidents occurred, and lawsuits resulted. But the conflicts in this part of Kansas were not as serious as elsewhere on the plains, and the most violent incident seems to have been one in which a cowboy intervened in the course of justice:

> Some very interesting events happened here in the fall of 69 and winter of 70. [Cattle grazing] was a source of trouble to the early settlers in eating up their feed that they had fought to raise on their new sod fields. Some were so stripped of feed to raise the next year's crop that they were compelled to raise what they could by grazing their oxen and horses on the buffalo grass or go back east and get a job of work . . . The settlers got together and concluded if possible they would find the responsible party or owner of the cattle to use the law. They succeeded in finding a party they thought they

> could fasten the claim on and proceeded to have [him] arrested and [to] bring him before Justice [of the Peace, Solomon] Clark's court. The day of the trial was set. Before the hour had arrived, a cowboy caught Mr. Clark unaware and slipped a rope over him and took him along the river and picketed him out. When the hour of court arrived, Mr. Clark was not there to call court, consequently the proceedings went defunct.[126]

Originally fencing was the responsibility of the person trying to protect cropland, but there were many settlers and relatively few cattlemen, so the political outcome was predictable. Between 1870 and 1872, the Kansas legislature passed a series of laws making fencing the responsibility of the herdsman. This forced the cattlemen to control the movements of their herds more closely, but this did not resolve the underlying problem. The legislature also passed laws giving bounties to farmers who created cattle-proof fences with hedge or rock walls, but neither was an adequate solution. Rock walls could be built around small areas, but the cost in time and labor for fencing in a quarter section of land in this fashion was prohibitive. Planting hedge trees also had its drawbacks in this relatively dry region where a hot dry summer could kill all the young trees and where they grew so slowly that cattle could penetrate the hedge lines for years.[127]

This is why wire fencing came to the fore. At first, farmers tried using smooth iron wire, but it proved inadequate. The metal sagged in hot weather and became stiff in cold weather, snapping readily. And the animals used fences as scratching posts, stretching and breaking the wires. The massive need for adequate fencing led to widespread experimentation and the development of barbed wire. The timing was fortuitous. No sooner had Joseph Glidden and others invented varieties of barbed wire that could be produced commercially that the Bessemer process for making steel came on the scene. Made from steel rather than iron, barbed wire did not sag or snap, and the barbs prevented livestock from rubbing against it and trying to crawl through it. It took over the western market after 1874. There was no bounty for erecting barbed wire fences, but it was economical to use, so long as one had fence posts.[128]

The western two-thirds of Kansas lacked adequate timber to provide posts for fencing and wood for other uses. The Timber Culture Act of 1873 was an attempt to deal with this problem. It provided an extra 160 acres to a homesteader for planting and maintaining forty (later ten) acres of trees.[129] Virgil Pangburn, who grew up in central Kansas, had a childhood memory of carrying water to his parents' trees until they earned their land bounty. Then they immediately stopped irrigating the trees, which all died

(Pangburn, personal communication). Another drawback to wooden fence posts in the early years were the prairie fires that could destroy them.[130]

At first the settlers in the region underlain by the Fencepost Limestone used whole slabs for some small fencing jobs, such as creating corrals. They occasionally used smaller pieces for hitching posts. The first indisputable use of the limestone to make fence posts was in 1876, when settlers erected a fence around the cemetery at Bunker Hill on the Saline River. Apparently the idea spread like a prairie fire. In 1878 the Sixth Biennial Report of Kansas State Board of Agriculture said of Ness County: "The fencing in this [southeastern] part of the county is mostly made with stone posts." The Ninth Biennial Report, for 1893 and 1894, noted that the bedrock "is known in geology as post rock." Apparently this was the usage of Kansas geologists, because the official name, "the Fencepost Limestone bed," was given in 1896 by F. W. Cragin of the U.S. Geological Survey. In regional usage, "post rock" has won out, but the official name is used in geologic reports.[131]

While post-rock fences were widespread in 1878, not all of the land was fenced that early. For individual homesteaders there was a considerable interval of time between staking the original claim and having enough stock to want to fence all of their land. In the intervening period, one had to make do with a few animals and no fences. Since he had cows but no fence, Henry Ise paid a neighboring family to run his cows with theirs. Rosie Ise went and got the cows every evening to milk them and returned them to the herd in the mornings. The movements of the horses were controlled by picketing them—roping them to a pin hammered into the ground in a spot that had not been grazed recently. In 1880 Ise fenced some of his pasture and reckoned that it marked the end of livestock picketing for his family.[132]

Townspeople had a similar problem if they wanted to keep a milk cow. Howard Ruede reported that families living in Osborne hired a man to herd their animals for "35 cents per month per cow." He would drive the animals to a corral in town so that their owners could milk them, and when the corral became soiled with mud and manure, they would just move it down the street a ways and start over.[133] Presumably, however, this was a corral with wood rather than stone posts.

Getting to the limestone to create posts and other products was relatively easy. Since it outcropped on the sides of hills, one merely had to remove the overburden, which was relatively thin at the edge of the outcrop. In the early days, men shoveled the dirt away; in later years they used horses and slips to drag it off.

Creating the fence posts involved breaking or splitting the stone to shape. A crude early process involved using a lever to raise a slab slightly, wedging rocks underneath to maintain the tilt, and using a sledgehammer to break off pieces at the outer edge. Because it was difficult to control the breaks in the rock, this method resulted in a lot of waste and was soon abandoned for a more controlled process.[134]

The more sophisticated technique involved drilling a line of holes eight to twelve inches apart most of the way through the ledge of rock. Then pairs of feathers were inserted into each hole. These were slender half cylinders of steel with one end that feathered down in thickness at the same time that they flared away from the flat side of the half cylinder. Two feathers, butted together on their flat sides, were inserted in each drilled hole and a wedge placed in the V created by the flaring ends of the feathers. The workman then went down the line of drilled holes, tapping each wedge once or twice and listening for the sound when the rock began to crack. When he heard the telltale ping at one hole, he would skip past it and continue to hammer on adjacent wedges until the rock split along the line of drilled holes.[135]

All this work had to be done as quickly as possible because the stone began to harden as soon as it was exposed to air. Even so, a good workman could create only twenty to twenty-four posts in a fourteen-hour workday. Once they were made, the posts were dragged or carted to the fence line, the mode of conveyance depending on the distance involved. A crude sledge made from a forked branch could handle two posts at a time, while ten made a pretty good wagon load.[136] Some of the resulting quarry sites are readily visible today; we mention some of them below. Also present are a few piles of fence posts.

Handling the posts was hard work. Each one was five to six feet long, with a cross section of eight by ten inches, and weighed from 350 to 400 pounds. To create a fence, the farmer dug holes eighteen to twenty-four inches deep at about a thirty-foot spacing. He then manhandled a post into a vertical position and dropped the heavy end into the hole. After tamping the post, he grooved it or drilled it in order to be able to attach the barbed wire.[137]

At a spacing of roughly thirty feet between posts, it would take 160 to 175 posts to create a mile of fence. Corner posts were braced with an additional two "leaners" so that the wire could be drawn tight. Since two miles of exterior fencing was required to enclose a quarter section, a homestead required about one hundred twenty-three thousand pounds of stone fence posts, just for the exterior fence. In 1950, there were over 3.7 billion

FIGURE 6.5 Section of limestone fence posts. The post in the foreground has a groove resulting from the use of drill and feathers in splitting the rock.

pounds of fence post still in use. Figure 6.5 shows one such line in Mitchell County.

In 1900 the quarrymen worked fourteen-hour days for a dollar to a dollar and a half per day. Since a good man could break out twenty to twenty-four posts a day, the cost of his labor came to less than a nickel per post. A farmer who did the job himself tended to do the quarrying in the wintertime, when the press of other duties abated. If he bought posts from a quarry, they cost him an average of a dime per post in the 1890s. The price rose gradually thereafter.[138]

In addition to fence posts, the same limestone was used for "stone foundations and footings, stone well curbs, stone walls, and hollowed-out slabs, . . . drinking vessels and feeding troughs for animals, not to mention . . . gate posts, hitching posts, clothesline posts, and a few telephone poles."[139]

From the beginning of his time on the claim in Osborne County, Howard Ruede intended to build a stone house. He wrote home saying, "Stone can be had for the asking; or by going on [as yet unclaimed] government land we can get it without asking. A man can soon learn to be a stone mason here. There is a man here named Dengler, who never laid a stone wall before, and he is putting up a little house, and it looks nice, too."[140] Later he wrote, "I intend to make the house as large as I can without going too

TABLE 6.1. Schoolhouse architecture in Mitchell County, Kansas

Date	*Number of schoolhouses made from:* *Stone*	*Frame*	*Log*	*Brick*	*Total*
1875	21	12	16	1	50
1880	31	55	3	0	89

much expense. My only expense will be the roof (shingles) and the floor and windows and door. The stone work we intend to do ourselves."[141]

Schools and other public buildings were also made from stone. Muilenburg and Swineford provide some interesting data about schoolhouse architecture in Mitchell County (Table 6.1). In 1875, after about five years of development, the county boasted fifty schoolhouses. Over 40 percent were built of stone, while another 32 percent were log structures. In the next five years, only ten more stone structures were built, and most of the log schoolhouses were replaced with frame structures.[142] Ise describes the discomforts and poor environment for learning provided by a log schoolhouse in which students faced the wall to use a shelf that passed for a communal desk.[143] The switch from stone architecture to wood frame was in part the result of a switch from a barter to a money economy. Previously homesteaders would pledge labor as their share in building schools and churches. Money allowed them to contribute in cash and save their labor for family gain.

Log cabins and soddies could be plastered with bentonite clay mixed with straw, but building with stone required the production of lime for mortar. Muilenburg and Swineford describe a limekiln on Mill Creek that was used by one of their elderly informants. It consisted of a well-like shaft eleven feet deep and twelve feet in diameter at the base. It was excavated into level ground beside the cut bank of the creek, and a horizontal shaft connected the bottom to the cut bank to supply oxygen for the fire. The base of the shaft was filled with firewood, over which chunks of limestone were placed. A hot fire calcined the limestone, providing lime for mortar.[144]

It sounds like a pretty impressive structure, but limekilns leave little in the way of archaeological remains. Because the shafts were not lined, the walls eventually collapsed, and being located immediately adjacent to creeks, flooding filled them with sediments. We found one kiln site in our survey. It consisted of a more or less circular scatter of burned lumps of limestone.

In contrast, some of the limestone quarries we found are impressive sites today. There are a series of them on the south side of the lake, and unlike most other archaeological sites, they are not likely to be harmed significantly by unaccompanied visitors. A walking trail and an interpretive sign or two would make them attractive to park visitors.

At the same time that the stone fence posts were being erected, the railroad came to the region. Creation of the Missouri Pacific Railroad along the river in 1879 brought the founding of Downs and the opportunity to ship agricultural produce to distant markets. It was a critical enhancement of the local economic infrastructure, and many towns on the plains that were bypassed by railroads simply ceased to exist.

When automobiles became widely available after the introduction of the Ford Model T in 1908, a new force was unleashed. Automobiles required better roads than horse-drawn wagons, and D. Ward King's Chautauqua presentation in 1910, "Good Roads . . . Right Now," was an early expression of an outcry that reached a crescendo after 1920. The result was the creation of the national highway system in 1926, the local expression of which was the eventual extension of Highway 24 west from Kansas City through the heart of the Waconda Spring vicinity.

Not all of the long-term effects of this were positive. The greater speeds

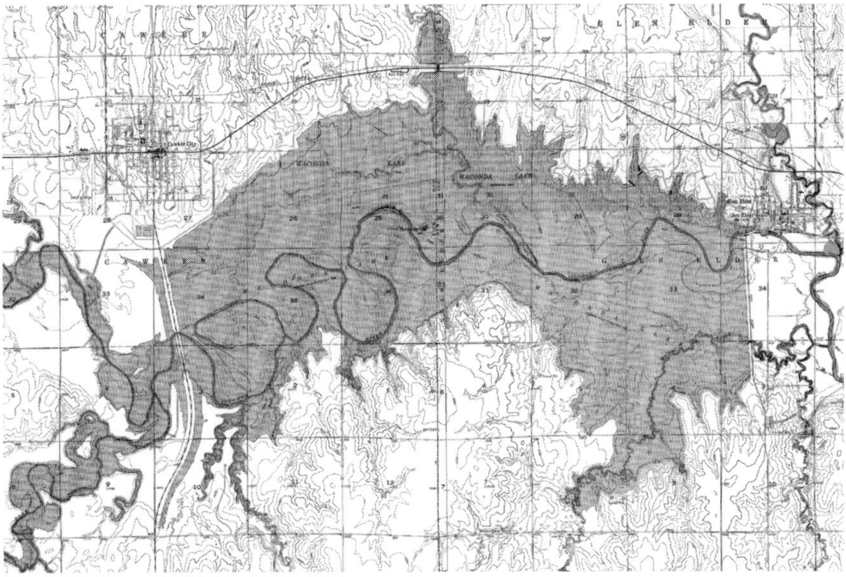

FIGURE 6.6 Glen Elder Dam (courtesy U.S. Bureau of Reclamation, Nebraska–Kansas office).

FIGURE 6.7 Visitors kiosk containing 'World's Largest Ball of Twine' in Cawker City, Kansas.

that automobiles allowed reduced the necessity of having towns as close together as they were in the horse-drawn era. A farm family that had to travel to town for business could go and return on the same day only if they lived within eight to ten miles, while a car could cover the equivalent distance in an hour. The economics of the situation meant that people could travel to more distant large towns where merchants (with increased volume) could sell goods more cheaply. This situation contributed to a long-term population trend all across region; since 1920, small towns have declined in population and only regional centers, such as Beloit, have seen any growth.

The construction of the interstate highway system, beginning in 1956, increased the problem. Towns and cities along the interstates had an advantage over those at a distance, and the Waconda Spring area is between I-70 and I-80, an hour's drive from the first and two hours from the second. Internal combustion engines also allowed the growth of larger farms, which along with government policies, further depleted the rural landscape of people.

The most important relatively new features in the cultural landscape are Glen Elder Dam and Waconda Lake (figure 6.6). The dam was built by the U. S. Bureau of Reclamation as part of the Pick-Sloan Plan for development of the Missouri River Basin. When the plan for the dam was published in 1961, it met with considerable local resistance from people who dreaded the loss of their farms and places important to them, such as cemeteries and Waconda Spring. In spite of that resistance, construction began in 1964, and the dam was finished in 1968. Today the dam and lake provide flood control, the municipal water supply for Beloit, recreation, fish, and wildlife conservation. Glen Elder State Park and the Glen Elder Wildlife Area draw hunters, fishers, and campers to the area, supporting a variety of local businesses.

Nevertheless, the total population of the area has continued to decline, and people are making attempts to draw more tourists. The Waconda Lake Association is working to enhance visitation to the lake with the Waconda Heritage Village, featuring the historic Hopewell Church, which was moved to the park in late 1994. In the future, they hope to build a full-scale replica of Waconda Springs. The Solomon Valley Highway 24 Heritage Alliance is a consortium of towns collaborating to interpret, preserve, and promote their heritage, each with a kiosk for visitors to learn about its attractions and heritage. Among them is the World's Largest Ball of Twine (figure 6.7), which in my opinion would be improved with the addition of the World's Largest Kitten.

7. Healing Water

ATTEMPTS AT EURO-AMERICAN settlement of the Glen Elder area began in the 1860s, but it was in 1870 that settlement began in earnest. In that year Charles C. DeRudio, lieutenant in command of Company G, U.S. Seventh Cavalry, under the provisions of the Preemption Act, purchased the quarter section that contained Waconda Spring for $200. He created a dugout and excavated a well there.[1] As we have seen, DeRudio and his command previously had been posted at a small blockhouse in the vicinity of the spring to guard settlers from Indian raids. Thus the passing of the spring from Native American worship to Euro-American ownership could not have been sharper. And with this act of preemption, Waconda Spring passed not only into a different economic system but also into a socio-cultural system vastly different in its beliefs from that of the Pawnees and their neighbors.

—New Myths

The first settlers in the region, those who had been exposed to raids by the Cheyennes, Arapahos, and Sioux, tended to be repulsed by all things native and viewed native religion as mere superstition. Thus Waconda Spring was called the "Devil's Washbowl" in an 1874 article in the *Cawker City Sentinel.* The anonymous writer of the article (who is clearly the A. L. B. who wrote a different piece for the *Republican Valley Empire* in 1872) said that he had camped by the spring for three months in the summer of 1854 and could "testify to the peculiar ideas that Lo had of this spring."[2] He said that he saw Indians bathe in and drink from the spring but offered no tribal identification. "Lo" was a code word used by Indian-haters on the frontier. Drawn from a line by Alexander Pope, "Lo! The poor Indian, whose untutor'd mind sees God in clouds, or hears him in the wind," the term "Lo" or "Mr. Lo" was meant to be ironic or sneering in tone. Use of the term indicated that the author had no sympathy at all for the natives, so this particular author's lack of interest in the identity of the nation whose rituals he observed should not be surprising. Neither should his use of the "Devil's Washbowl" for a sacred site.

In a later era, when the Dawes Act forced Native Americans to live on individual family allotments to and to sell "excess" lands, Ambrose Bierce, in his *Devil's Dictionary,* used "Lo" to double the irony and to aim it at the land grabbers: "Severalty, n. Separateness, as, lands in severalty, *i.e.,* lands held individually, not in joint ownership. Certain tribes of Indians are believed now to be sufficiently civilized to have in severalty the lands that they have hitherto held as tribal organizations, and could not sell to the Whites for waxen beads and potato whiskey." Bierce continued his satire with a poem:

> Lo, the poor Indian whose unsuited mind
> Saw Death before, hell and the grave behind;
> Whom thrifty settlers ne'er besought to stay—
> His small belongings their appointed prey;
> Whom Dispossession, with alluring wile,
> Persuaded everywhere every little while!
> His fire unquenched and his undying worm
> By "land in severalty" (charming term!)
> Are cooled and killed, respectively, at last,
> And he to his new holding, anchored fast![3]

A short time later, a new myth arose that involved a somewhat less debased vision of the native peoples. It makes its appearance in 1881:

> The reverence with which the Indians have always regarded the "Waconda" spring, is worthy of notice, as exhibiting in a marked degree some mental traits of a race destined to soon pass away. Upon this subject my knowledge is all second hand, but I am fortunate in having the following statement from one of the earliest settlers of Mitchell County, now a resident of Cawker City, a man whose character vouches for the truth of his words. In response to a request from me, he writes: "In answer will say, that through Indian interpreters I have the statement from various tribes visiting our

> spring, that Waconda, the daughter of a great Indian chief, at one time became infatuated with the son of another. The two tribes met at the spring, and being hostile to each other, the intimacy was strongly opposed by the parents, and a conflict ensued. The lover of Waconda, being wounded and weak from loss of blood, fell or was hurled into the pool, whereupon Waconda plunged in after him, and both were drowned. Ever since the spring has been called 'Waconda,' or the 'Great Spirit' spring, and the Indians believe that the spirit of Waconda still dwells in the mound, and sometimes becomes offended at bad Indians, and throws up vast volumes of water, drowning them."[4]

The tale of Princess Waconda is still being told. The Waconda Lake Association uses Princess Waconda in its logo, and the visitor center at Glen Elder State Park has a mural based on the story. But where did it come from? The attribution of the story to an anonymous but supposedly authoritative source is a rhetorical device commonly used in the nineteenth century to introduce a far-fetched story hatched by the author. So it would appear that it originated with G. K. Patrick, but it was hardly original. It is not a Native American story, but one of a type that the settlers brought with them. In a note that he inserted between pages 169 and 170 of his 1914 dissertation, Melvin Gilmore wrote: "A wholly fanciful Indian story of the spring has been invented by the white people, as usual, which has no manner of foundation in fact."[5]

As a local tale, it is the sort of story that folklorists call by a German term, *Sage* (plural, *Sagen*):

> This form of tale purports to be an account of an extraordinary happening believed to have actually occurred. It may recount a legend of something which happened in ancient times at a particular place—a legend which has attached itself to that locality, but which will probably also be told with equal conviction of many other places, even in remote parts of the world. It may tell of an encounter with marvelous creatures which the folk still believe in—fairies, ghosts, water-spirits, the devil, and the like. And it may give what has been handed down as a memory—often fantastic or even absurd—of some historical character. The story of the Pied Piper of Hamelin, of the wild horseman encountered by Ichabod Crane, of old Barbarossa sleeping in the mountain, and the dozens of tales of Indian lovers' leaps from cliffs all over America—all these are *Sagen*. It will be observed that they are nearly always simple in structure, usually containing but a single narrative motif.[6]

The story of Princess Waconda is pretty clearly just a variant of the lover's leap tale, with the spring standing in for the cliff. Stith Thompson says that the tale is found all over America, and that is not an exaggeration. Louise Pound published an article detailing the many variants of the tale told just in the state of Nebraska.[7] In fact, the modern local name for a Pawnee animal lodge in Nebraska, Ahkawita:ka (White River Bank), is "Lovers' Leap." It, too, is purported to derive from Indian legend.[8]

So widespread is this particular *Sage* that it has been given a proper name—the Winona myth—after a supposed Minnesota princess. Winona, at least, is an appropriate Siouan name for a first-born daughter; Waconda, or Great Spirit, is not. It's Princess Waconda in Kansas because the spring was called Waconda, not the other way around. In Tucumcari, New Mexico, it is Princess Cari—according to the local Chamber of Commerce—even though Tucumcari means "place of ambush" in Comanche. As Richard Dorson rather rudely put it, "White men have spun a kind of bastard folklore about the romanticized redskin, symbolized in the Lovers' Leap legend, but this synthetic folklore has become traditional and merits analysis."[9]

So what kind of analysis might be offered? One observation is that the Winona tale is often linked in the telling to the idea of the "vanishing Indian," as Patrick did in the account quoted above. In another local example, Marjory Hutton repeats a variant of the Princess Waconda tale in which the father kills the daughter. She ends her article with a piece of poetry purported to be an Arapaho song, addressed to Waconda, with the theme of the vanishing Indian.[10]

Another partial explanation for the newly invented *sagen* is that by connecting "ancient" and therefore Native American stories to landmarks, the Euro-American settlers were recreating something like the cultural landscape that existed in their homeland, one in which prominent features of the land had acquired their individual stories over the millennia. Why they drew so often on the lovers' leap motif is harder to explain.

Several other myths about Waconda Spring also developed, but they never had the popularity of the Princess Waconda tale. One, clearly derived from the form of the spring—issuing as it does from a circular vent at the top of a conical hill—is that it was formed by volcanic action. Another, based on the saltiness of the water and the fact that the water level rose and fell, is that the spring is connected to the ocean. In 1930, a geologist felt obliged to write, "Contrary to local belief the Waconda springs are in no way volcanic, and neither do they have any connection with the ocean. They are merely artesian springs and the water is mineralized because it comes from the saliferous shale lying at the top of the Dakota."[11] Both beliefs continue to be repeated.[12] The idea that the rising water would drown evil men has also been attributed to "Indians."[13] To the contrary, while Native Americans knew that the spring sometimes overflowed from the pool at the top of the hill, they felt their offerings were well received when this happened.

The idea that the spring is essentially bottomless and connected to the ocean has been the more popular and persistent of the secondary stories. It was even featured in Ripley's "Believe It or Not" in 1936 with the claim that the water rose and fell twice a day, just like the tides of the ocean.[14] According to local residents, the story was taken so seriously that when the dam was being constructed, a heavy equipment operator used a bulldozer to block the spring vent so that the new lake would not become as salty as the ocean.

A more reasonable observation, made by Carlos Bingesser, is that the level of the water rose and fell some ten to fourteen inches with the seasons. But on the Fourth of July, 1908, that good businessman G. F. Abrahams hired a deep-sea diver to make a public descent into the spring. He came up to announce that it was bottomless. He also brought up human bones, butts of guns, parts of tomahawks, pottery, arrowheads, and beads said to have been found on ledges.[15] The objects the diver brought up were probably real offerings left by Native Americans; as early as 1872 the *Concordia Empire* reported that people had pulled "muskets, beads, and blankets" out of the spring.[16]

A final story about the spring is being repeated. This one is the sort that is usually called a historical myth, meaning a misinterpretation of the past that is repeated so frequently as to pass for fact. When we began work at Waconda Lake, we were told that Sir William Johnson had apparently visited Kansas in the eighteenth century and had stopped at the spring. We eventually found essays that said this,[17] and so did a posting on the Kansas State Historical Society Web page. Sir William Johnson was an important figure in the early history of New York and once owned the springs at Saratoga. What was he doing in Kansas in the eighteenth century?

It turns out that the Sir William Johnson at Waconda Spring story derives from one of the early geological reports on the spring:

> This spring reminds one of the High Rock spring of Saratoga, N.Y., which was frequented by the Indians as early as the fourteenth century. It was called by them the "Medicine Spring of the Great Spirit." Professor Chandler, in writing of the High Rock spring, says: "The spring rises in a little

> mound of stone three or four feet high, which appears like a miniature volcano, except that sparkling water instead of melted lava flows from its little crater. When Sir William Johnson visited the spring, in 1767, the water did not overflow the mound, but came to within a few inches of the summit, some other hidden outlet permitting it to escape." This small mound was afterwards undermined in order to repair the spring, and under it were four logs, two of which rested on the other two at right angles, forming a curb. These rested on the black soil of a previous swamp. It was evident that the rock was built up by a deposit of water.[18]

So Johnson visited a spring in New York, not in Kansas. But there are similarities to both Waconda Spring and to its legends. Waconda Spring is a pretty good rendition, half in Siouan and half in English, of "Medicine Spring of the Great Spirit." Then there is the passing reference to the New York spring looking like a volcano, in keeping with the Waconda Spring as volcano idea. But perhaps more interesting is the clear evidence that the spring in New York was a sacred place for a very long time, time enough for a travertine cone to have built up several feet over the logs laid down in a square by early pilgrims to the site.

—The Spa Business

While they may have invented some new stories, the Euro-American settlers in the Solomon River valley brought with them elements of a very old European set of beliefs about health and spring waters. Springs were thought to be the abodes of major or minor deities (nymphs) who cured the ailments of visitors. Waters that were striking in color or taste (i.e., mineral springs), sparkled (i.e., contained carbon dioxide), had potent aromas (usually from hydrogen sulfide), or produced hot water typically were thought to be potent cures. In later years, when local deities and demiurges had been abandoned, the potency of the waters was still attributed to a mysterious or mystical "something" called the *Brunnengeist.*[19]

During the Roman dominion, baths at springs were common, but they were intended more for hygiene than for therapy. They included baths at various temperatures, including sweat baths, and there were facilities for exercise and sports, especially at the largest ones. Some public baths were endowed by gifts from the rich and famous. The Romans did treat some diseases at springs, particularly "chronic diseases and diseases of the joints and urinary tract." Votive offerings left by grateful visitors bear evidence that cures were sometimes obtained.[20]

By the time Europeans began coming to the Americas, European traditions regarding healing springs had been modified by centuries of Christianity and especially the emphasis on the future life rather than the present one. Bathing came to be viewed with suspicion. Still, common people visited springs. In the seventeenth and eighteenth centuries, drinking cures became popular even though bathing in the waters was not common.[21]

The English-speaking colonists in North America brought this tradition with them and were interested in springs both for curing and for business opportunities. Thomas Jefferson's *Notes on the State of Virginia* included ten paragraphs on medicinal springs and spas, especially the springs at Augusta.[22] He reported that the latter were said to be good for rheumatism. In New York colony, the great springs at Saratoga were first reported in a letter written in 1777 (but not published until 1793), which said that springs "have been considerably frequented by the poorer sorts of people, ever since their discovery."

That "discovery," in 1767, involved Sir William Johnson, a critically important figure in British interactions with the Iroquois.[23] After he had been wounded in a battle, his Iroquois friends brought him to the springs to treat his wounds. Johnson later owned the springs and eventually sold all but one that was reserved for public use.[24] The spa business was beginning in what would become the United States.

At first, the spas were fairly simple affairs. By 1750, Yellow Spring, Pennsylvania, had a "publick house of entertainment to the satisfaction and ease of the neighbors." In the 1790s, the business at Ballston, near Saratoga had a "pretty large house for entertainment, with near bathing houses and shower baths for the convenience of invalids." A full-fledged hotel was built at Sweet Springs, Virginia, one of the medicinal springs that Jefferson had described. Hotels also sprang up at Saratoga in 1803 and at Ballston in 1804. Thereafter spas sprang up as the line of settlement passed other notable springs. Hot Springs, Arkansas, had its first inn as early as 1820. Competition, evident in the fact that Ballston got its hotel a year after one was erected at nearby Saratoga, led eventually to finer and ever more elegant facilities.[25]

In July 1870, the town of Waconda was formed next to Waconda Spring, It had a population of only twenty-five in 1871, but Col. W. C. Whitney erected a stone hotel. Other businesses included a sawmill, brewery, and blacksmith's shop. The town added a school in 1872, and its population grew to a maximum of two hundred. But Waconda went into a rapid decline when the railroad was built through nearby Cawker City in 1882. The hotel at Waconda was abandoned to vagrants in 1887.[26]

Concurrent with the development of Waconda, another business venture was attempted. In 1875, Col. J. H. Cawker and R. F. Kshinka, with backers from Milwaukee, Wisconsin, formed the Cawker City Mineral Company to claim the spring under the Mining Act. They intended to make salt from the briny water.[27] They went so far as to hire workmen to clean out the spring and to have Dr. William H. McDonald analyze the mineral content of the water. The workmen were reported to have found "arrows, knives and other relics." Ultimately nothing came of this venture because (according to a note on a copy of the General Land Office survey map for the township) the mining claim was rejected.

Another money-making scheme proved somewhat more successful. A Mr. Burnham began selling the mineral water from the spring under the name Waconda Flier in the 1870s, and in 1884, in partnership with a Mr. McWilliams from Rochester, New York, he established a spa.[28] In 1902 Bailey provided a brief description of the spa in his report on mineral waters in Kansas:

"Hotel with accommodations for 25 guests. Hot and cold baths are provided. Grounds have been graded, and 600 shade trees planted. Ca.$ 10,000 spent on improvements. About 300 cases of water shipped last year, besides large quantities sent away in jugs and kegs."[29] The main structure was enlarged over the next ten years until it had forty-five rooms.[30]

The spa business evolved in a number of directions. One was that medical doctors come to own springs and run spas. In the nineteeth century, medical practice grew ever more competitive, and some doctors saw running spas as a fine way of enhancing both their incomes and their reputations. From 1906 until its purchase by the federal government, the spa at Waconda Spring was run first by Dr. G. F. Abrahams, then by his daughter Anna Abrahams-Bingesser and his son-in-law Carl Bingesser, and later by the Bingessers' son Carlos.

Another innovation was the sale of water from the springs, often to former patients who lived at considerable distances. As noted above, Mr. Burnham was selling his Waconda Flyer in cases, jugs, and kegs during the late nineteenth century. This was part of a widespread pattern that emerged first in Europe. Since travel to springs was more expensive than transporting the water from them, the owners of the popular springs bottled their water and shipped it to customers. The bottles, usually earthenware jugs, were carefully sealed to prevent evaporation. By the early nineteenth century, more than one and a half million bottles per year of Seltzer waters were exported.[31]

Some people tried manufacturing artificial mineral waters, especially after techniques for carbonizing water were invented. In 1774 a Swedish chemist published recipes for waters to match those from Seltzer, Pyrmont and Spa.[32] Owners of spas argued against the use of such "artificial waters," saying that the *Brunnengeist* was lost. The ultimate example of the entrepreneurial spirit shown in the shipment of water from spas occurred when the operators of the Blasing Springs spa south of Manhattan, Kansas, overcame the high cost of shipping water by offering dehydrated water (Bob Blasing, personal communication).

Another trend, fostered by the competition to offer finer facilities and more amenities than the competition, was for spas to draw customers more interested in relaxing vacations and mixing with other members of their social class than in matters of health. During the first half of the nineteenth century, touring spas became an upper- and upper-middle-class phenomenon:

"Significantly, for most of the travelers, the waters were only a pretext. What attracted them were not precisely medical problems, but the company of others, the multicolored world of a social life with promenades, clubs, cotillion, mask and other balls; races, hunting, sketching and later photographing; courting, serenades, romance, faro, prize euchres, champagne suppers, and the marriage market. Health and water, the excuse for all, had importance for only a few."[33]

Even water-cure establishments, which as we shall see, asserted a number of differences from ordinary spas began to emphasize pleasure along with their medical regimes. A brochure from the Round Hill water-cure brochure "invites to its enchanting retreats the pleasure-seeking, and those who wish for a season of recreation from the cares of business, where pure air, pure water, lovely walks and rides, and captivating scenery, may be enjoyed, without stint or measure."[34] This pattern was far more pronounced on the East Coast than in spots such as Kansas, however, where the facilities were not so luxurious nor the class differences as pronounced.

Instead Waconda Spring saw a period of use where it fit into an entirely different pattern that also had roots on the East Coast. Rather than existing "to the satisfaction of the neighbors," some spas began to be causes for concern. William Burke, writing of a spa in West Virginia in 1846, said, "There is one practice at this Spring so pernicious that it cannot be too severely reprobated; we allude to deep potations of mint julap [*sic*] and other spiritous mixtures, after coming from the bath that many of the cases said to have been injured by the water and bath may fairly be traced to mint julaps."[35]

At Waconda Spring the nature of the business changed from that of a spa to that of a house of ill repute. Under the management of one G. W. Cooper, between 1899 and 1905 Waconda Spring featured a dog track on the grounds and a bar in the basement. The latter was an ambitious affair in spite of its subterranean location. It featured a fifty-foot-long oak bar, carved from a single tree, that was nicknamed the "Blind Tiger." There was gambling in addition to drinking in the bar, and every night there was dancing in a structure called the "bungalow." This was in the same era as the development of the Lincoln Camp chautauqua described in chapter 8. The activities in the chautauqua were intended to be uplifting, but Gregg Dowd, a member of the family that ran the sanitarium in later years, assures us that some people attended the chautauqua by day and the so-called sanitarium in the evening. This was an era of fierce debate over the temperance issue. One advocate for abolition called Cawker City an "ancient cesspool of iniquity."[36]

The fun came to an end in 1905, when one of the operators shot his partner in a dispute over a woman. The local bank then induced Dr. G. F. Abrahams, the operator of a far more respectable spa in nearby Mankato, to buy the property and return it to a wholesome operation that would reflect well on the community. He did so, beginning in 1906. He, in turn, had his daughter Anna and son-in-law Dr. Carl Bingesser manage the place, and on his death the property passed to them. In time (1950) their son, Dr. Carlos Bingesser, and his wife Marjorie Sheahon Bingesser, took over management of the spa. It remained in the family until it was purchased by the Bureau of Reclamation.[37]

The operation came to have a post office (in 1905) and a swimming pool (in 1914). The latter is the concrete structure visible on the left side of Figure 5.3. Photographs of the pool and other structures at the spring were included in an advertising brochure that appears to date to the 1930s (Figure 7.1). The Bingessers continued to sell water directly as well as to take in customers, and by the mid 1920s, they were shipping 150 gallons per week.[38]

—The Medicine

The settlers also brought with them an evolving set of ideas about the causes of disease and possible cures. Some of the ideas went back to the ancient Greeks—that disease was caused by imbalance among four bodily fluids or humors. Although many practitioners had abandoned the humors as direct cause, the idea of imbalance still carried a good deal of force: "Nineteenth-century medical practitioners and laypersons . . . assumed

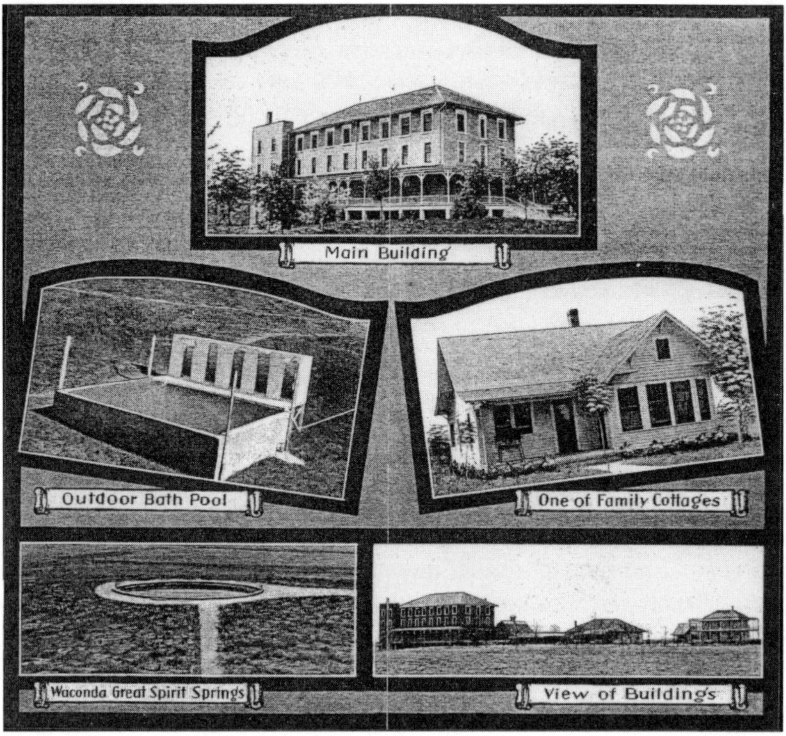

FIGURE 7.1 Images of the Waconda Spring Spa (courtesy Kansas State Historical Society).

that the body possessed a finite amount of "fixed energy," or "vital force." Physicians believed that health was achieved through an equitable distribution of this fixed quantity of life force. Consequently, illness resulted when one area of the body possessed too little or too much of the needed force."[39]

More specifically, American medicine had been influenced strongly by the ideas and practices of Benjamin Rush, the most prominent physician in North America at the time of the revolution. Rush recognized two kinds of causes for debility, but the result in both cases was a system vulnerable to over-response to any cause of excitation. Therefore treatment should take the form of removal of excess energy.

The outcome was a form of mainstream medicine in which physicians used venesection (bloodletting), local bleeding via cupping or the application of leeches, emetics, cathartics, and purges. Following Rush's lead—and he believed that too little bloodletting was a dangerous form of excitement of the patient—massive doses and extensive bloodletting became the norm. This was the age of "heroic" therapies in which the physician was supposed to intervene dramatically in the course of the disease. Given that four-fifths of the patient's blood might be drained, interventions were life-threatening.[40] So were some of the harsh drugs that were prescribed in the hope of destroying the disease without killing the patient—drugs that might contain mercury or arsenic. "Among the commonly employed emetics were tatar, antimony, zinc sulfate, and ipecac; regularly prescribed cathartics included tamarind, magnesia, jalap, and the highly poisonous calomel (Mercurous chloride)."[41]

In such a system, calling in a physician was seen as a last resort, and mainstream physicians and their "cures" were feared by many. Nevertheless, mainstream physicians adhered to science as it was then understood; the problem was that science had not evolved far enough to provide a better understanding of disease. Regular doctors had a meager supply of knowledge and usually very poor training. Still, mainstream medicine did evolve, and toward some more modern understandings. Rest was added to the list of treatments in the 1830s.[42]

As chemistry advanced, it was applied to the question of what constituents of mineral spring water might be curing people. Analysis of water from springs in Bristol, Pennsylvania, was performed in 1768, from Sweet Springs, West Virginia, in 1774, and from Saratoga in 1787. The latter included a list of medical indications and contraindications.[43] Analyses of the water from Waconda Spring were a part of this trend. Nevertheless, the continuing search for active ingredients, which began with anions such as iron or sulfur, proceeded through cations, especially iodine, to trace elements, and finally even radioactivity, without ever conclusively identifying an ingredient that cured a particular disease.[44]

While the chemical analysis of water from mineral springs never identified an obvious cure for any disease, such analysis did lead to another business concept. Various attempts, each more sophisticated than the last, were made to manufacture artificial (as opposed to dehydrated) mineral water. The science began in the eighteenth century and developed quickly in the nineteenth, becoming big business. Friedrich Adolf Struve, a Dresden doctor, built factories that bottled artificial but chemically accurate mineral waters in Dresden, Leipzig, Berlin, Brighton, Königsberg, Warsaw, Moscow, Kiev, and Petrograd. "Such competition made the owners and managements of many European spas nervous and led them to preach that the *Brunnengeist* which disappeared during bottling and could not be artificially reproduced, was the main effective constituent of water."[45]

—Sectarian Medicine

The mainstream physicians of the nineteenth century faced opposition from a variety of forms of alternative medicine. Sometimes called sectarian medicine, they bear some resemblances to alternative or New Age approaches of the present. Comprising roughly 20 percent of the medical practitioners in nineteenth-century America,[46] they included Thomsonian, eclectic, homeopathic, and hydropathic practitioners, or, as a mainstream physician raged in 1850: "Homeopaths . . . Hydropaths . . . Magnetic and Mesmeric doctors . . . Paw doctors, who profess to cure by friction with the hand . . . Indian doctors . . . Cancer doctors . . . Seventh-son doctors . . . Thomsonian doctors . . . Natural bone setters . . . Botanic doctors . . . oculists, and aurists, lung, liver, kidney, and urine doctors, dyspepsia doctors—pill doctors . . . and panacea doctors."[47] Amidst all this variety, there was a set of fairly substantial sects that shared elements of opposition to mainstream medicine. Among them were Thomsonianism, eclecticism, homeopathy, hydropathy, naturopathy, and osteopathy.

Dr. Samuel Thomson sold medicines in kit form for home use. He actually patented his system and then sold it to subscribers for $20 apiece. All of the medicines he promoted were based on botanical preparations, with none of the mercury and arsenic of mainstream medicines. He retained the large doses, however. An attractive element for many consumers was the concept of self-medication. Thomsonianism aspired to be big business; it had medical schools, stores, and infirmaries, and formed Friendly Botanic Societies to spread the word.[48]

Eclecticism grew from Thomsonianism, with, as its name implies, elements drawn from other sects. Founded by Dr. Wooster Beach, it took what he deemed to be the "redeeming traits" of other systems. Milder emetics based on vegetables replaced calomel, mercury, and arsenic, but they were still administered in large doses. One of eclecticism's most important innovations was the promotion of female doctors. This was in direct contradiction to the mainstream medicine of the time, which viewed women as inherently weak and unable to shoulder the responsibilities of a physician without endangering their own health. Indeed, women's natural reproductive passages were viewed as forms of illness, a succession of crises emanating from the womb.[49]

Samuel Hahnemann founded the homeopathy movement in 1825. He substituted very minute doses of medicines for the mainstream physician's heroic ones. And the drugs he recommended were supposed to produce the *same* symptoms as those that the patient already exhibited. He cited the "law of the cure"; that like cures like. He also believed that the smaller the dose, the more potent it was. In addition to medicines, he emphasized self-care, fresh air, pure foods and water, and avoidance of overstimulation. Finally, Hahnemann coined an epithet for the mainstream physicians, calling them "allopaths" to emphasize that they were just another sect.[50]

Still another popular medical sect in the latter half of the nineteenth century was phrenology. Remembered today only for being the quaint idea that a person's personality can be "read" by feeling the shape of the skull, phrenology was actually based on the newly discovered scientific understanding that various parts of the brain have different functions. It was popularized in United States by Orson Squire Fowler in the 1840s. Soon phrenologists flooded the lecture circuit. Their teachings included rectifying health problems through prescriptions based on the shape of the patient's skull. Based on their approach, they also denied women's inferiority, and their prescriptions included temperance, exercise, fresh air, and dress reform.[51]

In these suggestions they were aligned with hydropathy, a medical sect that (along with naturopathy and osteopathy) clearly influenced treatment at Waconda Spring under the management of the Bingesser family. This might seem contradictory, since the proponents of hydropathy emphasized the use of pure soft water as opposed to mineral water, and hence were opposed to the use of mineral springs for therapy. In spite of the vocal conflicts, however, all of the forms of alternative medicine, including treatment at spas, borrowed heavily from one another and tended to share other reformist tendencies as well.

Hydropathy was founded in the early 1830s by Vincencz Priessnitz, who opened a treatment center at Gräfenburg. An uneducated peasant who began by treating himself for various ailments, Priessnitz decided that the panacea for all human ailments was cold, pure water. Preissnitz had his patients drink twenty to thirty glasses of cold water a day and urged them to exercise, to behave temperately, and to avoid flannel and cotton, which he thought weakened the skin. There were to be no medicines, no reading or other intellectual effort, no gambling, and no "immoral excitement."[52]

Father Sebastian Kneipp, the founder of what came to be called naturopathy, prescribed similar treatments: soaks and showers along with wading in the dew or in shallow pools, herbal baths, a vegetarian diet, and exercise in the fresh air. Both men called for a return to simple, natural cures as opposed to unnatural and harsh drugs, and argued that pure water was the source of most cures. And given Priessnitz's lower-class origins, their movement was a challenge to the medical establishment, which in both Europe and the United States was of, and served, the upper and upper middle classes. Early on, Priessnitz was charged with practicing medicine without a license, but because he prescribed only water, he was found innocent.[53]

Hydropathy was carried from Germany to England in 1842 and to the United States in 1843, when it was introduced in New York City by Dr. Joel Shew. Its main tenet was that internal consumption and external application of "pure," soft water, when combined with a carefully prescribed regimen of fresh air, exercise, diet and the elimination of various excesses and artificial habits of "civilized" life, could prevent illness and cure all known diseases. It was what today would be called holistic medicine, as it involved not only the ingestion and application of water but also consideration of diet, exercise and other aspects of behavior.[54]

Spas that treated patients according to Priessnitz's system were called water-cures, never spas. American cold-water cures disdained the lifestyle they associated with mineral springs because it emphasized indulgence and frivolity in lieu of restraint and commitment. But in order to draw customers, the managers of water-cures soon learned to advertise luxurious accommodations and serene pastoral settings, just as spas did. The differences were more in the rhetoric than in actuality. Like the spas, water-cures wanted a resident physician, who was often a physician-owner, and the larger ones wanted a woman physician as well.[55]

Hydropathists developed a theory that attributed all diseases to two sources: hereditary lack of vital force in either the germ (egg), sperm, or both, and violation of basic laws of hygiene. They consistently saw disease as a negative—a lack of health—rather than an entity as in mainstream medicine. Thus their treatments never involved the removal of anything from the body by purges, emetics or bleeding. They also differed from the mainstream of the day in denying that women's health problems are derived from an inherent weakness in that sex.[56]

In this country, hydropathists advocated a reformed way of life that included at least an approximation of a vegetarian diet and, for women, dress reform. Dress reform did not involve avoidance of cotton and flannel as in Germany but avoidance of corsets and other restrictive dress in favor of what was called the American costume. This style featured a relaxed waist and bloomers or trousers or at least a simple, relatively short skirt in place of the long heavy skirt and numerous petticoats that fashion then demanded.[57]

Indeed, hydropathy was allied with a wide range of reform movements that included early feminism, calls for a vegetarian way of life, temperance, and the like. The *Water-Cure Journal* promoted vegetarianism, temperance, physical education, and, most important, dress reform and an expanding domestic and social realm of influence for women.[58] One allied reformer was Dr. James Caleb Jackson, a leader of the Seventh-Day Adventists and inventor of Granula (not granola), a cold breakfast cereal. Jackson was a reformer first and only later a hydropathy advocate. He began his career in the 1830s as a lecturer on abolition and temperance, and turned to hydropathy only in 1850 after undergoing a cure.[59]

Another co-reformer was John Harvey Kellogg, who invented Grape Nuts and wheat flakes, two other cold breakfast foods that he hoped would moderate sexual drives.[60] A third was Sylvester Graham, who advocated frequent bathing, fresh air, regular exercise, vegetarian diet, dress reform, sunlight, and sexual hygiene while also inventing Graham crackers as a vegetarian food.[61]

Water-cure advocates often argued against taking coffee, tea, and tobacco as well as stronger stimulants, arguing that once a person was inured to mild stimulants, hard-core intoxicants were sure to follow. Substitute marijuana for coffee and tea, and you have a present-day argument. One of the reasons for their opposition to medical drugs is that most patent medicines contained high levels of alcohol. Medicines, therefore, were a surreptitious delivery system for alcohol. A poll of fifty temperance workers by the *Ladies' Home Journal* in the 1890s found that 74 percent regularly imbibed medicines that contained alcohol.[62]

Given their attitude toward women's health, the hydropathists, like the eclectics, supported the careers of women physicians. When they developed their own medical school, it was open to both sexes, and women earned medical degrees there. The larger water-cures wanted to have a woman physician on staff to treat the female patients, and a consequence of this was the creation of jobs and careers for at least a few women. And naturally such institutions drew women's rights advocates as patients.

Naturopathy came to the United States with Benedict Lust, who was sent to spread the word by Father Kneipp. Lust founded the American School of Naturopathy in New York, the first naturopathic college in the United States, and promoted the specialization so that it was eventually licensed in several states. Carl Bingesser, Anna Abrahams-Bingesser and Carlos Bingesser all carried the title ND, Doctor of Naturopathy. As such, they adhered to its basic treatments, which rely exclusively on natural remedies, such as sunlight, air, and water, supplemented with diet and therapies such as massage. They believed that the mineral properties of the spring water, combined with a diet prepared by Anna—a diet they claimed harmonized with the ingredients of the water—along with plenty of rest could cure or alleviate many conditions.[63]

Carl Bingesser also held a DC degree, Doctor of Chiropractic. Chiropractic medicine was founded in the late nineteenth century by Daniel David Palmer. He came to believe that all health problems could be cured or prevented through spinal adjustments. He developed a vitalistic theory that involved what he called vertebral subluxations that interfered with the body's ability to deliver "innate intelligence" to one or more organs. Although chiropractic began as one holistic approach among many, it survived when other movements died away. Manipulation of the spine has been shown to be helpful, not with all diseases, but with some. Its utility for alleviation of lower back pain has been demonstrated.[64]

Another long-term survivor is osteopathy, and Carlos Bingesser earned a Doctor of Osteopathy degree. This approach to medicine was started by Andrew Taylor Still, who practiced medicine in Kansas for part of his career. He served as a physician in the Union Army during the Civil War and returned to the frontier. He lost faith in mainstream medicine when he lost two sons to infectious disease, and unencumbered by an advanced education (he had become a doctor through apprenticeship, not formal schooling), he developed his own idiosyncratic approach to healing. Still believed that the human body was capable of curing itself and that the physician's role was to remove impediments to proper somatic function. He asserted that diseases were caused by mechanical interference with nerve and blood supply, and were curable by manipulation of "deranged, displaced bones, nerves, muscles—removing all obstructions—thereby setting the machinery of life moving"—a method that came to be called Osteopathic Manipulative Treatment (OMT). He also recommended that his patients develop a healthy lifestyle with proper nutrition and abstain from alcohol and drugs. These treatments and prescriptions were informed by a philosophy that emphasized a holistic view of the person—body, mind, and spirit. Still founded the first osteopathic college in Kirksville, Missouri, in 1892.[65]

If osteopaths had adhered strictly to Still's beliefs, the practice probably would have died out long ago. He wrote in his autobiography that he could "shake a child and stop scarlet fever, croup, diphtheria, and cure whooping cough in three days by a wring of its neck." In the twentieth century, however, schools of osteopathy in the United States incorporated more and more mainstream medicine into their curricula, and modern osteopaths apply OMT to a minority of their patients.

It is a fair question as to whether spas or water-cures, homeopaths, naturopaths, early osteopaths or chiropractors, or even mainstream physicians, actually cured many patients in the nineteenth century. The honest answer, for all of the above, is probably no. Certainly they could not cure acute diseases, but this is not to say that they did not make their patients feel better. "Particularly in an era when the therapeutics themselves held only minimal hope of curing disease, the symptomatic relief offered by water-cure therapies, because they emphasized the relief of suffering [as opposed to sometimes horrific effects of heroic allopathic interventions] was significant and accounts in large part for their efficacy."[66]

In addition to relieving symptoms directly, spas and water-cures, naturopaths, and others tried to teach their patients good hygiene, and the patients probably benefitted from the placebo effect:

> A spa is a place away from home, away from business and routine worries, away from tensions; it is a place where (unpleasant) news arrives late or unobtrusively; it is a place where the scenery and diversions are pleasing, where someone else does the marketing, cooking, and cleaning, where business associates have difficulty establishing or maintaining communication. At a spa, the patient meets many others with complaints similar to his own; he may compare and commiserate. Some persons, physicians, for example, are loath to discuss their symptoms; but there are large numbers of people who derive deep satisfaction from recounting their ailments and treatments. A spa is a place to talk about symptoms—in the pump room, after a concert; there is always time at a spa.
>
> A spa is a place where people of limited means may enjoy luxurious living for a while. They may bathe in marble pools, walk in elegantly flowered parks with fine statues and fountains. Always, they may take their time. Even the physicians at a spa have more time for the patient than do busy physicians in a city. For the patient from the small village, there are medical facilities that may not be available back home. Most people who visit a spa for their health go in high expectation of regaining it. Motivation is very high; it would be difficult to find a better psychologic setting for medical care than a spa.[67]

Most of the various medical sects did not survive long into the twentieth century. As science advanced, the scientifically based mainstream physicians began to claim some real cures. These came first with vaccines, then with the germ theory of disease, the application of hygiene to hospital settings, and finally to the development of penicillin and other effective drugs. The emergence of public health professionals allied with scientific medicine undercut the various sects, and there were closings and mergers of homeopathic, eclectic, and other schools between 1906 and 1910. Schools of osteopathy incorporated more and more mainstream medicine in their curriculum, and the original emphasis on physical manipulation of the patient faded away. A few water-cures survived into the twentieth century by broadening their range and including water as just one of a set of therapies.[68]

Thus when the Abrahams-Bingesser family took over the operation of Waconda Spring in 1906, it was at the end of the era in which spas and water-cures had thrived. Their operation, however, drew on the best that the various reform traditions had to offer. Dr. Carl Bingesser treated patients for rheumatism, gout, sciatica, arthritis, lumbago, neuritis, stomach and intestinal disorders, and non-infectious skin diseases—the same suite of ailments for which other spas and water-cures offered hope. For the most part these are chronic problems that rest, relaxation, and a good diet would probably help, at least temporarily. Hot baths in the mineral water and massages were part of the daily regimen.[69]

Anna Bingesser, the female presence on the staff, was in charge of the gardens and the kitchen. Only natural foods, much of them grown on the grounds, supplemented the intake of mineral water from the spring. Even the use of pepper was prohibited, generating the bland "hospital food" that Perry Weston (see below) complained about. The spa at Waconda Spring, with elements from the hydropathy movement and other reform movements, continued to be successful and reputable until the very end

—Inside the Waconda Spring Sanitarium

A personal look at the operation of the Waconda Health Resort comes from the papers of Perry Weston who was a patient there at intervals between 1916 and the 1930s. He, his wife, and his father (who also was a patient at one time) wrote letters home that contain snippets of information about everyday life there and about the kinds of treatment received.[70]

In 1916 the spa averaged forty patients, with three to four arriving and departing every day. There was the hotel and the cottage plus another building near the road. During the time his wife was with him, Perry had a room in the hotel, but once she left, he was transferred to the cottage. Weston also mentions a swimming pool (Figure 7.1). In 1917 he mentions hundreds of tourists visiting the spring every day.

Weston suffered from a heart condition for which angina (chest pains), jaundice, and edema (swelling) were some of the symptoms. The treatments he received included rest, bath treatments, and a restricted diet. The enforced rest included lots of afternoon naps and other relaxing activities. Perry spent some of his time in the card room playing pitch. Another activity was fishing on the Solomon River. In a letter dated June 4, he reported taking an automobile ride up the valley. This departure from his normal life seems to have been on his mind, as his letters home were filled with inquiries about the farm work that he normally would have been pursuing.

Occasionally he mentioned the baths, both hot and cold, in the mineral water. Perry mentioned "fairly cool baths, but hot enough to sweat," followed by cold. The hot baths became increasingly hot, and on June 7, he wrote, "stood the water at 115 1/2 today." One day he fell asleep after a hot bath, when he had been put on a bench to cool. While he was sleeping, Dr. Bingesser wrapped him in hot rags to prolong the sweat.

Patients drank only rainwater and mineral water from the spring . Perry did not complain about this, but his wife did. In one letter, she mentioned looking forward to being back home where she could have a drink. Perry did complain about the diet, however. When his wife left, he wrote to his parents to ask her to tell them about life at Waconda Spring, "especially the hospital food." In another, he refers to "hospital food, in small amounts." Later, he reported, "They have put me at the diet table and by God I don't get nothing to eat to amount to anything. All I get is toast and soup."

Perry had an aversion to tomatoes, so some later letters had special poignancy: "I had tomato soup for supper. Grand ain't it. I won't fill on trash." In a 1937 visit he wrote, "They put me on a juice diet today. It will last three days. Of course tonight it was tomato juice. I never touched mine." The statement "I won't fill on trash" is probably a repetition of Anna Bingesser's advice regarding diet. She was in charge of the gardens and kitchens at Waconda Spring, and her advice regarding food (no meat is mentioned except fish) is in keeping with the broad pattern in the various medical reform movements of a primarily vegetarian diet, without strong spices, taken in moderate amounts. One of Perry's last letters from the 1916 visit says, "You must have quite a garden by this time. Just keep on setting out cabbage plants. The Doctor said I ought to eat slough [slaw] by the peck to get more blood into me." In a later (1937) visit, the restrictions on drink seem to have been relaxed. Perry reported that the doctors "told me when I get home I must take a tablespoon full of whiskey every night and every morning for at least eight months. To build up my heart."

The work seems to have taken a great deal out of Anna Bingesser. On his next visit, in February 1917, Perry Weston wrote: "Mrs.—and the two girls left last night for Los Angeles. It is the first night she has spent away from here in three years. She was getting nervous and Dr. made her leave.

She expects to be gone for a month or two. Doc says she will be back in two weeks."

The letters also give some hints regarding the economic aspects of the operation. Occasionally they mention the farm attached to the spring, saying that "the Doctor has 340 acres, part in crops and part in pasture." There Bingesser planted wheat, corn, and oats, and raised stock. In the early years—up to 1928—the operation seems to have been quite successful, with thirty to forty patients in residence. In 1927 Doctor Bingesser confided to Weston that he was considering putting up a broadcasting station to take advantage of the advertising possibilities that radio offered.

Then came the stock market crash, the economic depression, and drought. Times were harder, but Weston's letters from visits in 1937 and 1938 mention only a dust storm, and do not refer directly to the economics of the resort. The Westons, however, saved some of the mailings they received from Waconda Spring, and these give an impression of relative urgency. During the holiday season in 1931, there was a letter offering Georgia pecans for sale. A second mailing the same year noted that the resort was open for business during the winter and offered a 10 percent seasonal discount. In 1932 a letter offered a permanently reduced rate and solicited a return visit from Weston. A final mailing, dated December 25, 1938, was a form letter gently requesting the patron to give an enclosed postcard to a prospective patient.

The Weston letters offer a small trove of further information about the Waconda Spring operation in the form of letterheads, photos, and a brochure from the resort. The letterheads and one envelope show a progression of names, emphases, and designs that reflect the changing tastes of Middle America. The earliest letterhead and accompanying envelope (Figure 7.2, middle and bottom) call the operation a sanitarium and offer the slogan *Deutsche Wasser fur Anstalt,* "German water for Health." This appears to be a reference to the hydrotherapy movement, which began with Preissnitz in German-speaking Europe and spread to America. Like the hydrotherapists, the Bingesser family carefully avoided using the word *spa* in their advertising; instead, they used the term *nature cure,* parallel to the hydrotherapists' *water-cure.*

Later letterheads place greater emphasis on the supposed Native American roots of the cure, with romantic images (Figure 7.3, top) and prominent use of the term, "Great Spirit Springs" (Figure 7.3, middle and bottom). That is, the Bingessers took up the pseudo-legend of Princess Waconda and used it in their promotional literature. By the 1930s, Native Americans were no longer the feared and ferocious savages of the frontier

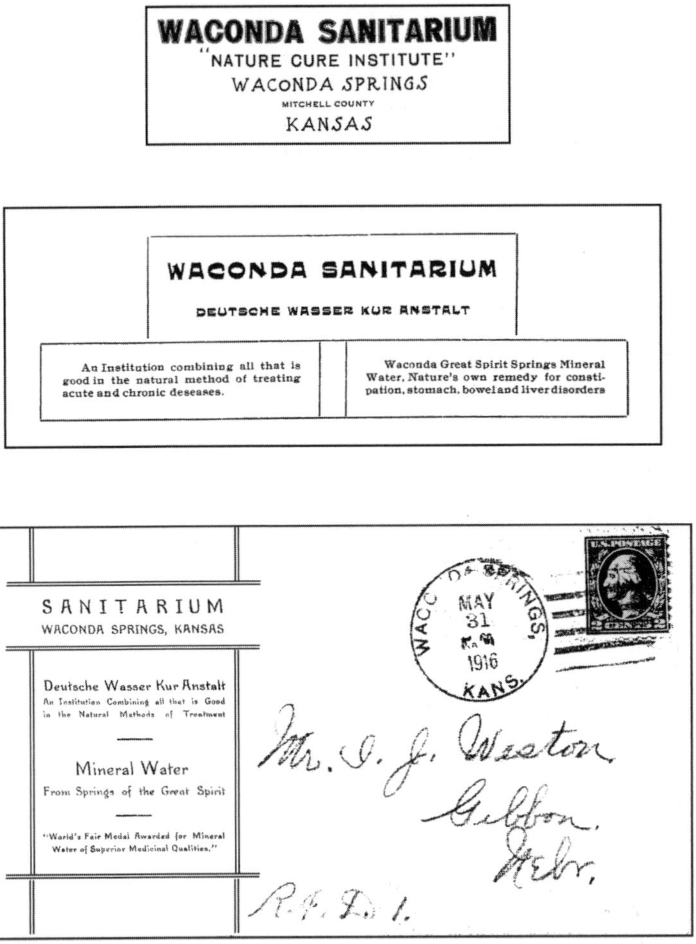

FIGURE 7.2 Envelope and letterheads from Waconda Springs (courtesy Kansas State Historical Society).

imagination but were becoming remote and romantic—the ecologically minded noble savages of today's imagined world.

An early letterhead (Figure 7.2, middle) mentions treatment for constipation, stomach, bowel, and liver disorders. Of these, constipation was a common and serious complaint in the late nineteenth and early twentieth centuries. This was the result of a diet that often included very few vegetable foods rich in fiber. Anna Bingesser's vegetable-rich diet probably generated many cures for as long as the patients kept to the recommended diet.

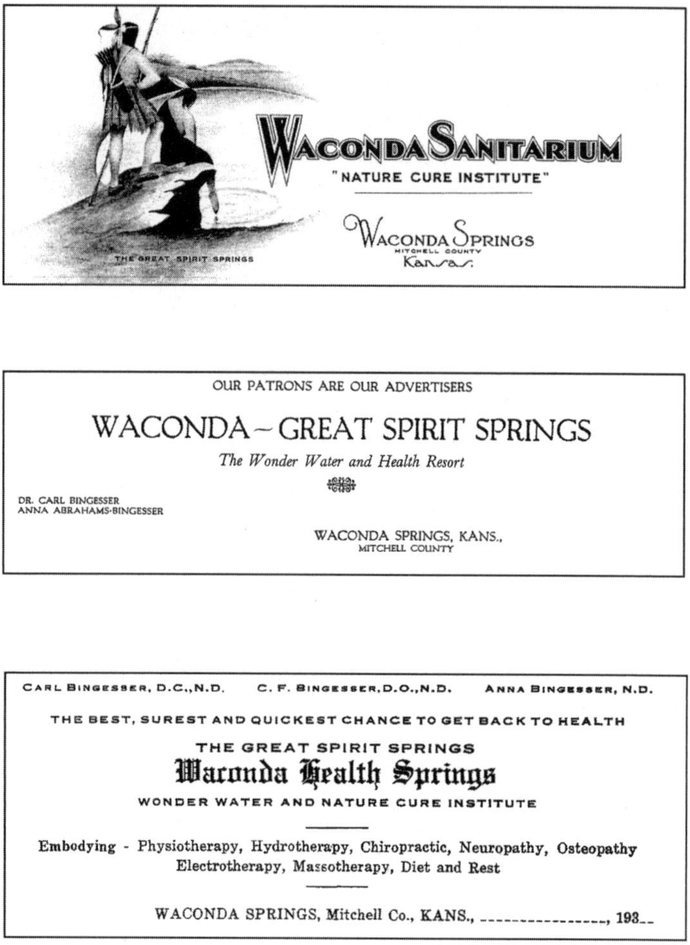

WACONDA SANITARIUM
"NATURE CURE INSTITUTE"
WACONDA SPRINGS
MITCHELL COUNTY
KANSAS.
THE GREAT SPIRIT SPRINGS

OUR PATRONS ARE OUR ADVERTISERS
WACONDA–GREAT SPIRIT SPRINGS
The Wonder Water and Health Resort
DR. CARL BINGESSER
ANNA ABRAHAMS-BINGESSER
WACONDA SPRINGS, KANS.,
MITCHELL COUNTY

CARL BINGESSER, D.C.,N.D. C. F. BINGESSER,D.O.,N.D. ANNA BINGESSER, N.D.
THE BEST, SUREST AND QUICKEST CHANCE TO GET BACK TO HEALTH
THE GREAT SPIRIT SPRINGS
Waconda Health Springs
WONDER WATER AND NATURE CURE INSTITUTE
Embodying - Physiotherapy, Hydrotherapy, Chiropractic, Neuropathy, Osteopathy Electrotherapy, Massotherapy, Diet and Rest
WACONDA SPRINGS, Mitchell Co., KANS., ________________, 193__

FIGURE 7.3 Letterheads from the Waconda Springs Sanitarium (courtesy Kansas State Historical Society).

The last letterhead (Figure 7.3, bottom), dating from the 1930s, provides the most information about the training of the doctors and the nature of the treatments offered. It lists Carl Bingesser, D.C., N.D.; C. F. (Carlos) Bingesser, D.O., N.D.; and Anna Bingesser, N.D. Thus Carl had two degrees, in chiropractic and naturopathy, while his son had degrees in osteopathy and naturopathy, and his wife had a degree in naturopathy. The list of treatments offered covers just about the whole range of alternative therapies then available—Physiotherapy, Hydrotherapy, Chiropractic, Neuropathy, Osteopathy, Electrotherapy, Massotherapy, Diet and Rest—

everything except drugs and surgery. Of the list, the only item that is difficult to assess is Neuropathy, a term that today refers to a disease state, not to a form of treatment. The Bingessers seem to have meant a treatment that focused on the nervous system.

Among the items in the Weston collection at the Kansas State Historical Society is an undated brochure that appears to have been sent in the early 1930s. It includes a testimonial letter from a Dr. A. H. Ball of Chicago, who had served on the staff at Waconda Spring in 1928 (Figure 7.4). The full text of the brochure can be found in Appendix A. It also included a page of photographs of the Sanitarium (Figure 7.1).

The institution that Dr. Bingesser and his family developed at Waconda Spring thus was eclectic. They drew selectively from the various reform-minded medical movements of the nineteenth century to treat chronic illnesses as best they could. Although Dr. Ball probably received something in return for his kind words used in the brochure, he may not have

WACONDA
HEALTH RESORT

Devoted exclusively to the correction and cure of chronic states of ill-health thru natural, non-surgical, non-medical methods of treatment.

YOU CAN REGAIN
GOOD HEALTH

Come, receive the benefits of these most wonderful curative spring waters, nature's health building, vitalizing mineral baths, corrective diets and up-to-date non-surgical treatment.

GREAT SPIRIT SPRINGS

In the heart of the famous Solomon River Valley. On U. S. Highway No. 40 North, 16 miles west of Beloit.

For further information
write

WACONDA HEALTH RESORT
WACONDA SPRINGS, KANSAS
Dr. Carl A. Bingesser, Director

This Letter Indicates the Exact Reason for Our Remarkable Success

DR. A. H. BALL
4626 Dover St., Chicago, Ill.
February 3, 1929

Dr. Carl Bingesser,
Waconda Springs, Kas.
Dear Doctor:

Just a few lines relative to your Institution and its methods. Last summer was indeed a most pleasant surprise in many ways, perhaps most outstanding being your very effective method of treatment.

Several hundred patients were treated during my stay with you. They came with rheumatism, neuritis, sciatica, arthritis, liver-gall-bladder, stomach disorders, only to be relieved in a comparatively short time.

Other Institutions are not getting results in twice the time taken at your Sanitarium.

Your method of treatment is decidedly unusual, since such an ideal combination does not exist elsewhere, because you tave taken the best in healing modes and have so evolved such a unique form of application together with marked personal skill, that sickness seems literally to melt away.

You are indeed to be congratulated in evolving such a form of treatment, also your neighborhood is to be considered most fortunate in having such an Institution in its midst.

I can only wish you every success and trust that you will carry on the excellent work you are now doing.

In conclusion I shall always pleasantly recall the relations between us while a member of your staff in the summer of 1928.

Sincerely,
DR. A. H. BALL

Great Spirit Springs

WACONDA HEALTH RESORT
Waconda Springs, Mitchell Co., Kansas

FIGURE 7.4 Selected text from a Waconda Spring advertisement (courtesy Kansas State Historical Society).

been far from the mark in his emphasis on Bingesser's use of a combination of healing strategies in his attempts to help the people who came to Waconda Spring. While mainstream medicine, then and now, might look askance at the theories behind the methods, there is nothing in the record to suggest that the Bingessers ever violated the medical principle: "first, do no harm."

8. Lincoln Camp

A SHORT DISTANCE above the mouth of Oak Creek stood an enormous grove of trees from which the creek took its name. It extended from just north of the modern highway to beyond the boundaries of the federal property. After the land was homesteaded by a Mr. William Belk, the grove became known as Belk's Grove. This enormous grove, some fifty acres in extent, was a critical resource in an otherwise fairly treeless environment, and its importance to the inhabitants of the region cannot be underestimated.

There were other such groves in the general area. Bartsch's Grove on Dry Creek and Stone's grove on Twelve-Mile Creek are two others. Bartsch's Grove served as a campground for settlers on their way west, for religious meetings, picnics, and other celebrations. Yet it featured only some trees with swings.[1] Belk's Grove, located near the river and the main route of travel, came to have much more.

Its story begins in the prehistoric period. Archaeological survey of the portion of Belk's Grove on federal property disclosed the largest set of Solomon River Phase sites recorded at Waconda Lake. Mr. Gerald Dubbert, who owned the adjoining land, encouraged survey of a nearby hillside, which yielded another site, and he told us of one that had been destroyed when the railroad was relocated. It seems clear from all of this that the grove existed in the twelfth and thirteenth centuries and that it had persisted to the present day. That it was important to the prehistoric inhabitants of the region for shade, fuel, raw material, and horticultural land cannot be doubted.

After Euro-Americans took the land, its importance continued. In a region where timber resources were relatively scarce, Mr. Belk's homestead was valuable property. Stands of trees were important sources of firewood, and old maps that show property lines often disclose where groves of trees were to be found. Because of the Homestead Act and the amount of land it allowed each settler, most of the property in this region was held in eighty-acre pieces or in multiples of eighty. Well-to-do farmers might hold 320 or 160 acres, and few people held forty acres or less. But on the old county atlases that were published near the turn of the century, one can find along certain creeks and rivers pieces of property of three, five, and ten acres. The landowners' names on them turn out to be the same as those on nearby farms of ordinary sizes.

These little pieces of ground are the woodlots, purchased by the farmers of the area from the lucky homesteader whose property included substantial amounts of trees. The woodlots produced by this process were critical to the early farmers. Almost all heat was produced from wood stoves, and in a region of bitter winters, a fuel supply was absolutely critical. Fuel was also needed for cooking, and in a region where economic survival was difficult, purchasing fuel for everyday use was out of the question. The local people simply had to have a supply of wood.

The early history of Belk's Grove is recounted by Tula Draher Emigh in a report compiled from early newspaper stories. According to her, the grove became an important public meeting ground after 1882. In that year, Col. C. W. Whitney of Cawker City leased the full grove, fifty acres, from Mr. Belk for a pleasure resort. He immediately began a series of improvements, and announced the availability of what he named Lincoln Park in August 1882. He arranged a simple depot on the railroad that ran twenty rods south of the park, where the trains could stop when special events were scheduled.[2]

The effective grand opening of the park was in 1883. By that time, Whitney could advertise that the park featured winding drives, swings, fountains, and boats. He had the creek dammed, and a stern-wheeled boat offered rides a mile up the creek and back for twenty-five cents. In June of that year, a reunion of Civil War veterans was held at the grove. Whitney persuaded the local post of the Grand Army of the Republic to invite the other posts in this region of the state to attend.

Other events the same year included a Union Sunday School picnic and, in September, the Lincoln Park Fair. This event, also organized by Whitney, was the equivalent of a county fair. The admission was twenty-five cents. Attendance was good, as one report mentioned four hundred teams on the grounds at one time. In addition to the entertainment provided by several orators, Colonel Whitney had two crates and one barrel of goods hauled high in an oak tree, and he tossed them out for fairgoers to scramble for.

The land leased to Whitney for his park soon became a focal point in the social life of the region. It was used for church outings, picnics, and a wide range of other activities described below, to which people came from surrounding towns and farms. This is a pattern repeated widely over the relatively treeless and waterless plains. Certain features of the landscape, be they groves of trees, water holes, or simply picturesque spots became important to the Euro-American settlers and remained so until fairly recently. They became focal spots in the cultural landscape.

I have worked in a wide variety of localities in the Great Plains, and in each project performed since I noticed the pattern, I have never failed to learn from some of the older local people where these spots were. At Hillsdale Lake in eastern Kansas, it was Rocky Ford, a natural crossing of Bull Creek that created a swimming hole. On the Cimarron River in the panhandle of Oklahoma, one such spot was Castle Rock, and the petroglyphs in its vicinity included the names of some of the surrounding towns, apparently carved during a Fourth of July picnic or other such event. Along the edge of the Llano Estacado in Texas, the upper canyons that dissect the rim of the plateau drew people like magnets, and today there are Boy Scout camps, church camps, and private developments in these spots.

Such was Lincoln Park. From 1882 the park continued in constant but changing use until 1964, when it was purchased by the Bureau of Reclamation. When the University of Nebraska crews excavated Solomon River Phase sites in the vicinity, they documented their location with respect to what was then called Lincoln Camp, which they identified as an old Civilian Conservation Corps facility. Shortly thereafter, the buildings were bulldozed, and when we surveyed the site, it was extremely difficult to find any trace of what had previously been so important.

At first Lincoln Park was the scene of fairly informal activities by groups from the immediate vicinity. Church groups and other social organizations from Cawker City and Downs used the park for summer events such as picnics and revivals. In 1884 the Fourth of July celebration at the park included races, driving contests, boating, and dancing. In 1886 the Grand Army of the Republic returned for a four-day reunion. Then, in 1896, the Ministerial Association of the Methodist Church took up the idea of sponsoring a chautauqua, copying it from the Ottawa, Kansas, assembly.

The Lincoln Camp Chautauqua is an example of a nationwide phenomenon, the chautauqua movement. The latter began, very simply, in an attempt to improve the quality of Sunday school teaching. John H. Vincent, who was concerned about the training of Methodist Sunday school teachers, joined with a friend, Lewis Miller, who was a trustee of a defunct revival camp on Lake Chautauqua, New York. In 1874 they opened a summer camp for young people in order to train them as Sunday school teachers. It very quickly became a success, and almost as quickly the focus turned from bible instruction alone to more general forms of education.[3]

Vincent was no ordinary person. Although he was an ordained Methodist minister, he did not share the narrow, sectarian perspective that was common in his day, and he opened the chautauqua grounds to all Protestant sects. He also promoted diverse forms of education, with the result that the chautauqua grew from a two-week event in its first year to a two-month affair in later years. From a few dozen young people in 1874, it grew to accommodate thousands, most of whom lived in tents.[4]

The institutional framework grew as the educational opportunities expanded. In 1878 Vincent added a home study course for the rest of the year, organized in local "Chautauqua Literary and Scientific Circles." This eventually grew into a four-year course of study, the closest thing to a college education that was available to many Americans. In 1879 he added the Chautauqua Teachers Retreat for public school teachers, and the Chautauqua School of Languages. In 1881 he founded the Chautauqua School of Theology, and in 1883 the Chautauqua University. University extension courses were added in 1889, and in 1893 a magazine, the *Chautauquan,* which had a nationwide circulation. Finally, in 1900, the Chautauqua Press opened.[5]

The rapid development of the "Mother Chautauqua" fostered the growth of copycat assemblies all across the country. Vincent and Lewis made no effort to restrict the use of the name of their institution nor its ideas, and local communities soon began to institute their own summer shows. The chautauquas were especially popular in the new states of the Midwest, where other educational and cultural opportunities were rare.

The growth of the local chautauquas began after the second season of the original one, when a visit to it by President Grant was publicized nationally. The first copy sprang up in Ohio in 1876, and the next year two more appeared, in Iowa and Michigan. By 1900 there were two hundred of these institutions scattered across the American landscape.[6] Their popularity can be attributed to a variety of factors, including the general lack of other forms of entertainment, and the themes they developed struck a chord in the American psyche. Chautauquas came to mean respectability, integrity, self-improvement through study, healthy fun, wholesome recreation, non-denominational religious reverence, good taste, and honest inquiry. Theodore Roosevelt is supposed to have said that they were "the most American thing in America."[7]

As opportunities for self-improvement through education, they were not new. Instead they developed in part as a summer and rural version of what had been an urban and winter institution: the lyceum. The lyceum movement began in 1826, when Josiah Holbrook organized a group of neighbors for mutual intellectual improvement. The idea spread, and by 1850 there were three thousand lyceums in the United States, supported by local towns and cities.[8]

Initially scholars and cultural figures provided their services for nominal honoraria, but as the demand for their services grew they began to ask for more money. At the same time, they had difficulty developing rational schedules, as they responded to requests from lyceums scattered more or less randomly across their regions. These problems were cured by a man named James Redpath, but his prescription killed the patient. He developed the Redpath Lyceum Bureau to arrange both speakers for the lyceums and speaking opportunities for the scholars and orators. Eventually bureaus like his took over the whole business, and the local self-improvement clubs faded from the scene. The same thing was to happen to the chautauquas, but first they had a period of spectacular success.

By the turn of the century, the Lincoln Park Chautauqua was one of the most successful permanent local chautauquas in the Midwest. All of the permanent chautauquas consisted of open-air assemblies dedicated to education, worship, personal improvement, rest, recreation, and amusement. All repeated the basic scene found in the original: tents in a grove of trees next to a body of water. Belk's Grove on Oak Creek provided one of the most beautiful of the chautauquas.

The association that ran the Lincoln Park Chautauqua first organized in 1897. It took a year to write by-laws, sell shares, and purchase the large tent under which the main meetings were to be held. The first chautauqua was held in 1898. The newspaper articles reviewed by Emigh allow us to trace the development and subsequent decline of the institution.[9]

As the years went by, the facilities offered in Lincoln Park became more elaborate. In the first year they included the assembly tent, or tabernacle, a tent hotel, a lunch counter, and fifty tents that families might rent if they wished to camp for the duration of the Chautauqua. The next year the number of rentals increased to eighty tents. In 1901 plans were made to dig wells and install windmills to eliminate the expense of carting water from town to the park. In 1901 the Women's Hesperian Library Club added a reading-room tent, and, by 1902, newspaper articles mention tents of various organizations: the Women's Relief Corps (the women's auxiliary of the Grand Army of the Republic), the Secretary of the Chautauqua, and the Masons. In the same year, a permanent sign over the gate was added.

The year 1903 saw a fundamental change in the park. That year the Chautauqua Association prevailed on Mr. Belk to sell part of the grove to the association so that permanent improvements would have a legal footing. He agreed to part with the southern section of the grove, some thirty acres, for $100 per acre or $3,000 in all. The sale quickly led to the construction of a series of permanent buildings.

By 1904 a new suspension bridge was hanging where the old dam used to be. In the same year private lots that families could use year-round sold for fifty dollars each. There were only a few takers. In 1905 the Women's Christian Temperance Union (WCTU) began plans for a permanent building to replace their tent, and some families announced their intention to build cottages on their private lots. A new dining hall was raised in 1905, and 1906 saw both the dedication of Lillian Stevens Hall, named for the president of the WCTU, and the completion of the first private cabin. This was followed by a Federation of Women's Clubs building, and, in 1907, a Women's Rest Cottage for female performers.

By 1908 another cottage was completed, and some families brought wagon houses, an early form of camper, to their lots. A tennis court was added the same year, and for the first time a sand pile for children was mentioned. By 1909 there were six summer cottages on the grounds, and another cottage being built. A roofed stage and dressing rooms for the performers were added the same year.

As the years went by, the focus of the gathering also changed somewhat. In the earliest years, the chautauqua proper was preceded by a meeting of the Epworth League Assembly, primarily a church-related affair that featured training for league leaders, that also offered bible study, spiritual lectures, and psalm singing. Thus the Lincoln Park Chautauqua had a history very similar to that of the original or "Mother" Chautauqua. In 1903, however, the Epworth League meeting was moved to Beloit Park, separating it from the chautauqua. Moral rectitude continued to be stressed, however, and in 1910 the newspaper editor was making fun of people who applied to the Lincoln Park Chautauqua Association for concessions so that they might offer bowling alleys, wild west shows, prize wheels, merry-go-rounds, and fortune-telling parlors.

While the chautauqua never became a mere carnival, concessions in the park offered a variety of goods and services. In 1903 there were only a grocery store and a boarding tent that offered meals for $3.50 per week. Other concessions mentioned over the years include ones for Hires Root Beer, popcorn, cotton candy, taffy, photography, novelties, cigars, orangeade and peanuts, popcorn, and ice cream. For years meats and milk were delivered for sale at the park, and by 1906 a newspaper, the *Day Book,* was being offered on the grounds.

The main focus was on socially and morally uplifting education. The themes of progress and optimism were stressed, and one chautauqua official was described as being so optimistic that he never saw a shadow. Politics, in the form of orations and debates, were part of every chautauqua, and some of the largest crowds ever at Lincoln Park were drawn by William Jennings Bryan in 1901 and Robert LaFollette in 1906 and 1907. Governors, senators, and congressmen all attended, but an attempt to get Teddy Roosevelt to attend in 1902 failed.

Other activities included music, both bands and individual performers. Bands played, at least for several years, while seated in a large oak tree. Elocutionists, magicians, and preachers rubbed elbows with scientists. A speech by Booker T. Washington appears to have been the single best-attended event in the history of the Lincoln Park Chautauqua. Organized activities included kindergartens, boys' and girls' clubs, baseball and basketball tournaments, poetry and short story readings, and oratory contests. In 1902 the moving picture *The Passion Play* was featured.

Attendees could obtain training in arts, crafts, domestic and physical science, and literature. Eventually local people joined the Chautauqua Literary and Scientific Circles, and the involvement in these by attendees of the Lincoln Park Chautauqua was said to be the highest in the region. In 1907 John H. Vincent, the founder of the original chautauqua, presented the diplomas at Lincoln Park.

Several of the newspaper articles quoted by Emigh, beginning in 1906, make passing references to the "Seton Indians."[10] They were part of a movement that eventually was swallowed up by the Boy Scouts. Ernest Thompson Seton was an Englishman who had been raised in Canada before immigrating to the United States. He was the primary source of the "back to nature" movement that is still influential in American culture. An avid outdoorsman, Seton became convinced that training in woodcraft could save young people from the deleterious effects of town life. In 1902 he formed the Woodcraft Indians, using James Fennimore Cooper's version of the noble savage as his inspiration.[11]

His main focus was on children, but he realized that the activities and training had to address whole families, and he established the Little Lodge for children under the age of twelve, the Big Lodge for their older siblings, and the Medicine Lodge for their parents and other adults. The purpose of the activities was training in outdoor skills and fostering high principles, but these were dressed up in beaded shirts, feathered headdresses, and the mysteries of the "Cariboo Dance."

Seton made no attempt to control the growth of his organization. Instead he announced its formation in the *Ladies' Home Journal* and made available to all interested parties its games and ceremonials. The Woodcraft Indians movement was quickly adopted by the local chautauquas, which needed activities for the children in attendance, and this appears to have been the case at Lincoln Park. In later years, however, the tent chautauquas described below came to dominate the scene, and because these visited each town for only one week a year, they soon stripped the Woodland Indians of all substance, leaving only the empty trappings. As a result, when the Boy Scouts organization was introduced from England, it soon overtook and swallowed up Seton's earlier movement in spite of the objections of many to the military character of the Scouts.[12]

As was the case with the Seton Indians, the Lincoln Park Chautauqua was tied so intimately to the social life of the region that some of the changing details of the Chautauqua are a précis of the local history. In 1902 the windmills that provided the drinking water were dismantled, and a gasoline engine was brought from town to pump water into the tanks. In that year horse-driven hacks made regularly scheduled trips to the campground from adjoining towns. Also in that year three moving pictures were shown. In 1903 the Grand Army of the Republic and the Women's Relief Corps sponsored an Army and Navy Day, the first event in the area to be filmed with a movie camera.

In 1906 a sermon was illustrated with a stereopticon show, and in 1908 the park was fitted with one hundred electric lights. In the same years, the first automobiles began to show up in the area, and in 1909 the chautauqua was advertised with two automobile booster trips to surrounding regions. One with six cars went up the South Fork of the Solomon as far as Stockton. Another to Concordia, Burr Oak, and Kensington, to Smith Center and home via Downs, had seven cars. The local papers reported the miraculous fact that this monumental journey was accomplished without a single flat tire or engine breakdown. The next year drivers of autos to the chautauqua had to be warned to keep from frightening the horses, and traffic was so heavy that they had to be advised to avoid running into each other.

In 1910 the rapidly increasing impact of automobiles could be seen in both the facilities and the content of the program. The newspaper editor noted that while only a few years previously it was almost impossible to care for all of the teams of horses taken to the campground, now nobody wanted to bid on the concession to do just that. A featured speaker was D. Ward King, whose topic was "Good roads without money, right now." Training in photography was also offered for the first time.

For about a generation, the Lincoln Park Chautauqua was a roaring success. It grew in numbers of people attending, in the length and variety of its program, and in the costs involved. From fifty tents of people the first year, to 152 tents occupied by members of 174 families by 1903, the number of people who stayed for the whole program grew. In 1905, two hundred tents holding five to six people each were in use. One-day attendances also grew, reaching thirty-five hundred in 1903, five thousand in 1904, and seven thousand in 1908. The programs grew from ten days in 1900 until they finally stabilized at sixteen days after 1908.

In 1899 the total expenses for the Chautauqua Association were $400. In 1900, with a much-expanded program, they increased to $1,800. In 1902 admission was charged: $2.00 for adults, $1.00 for minors, with children under ten free. In 1907 the total indebtedness of the Association was $6,000. As a result, admission was raised to $2.50 for everyone except children under the age of ten. That year the Association showed a profit estimated to be $600, but the other permanent chautauquas in the state all showed losses.

The end for the Lincoln Park Chautauqua came very quickly, as Mother Nature, increasing competition, and the changing national culture combined to undercut it. In 1911 a severe flood on the first day of the meeting did fairly little damage to the campground, but it knocked out bridges that provided access to Lincoln Camp from surrounding communities. Attendance dropped, and free admission on one Sunday to demonstrate how the campground had recovered added to the deficit. At the end of the meeting, the debt was $6,300. The directors of the association pledged to pay it off, and the next year, advance sale of season tickets was tried.

In 1912, however, only eighty tents were rented to go along with the ten permanent cottages and ten privately owned tents, and only five to six hundred people stayed at the grounds for the duration of the chautauqua. In 1913, foreclosure proceedings were begun when the association failed to meet an interest payment. Eventually the park was purchased by G. W. Dockstader for $2,050.

One of the main elements in the decline and fall of the Lincoln Park Chautauqua was the development of a new form of chautauqua. As the permanent chautauquas became popular, they turned to the lyceum bureaus to provide talent.[13] At first this was mutually beneficial because the lyceums were urban institutions that were active primarily in the winter season. Thus the chautauquas not only did not compete with them directly, they provided additional income to the speakers and other entertainers who had come to depend on the lyceums for a great deal of their livelihood.

Individuals in the lyceum bureaus, however, soon saw business opportunities in the problems that arose. Scheduling of the performers was incredibly difficult, as each permanent chautauqua was held at a traditional time of the summer, and the local associations saw no reason why they should change their schedules to fit the needs of a booking agent. Further, each local association chose the performers they wanted, and the booking agents had little luck in arranging a rational schedule of travel for each performer on the circuit.

In 1903 two people with experience in the lyceum bureaus solved this problem and in so doing turned an enormous profit. In that year, Keith Vawter and J. Roy Ellison started up the tent chautauqua business. What they did was bypass the permanent chautauquas and sell whole slates of performers to towns that previously had held no chautauquas. In return for guaranteed ticket sales provided by local businessmen and community leaders, they provided not only the entertainers but also a large tent in which the show could be held. By signing up a series of towns along a railroad line, they were able to send the show from town to town in a cost-effective manner.[14]

By 1904 the success of these tent or circuit chautauquas was assured, and the permanent chautauquas such as Lincoln Park went into a decline. Now every town could have its own show, each scheduled for a single week.[15] This meant two things. First, people from the surrounding region were not as apt to support regional permanent chautauquas such as that in Lincoln Park. Second, the Lincoln Park Chautauqua with its sixteen-day run, did not fit into the schedule. While the booking agents were still happy to sell talent to Lincoln Park, it became easier and easier for them to fit the best performers into their own tent chautauqua schedules. Complaints in the Glen Elder papers about certain unnamed upstart chautauquas and lyceums document the effects of the new competition, and by 1913 the Lincoln Park Chautauqua was dead.

The tent chautauquas were not the only force undermining the permanent ones, and they lasted only a decade longer. In 1924 they celebrated the jubilee year of the chautauqua movement, but this was also the last year that the bureaus made a good profit. Blame for their demise has been given to the spread of the radio, to mass-produced automobiles and improved roads, and to talking pictures.[16] Others blame a decline in the quality of the shows as their numbers increased, and still others are of the opinion that it was the imposition of an amusement tax on ticket sales that finally made clear to local backers that they were supporting entertainment rather than education.[17] An insider, however, attributes it to the beginnings of the Great Depression, which were felt in the countryside years before the Wall Street debacle.[18]

The effects of the chautauqua movement on the nation and of the Lincoln Park Chautauqua on the region were immense. Chautauquas provided education, entertainment, and connection to the political life of the nation for the publicly educated citizens of remote rural areas. They led to the breakdown of inter-denominational suspicions, to the growing legitimacy of theater, and to the popularity of classical music. The Chautauqua Literary and Scientific Circles that were so popular at Lincoln Park were forerunners of reading societies, book clubs, correspondence schools, and extension courses. In particular, they provided a new chance for personal growth for women who had few opportunities for higher education.[19]

Chautauquas introduced new ideas and new programs here and elsewhere; they brought the graduated income tax, slum clearance, juvenile courts, pure food laws, school lunch programs, free textbooks, balanced diet, physical fitness, the Camp Fire Girls, Seton's Indians, and Boy Scouts to communities that otherwise might not have heard about them.[20] The Chautauqua Press published pieces of poetry, science, and literature—the first paperbacks printed in this country.[21]

The Mother Chautauqua was even tied to the creation of the University of Chicago. The first president of the university, William R. Harper, had been in charge of instruction in Hebrew at the Mother Chautauqua and had been responsible for introducing the idea of extension courses there. His choice for the university's first head football coach, Amos Alonzo Stagg, became director of physical education at the Mother Chautauqua. The university's extension division and the University of Chicago Press grew directly out of Harper's chautauqua experiences.[22]

The decline of the Lincoln Park Chautauqua was a tragedy for the region. G. W. Dockstader purchased the park in order to keep its assets from being divided among creditors. He then donated the park to a consortium of local Protestant churches, and they formed an association to run it. In February 1914, they planned for a two-day Sunday school convention, a one-week chautauqua, and a gospel meeting to be held that summer. Doing so proved very difficult, and the president resigned in April, to be followed by the secretary in May. Attendance at the Sunday school convention was two hundred, while only thirty families camped at the chautauqua, and total attendance was between two thousand and twenty-five hundred. Although it was declared a financial success, apparently because only local talent was used, the Church Association decided not to try to hold another Chautauqua in 1915.

Lincoln Park was sold again in 1920, to the Young Men's Christian Association, which used the Women's Christian Temperance Union building as its headquarters.[23] Use of the park continued to be sporadic until the Great Depression brought a new function. In 1934 the land on the west side of Oak Creek was used for a Civilian Conservation Corps (CCC) camp. The purpose of the CCC was to provide work for the unemployed, and in Osborne and Mitchell counties the CCC constructed farm ponds, watershed dams, and bridges. To accommodate the workers, a series of buildings were constructed in the western part of the park.

After the CCC left the area, Lincoln Park came into the hands of a regional 4-H organization. The 4-H organizations of the surrounding eight counties joined together to clean and operate the park. They tore down some of the poorly constructed CCC buildings but sold the ones that were in fairly good shape in order to raise funds to cover the clean-up costs. They then made the park available to the public, and charged a minimal daily fee to individuals, campers, and groups that wished to use the park.

This use of the park lasted only a fairly short time, because the government soon needed the land again, this time for a prisoner of war camp. When the North African campaign of 1943 succeeded, the Allies captured large numbers of German and Italian soldiers. In order to remove them from the theater of operations and in order to replace the manpower diverted from other activities to the war effort, a series of prisoner of war camps were established in the United States.

In Kansas, three main camps were established. They were Camp Phillips, which was located near Salina; Camp Riley, in the vicinity of Fort Riley; and Camp Concordia, near the town of the same name. These main camps housed seven thousand German prisoners of war. In Nebraska there were three other main camps, at Scottsbluff, Fort Robinson, and Atlanta. The first two held three thousand Italian prisoners each, while the latter contained one thousand German POWs.[24]

The prisoner of war camps were run strictly according to the Geneva Conventions.[25] Adequate food was provided along with opportunities for physical and intellectual development. There were sports, movies, and art and literary events, mostly organized by the prisoners. Camp Concordia had three German-language newspapers published by the prisoners.

Some camps even provided classes, with college offered by the University of Kansas.[26]

Nevertheless, life in a prisoner of war camp necessarily featured a great deal of tedium. Many of the prisoners, therefore, welcomed the opportunity to work outside the camps when it was offered to them. Because the war effort drew most of the able-bodied young men from the region, such an opportunity was not long in coming. In 1943 regulations were created to allow the use of prisoners of war as farm laborers under certain conditions:

> there had to be a local farm labor shortage,
> prisoners could not work more than ten hours per day,
> prisoners had to be treated in the same fashion as regular farm workers, and
> farmers had to pay the government wages equal to those normally given to regular farm laborers.

In areas distant from the previously established prisoner of war camps, local communities had to provide housing and food, and the sub-camps so created had to have security so that escapes would not be possible.[27]

Lincoln Camp was perfect for such an operation, and in 1944 what was left of the former Civilian Conservation Corps camp became the Cawker City Prisoner of War Camp. It was filled with German soldiers from Camp Atlanta in Nebraska. Some local oral traditions now assert that the prisoners came from Camp Concordia, but the official records tell otherwise. Local stories also assert that the camp held 250 men, but the official weekly list of prisoners never went above 169 men.[28]

The Cawker City Prisoner of War Camp was in use from the summer of 1944 until October 1945. In that short interval of time, however, some important friendships developed between prisoners and the farm families they worked for. The prisoners were young men of the same age as the American youths who had been drawn away from home to participate in the war. Many of the prisoners came from farm backgrounds and were happy to work in the fields next to the American farmers. Many learned enough English to converse with Americans, and the result was that the stereotypes created by the propaganda machines of both governments tended to be broken down. After the war, some prisoners chose to remain in the United States, others kept up correspondence from home with their American friends, and a few prisoner of war reunions have been held in the United States and abroad.[29]

When Gerald Dubbert returned to his home from the war, he found the camp still in operation. He said it was disconcerting to find the enemy so well treated and so well liked by his family and acquaintances. He mentions also hearing the music coming from the camp at night and describes some of the paintings made by the prisoners to decorate their barracks. One that he particularly remembers was done on a piece of cardboard and was of a German tank in front of a North African sunset (Gerald Dubbert, personal communication). Another, painted on a towel, was a sunset scene in the Bavarian Alps. What happened to the pieces of art after the camp was abandoned is not known.

After the closing of the Cawker City Prisoner of War camp in 1945, the land was returned to the Cawker City YMCA. A fee of seventy-five cents per person per day was being charged in the early 1960s for use of the park, and the money accrued from the fees was used for cleaning and maintaining the park. The YMCA ran the park until 1964, when it was purchased by the Bureau of Reclamation.

When the land was purchased by the federal government, all of the old buildings were bulldozed so that they would not create safety hazards for visitors to the lake. When Belk's Grove was surveyed by crews from Wichita State University beginning in 1989, hardly any physical trace of its long history was evident. In 1991 we had Gerald Dubbert lead us through the ground on the west side of the creek where the prisoner of war camp and the earlier Civilian Conservation Corps camp had stood. He pointed out the locations of the buildings, but the only trace of them visible on the surface was a single limestone foundation block. Essentially the only visible trace of the earlier chautauqua era was the end of one of the cables for the old suspension bridge that used to hang above the now-dry creek. Then in 1993 a tremendous flood on the Solomon River filled Waconda Lake to its peak capacity, flooding Belk's Grove. The standing water, held in the lake to reduce severe flooding downstream, killed the trees, and today only some of their skeletal remains still stand.

While Belk's Grove certainly had a rich and varied history, it is but one of dozens of such spots across Kansas. Groves of mature trees, natural fords across streams, swimming holes—all were important to the rural communities that surrounded them. Today, however, only the old folks remember them well. The places are still there, but we have removed ourselves from them.

9. Perspectives

THE GREAT TRANSFORMATION that has been the subject of this book started with Charles C. DeRudio (née Carlo Camillo di Rudio) on July 6, 1870. For the first time in this region, land was treated as a commodity, and two hundred dollars bought the rights to a quarter section of land. The most profound change on that day was the transformation of Waconda Spring from a place where pilgrims communicated with the spirit world to a potential source of wealth.

The previous cultural landscape had ancient roots. This is not to say that it was unchanging; the physical landscape itself changed as climatic regimes came and went, and the archaeological records shows that the human cultures underwent many profound transformations. James Sherow's "geodialectic" was surely at work.[1] But the native routes of travel became adjusted to the landscape through a pattern of trial and error, so that the primary trails were those that provided all of the necessities of life, while others may have been used only during wet seasons. Even when one population replaced another, as when the Apaches entered the region, the knowledge of the landscape passed to the newcomers. This was true even for the sacred places, as all of the peoples of the region, even though they had their own specific rituals and beliefs, nevertheless shared in a continent-wide religious tradition with a single underlying cosmology.

Most of that changed practically overnight. After 1870, the landscape became both physically and culturally different. The native nations were driven away, and the physical changes were just as profound. Bison were hunted to the edge of extinction, which led to changes in the species of grass, which in turn caused the local extinction of prairie dogs.[2] Farmers broke the sod in order to plant, fenced the land, and introduced new species of plants, both intentionally and unintentionally. What had been clear-flowing streams with beds of sand or rock became choked with sediment that eroded from the fields. Windmills and then irrigation pumps drew down the water table, causing many springs and even some rivers to stop flowing. Routes of travel became more artificial, with most local traffic flowing along section-line roads.

The intangible changes were just as profound. The "spirit of the place" had changed.[3] Land instantly became a commodity, with its value subject to market forces. Mineral rights became a consideration. Immigrants who did not share the old cultural understandings formed new communities and developed new myths and legends. Some of the myths persist to this day, in service of the market. One commonality with the old order was the presence of special places like Lincoln Camp, places that helped to unite communities and that provided a space for moral instruction. But these have gradually faded into disuse.

In the present-day order of things, everything—even religion—becomes a commodity. People have little interaction with the land and tend to live indoors. Even in rural areas, the interaction is primarily with the plowed fields, and people enter the natural world only to hunt or fish. The main routes of travel are now designed primarily with cost in mind, so that the interstates lie away from the visually interesting spots, with their hills and stream crossings.

How can I sum this up? It is hard to write about the losses I perceive with regard to the modern disconnection from the landscape without sounding like a grumpy old man, but we have become unmoored, with no meaningful connection to the land. We are now adrift in a way that no one has ever been before. Even the nomadic societies that existed in this region more than a thousand years ago had a stronger connection to the land than we do. Nomads do not wander randomly but move between places they know on a fairly regular basis, carrying their knowledge of and beliefs about those places with them. Today many people meet, not at a specified place within their familiar surroundings, but on the Internet, an entity that substitutes for real space. Places are now Web pages, and the meetings lack face-to-face contact with physical human beings.

So let me end with a question: What does it mean for a society to live without place?

Waconda Health Resort Brochure

—Waconda Health Resort

The purpose of Waconda Health Resort is to provide a place where people in ill health can obtain a thorough and dependable examination and diagnosis; mineral waters and baths best suited for their needs; correct meals made up of foods that work in harmony with the mineral waters; a complete course of non-surgical treatment when necessary; rest, relaxation, recuperation and a general upbuilding of the body.

The Waconda Health Resort is not a hospital or sanitarium as these terms are commonly used and understood but rather a big comfortable homelike place where one has all the convenience, accommodations and freedom of a comfortable hotel and the facilities and service for treating and curing the chronically sick, all under one roof and one direction, on a plan that is reasonable and efficient.

The principal diseases that we are called upon to treat every day and for which we are especially equipped and qualified to cure include rheumatism, gout, sciatica, arthritis, lumbago, neuritis. Stomach and intestinal disorders including indigestion, gastritis, bowel impaction, colitis, ulcers, appendicitis and chronic constipation. Liver disorders, kidney trouble, piles, female disorders, skin diseases, blood poisoning, nervous run down condition, malnutrition and general toxemias.

—Waconda Great Spirit Springs

The wonderful medicinal value of Waconda Springs' cool, sparkling waters was discovered and used by the great tribes of Western Indians who made yearly pilgrimages to the springs from every section of the west, east, north and south to avail themselves of its benefits. The spring was worshiped by the Indians and regarded as a gift from the Great Spirit, and from the Chief of the Kansas Tribe, it received its present name of Waconda Great Spirit Springs in honor of his beautiful daughter.

That the Indians were not mistaken in their discovery of "Medicine Water" has been proved by authentic chemical analysis made by the University of Kansas which show that these springs possess the same rare qualities that have made famous the world renowned European Springs at Carlsbad, Vichy, etc. Waconda Water is palatable and pleasing to the taste. It has no odor and it is absolutely free from the disagreeable after effects common to most medical preparations.

—Health Building Baths

Waconda mineral water baths are almost miraculous in their ability to correct the causes and relieve the symptoms of many chronic maladies. We use various types and kinds of baths, depending on the requirements of the case in hand; however, the primary purpose of all baths and other forms of hydrotherapy is to cleanse and purify the system by dissolving, absorbing and eliminating impurities and toxemic poisons that have accumulated to clog the cells, tissues and blood stream. All forms of treatment are given with the one idea and purpose of helping the vital life sustaining blood stream to perform its function and the baths and other forms of hydrotherapy do this better and quicker than nearly any other form of treatment known.

It is difficult to describe the fine feeling of rest, relaxation and freshness which follows one of these baths and massage and they have been the means of giving thousands of painful, long suffering cases complete and lasting relief.

—Corrective, Wholesome Diets

The reason Waconda Mineral Waters are able to correct so many chronic ailments is because they contain certain chemical elements that are absolutely essential in the body. There are certain types of food that contain the same chemicals as the mineral waters, therefore to get the best results the patient should eat foods that harmonize with the waters. It costs no more to eat the right types of food than the wrong and unless the patient does eat the right foods there is no certainty of them ever getting well, no matter how much treatment they take. Special diets are prescribed for such cases as Diabetes, Bright's disease and other nutritional disorders. There is no extra charge for corrective diets.

—Modern Treating Facilities

When you come to Waconda Health Resort you will have the benefits and advantages of the most modern non-surgical treatment facilities and equipment it has been possible for us to secure. The best of all systems of proven merit, combined with the mineral waters, baths, massages, corrective meals, electrotherapy, manual manipulation, and hydrotherapy are utilized to correct the causes and symptoms of your trouble. Many cases that are considered incurable, and that have failed to get cured when treated in the usual way at home are promptly and entirely cured when given this treatment.

—Year Round Service

Waconda Health Resort provides a year round service. Everything you want or need including comfortable steam heated rooms, meals, mineral waters fresh from the springs daily, baths and all professional non-surgical treatment, as well as entertainment and pleasure is here for you under one roof. No matter what sort of weather we may be having, your treatment schedule goes on without interruption until you are well and ready to return home.

—Rates

Rates for patients include room, meals at the table, mineral waters, bath treatments at an average cost of $30.00 per week for a course of treatments of two weeks or more. For lesser period that rate is $3.00 for the treatment and $2.50 per day for Hotel charges, or $35.00 per week.

Bedfast patients must provide their own attendant or in minor cases they may have nurse service for a small extra charge. Hotel rate for such attendant is $2.00 per day. No charges are made for auto storage.

We do not take contagious, infectious or obnoxious cases.

—How to Come to Waconda Springs

Waconda Springs is located in Mitchell County, Kansas on the Northern Kansas branch of the Missouri Pacific Railroad. U. S. Highway No. 40 north passes directly in front of our grounds. Regular bus service from all points east, west, north and south is maintained on highways No. 40, No. 9, No. 8, No. 14 and No. 18. Regardless of the time of day or night you arrive you will be taken care of promptly.

NOTES

CHAPTER 1

1. An excellent general introduction to the life of Carlo di Rudio is Cesare Marino and Ken Comery, "Carlo deRudio: A Survivor of the Little Bighorn," http://www.derudio.co.uk.

2. "De Rudio Served with Gen. Custer," *San Francisco Call,* September 30, 1908.

3. Paul Wilhelm, Duke of Württemberg, *Travels in North America, 1822–1824,* trans. W. Robert Nitske, ed. Savoie Lottinville (Norman: University of Oklahoma Press, 1973); Charles Augustus Murray, *Travels in North America during the Years 1834, 1835, & 1836* (London: Richard Bentley, 1839); Maximillian Wied, *Maximilian, Prince of Wied's Travels in the Interior of North America, 1832-1834* (New York: AMS Press, 1966); Hal Schindler, "Sir George, The Buffalo Slayer" (*Salt Lake Tribune,* Febrary 16, 1997); John M. Carroll, ed., *The Grand Duke Alexis in the United States of America* (New York: Interland Publishing, 1972).

4. Goodman, George J., and Cheryl A. Lawson, *Retracing Major Stephen H. Long's 1820 Expedition: The Itinerary and Botany* (Norman: University of Oklahoma Press, 1995); George Catlin, *Letters and Notes on the North American Indians* (New York: Clarkson N. Potter, 1975); Robert J. Moore, *Native Americans: A Portrait: The Art and Travels of Charles Bird King, George Catlin, and Karl Bodmer* (New York: Stewart, Tabori & Chang, 1997); Alfred Jacob Miller, *The West of Alfred Jacob Miller (1837), from the Notes and Water Colors in the Walters Art Gallery* (Norman: University of Oklahoma Press, 1951).

5. John Treat Irving, *Indian Sketches Taken During an Expedition to the Pawnee Tribes* (Norman: University of Oklahoma Press, 1955); Washington Irving, *A Tour on the Prairies,* ed. John Francis McDermott (Norman: University of Oklahoma Press, 1956); Frederick A. Wislizenus, *A Journey to the Rocky Mountains, 1839* (Glorieta, N.M.: Rio Grande Press, 1969); Edmund C. Bray and Martha Coleman Bray, *Joseph N. Nicollet on the Plains and Prairies: The Expedition of 1838–39 with Journals, Letters, and Notes on the Dakota Indians* (St. Paul: Minnesota Historical Society Press, 1976).

6. Donald J. Blakeslee, *Waconda Lake: Prehistoric Swidden-Foragers in the Central Plains, Central Plains Archaeology* 7, no. 1 (1999).

CHAPTER 2

1. Rolfe D. Mandel, "The Effects of Late Quaternary Landscape Evolution on the Archaeological Record of Kansas," in *Kansas Archaeology,* ed. Robert J. Hoard and William E. Banks (Lawrence: University Press of Kansas, 2006), 28–45; David W. May, "Geoarchaeology of Four Sites at Lake Waconda, Kansas," (report submitted to the Bureau of Reclamation, Grand Island, Nebraska, 1991); David W. May, "Holocene Fluvial Landforms and Alluvial Stratigraphy in the Solomon River Valley, Lake Waconda, Kansas" (report to the Bureau of Reclamation, Grand Island, Nebraska, 1991).

2. Steven R. Holen and David W. May, "The La Sena and Shaffert Mammoth Sites: History of Investigations, 1987–1998," in *Medicine Creek: Seventy Years of Archaeological Investigations,* ed. Donna C. Roper (Tuscaloosa: University of Alabama Press, 2002), 20–36.

3. P. V. Wells and J. D. Stewart, "Spruce Charcoal, Conifer Macrofossils, and Landsnail and Small Vertebrate Fauna in Wisconsinan Sedimentation in the High Plains of Kansas," in *Quaternary Environments of Kansas,* ed. W. C. Johnson (Lawrence: Kansas Geological Survey, University of Kansas, 1987).

4. Gary Haynes, *The Early Settlement of North America: The Clovis Era* (Cambridge: Cambridge University Press, 1980); Eileen Johnson, "The Lubbock Lake Paleoindian Record," in *Guidebook to the Central Llano Estacado,* ed. Vance T. Holliday (Lubbock: Friends of the Pleistocene, South-Central Field Trip, ICASALS and the Museum, Texas Tech University, 1983), 81–105.

5. Frederick H. West, "The Antiquity of Man in America," in *Late Quaternary Environments of the United States, Vol. 1: The Late Pleistocene,* ed. S. C. Porter (Minneapolis: University of Minnesota Press, 1983), 364–82.

6. Paul S. Martin, "Prehistoric Overkill," in *Pleistocene Extinctions: The Search for a Cause,* ed. Paul S. Martin and H. E. Wright, Jr. (New Haven: Yale University Press, 1967), 75–120; Paul S. Martin, "Prehistoric Overkill: The Global Model," in *Quaternary Extinctions: A Prehistoric Revolution,* ed. Paul S. Martin and Richard G. Klein (Tucson: University of Arizona Press, 1984), 354-403.

7. Donald K. Grayson and David Meltzer, "A Requiem for North American Overkill," *Journal of Archaeological Science* 30 (2003), 585–93.

8. Colin Nickerson, "Cosmic Blast May Have Killed Off Megafauna," *Boston Globe,* September 25, 2007.

9. George C. Frison and Lawrence C. Todd, *The Colby Mammoth Site: Taphonomy and Archaeology of a Clovis Kill in Northern Wyoming* (Albuquerque: University of New Mexico Press, 1986).

10. Douglas W. Owsley and David R. Hunt, "Clovis and Early Archaic Period

Crania from the Anzick Site (24PA506), Park County, Montana," *Plains Anthropologist* 46 (2001): 125–48.

11. Michael D. Stafford, "The Powars II Site (48PL330): A Paleoindian Red Ocher Mine in Eastern Wyoming" (master's thesis, University of Wyoming, 1990).

12. George C. Frison, *The Mill Iron Site* (Albuquerque: University of New Mexico Press, 1996).

13. Paul A. Mayewski and Michael Bender, "The GISP2 Ice Core Record—Paleoclimate Highlights," in *U.S. National Report to IUGG, 1991–1994, Review of Geophysics* 33 suppl. (1995).

14. George C. Frison, and Dennis J. Stanford, eds., *The Agate Basin Site: A Record of the Paleoindian Occupation of the Northwestern High Plains* (New York: Academic Press, 1982); Edwin N. Wilmsen and Frank H. H. Roberts, Jr., *Lindenmeier: 1934–1974; Concluding Report on Investigations* (Washington, D.C.: Smithsonian Institution Press, 1978).

15. George C. Frison and Bruce A. Bradley, *Folsom Tools and Technology at the Hanson Site* (Albuquerque: University of New Mexico Press, 1980); Cynthia Irwin-Williams, Henry T. Irwin, George A. Agogino, and C. Vance Haynes, Jr., "Hell Gap: Paleo-Indian Occupation on the High Plains," *Plains Anthropologist* 18 (1973): 40–53.

16. Robert L. Kelley and Lawrence C. Todd, "Coming into the Country: Early Paleoindian Hunting and Mobility," *American Antiquity* 53 (1988): 231–44.

17. L. C. Bement and B. J. Carter, *Bison Hunting at Cooper Site: Where Lightning Bolts Drew Thundering Herds* (Norman: University of Oklahoma Press, 1999).

18. B. R. Harrison and K. L. Killen, *Lake Theo: A Stratified Early Man Bison Butchering and Camp Site, Briscoe County, Texas* (Canyon, Tex.: Panhandle-Plains Historical Museum, 1978).

19. Bement and Carter, *Bison Hunting,* 37–39, 176–82.

20. Jack L. Hofman, R. L. Brooks, D. W. Owsley, R. L. Jantz, M. K. Marks, and M. H. Manheim, *From Clovis to Comanchero: An Archaeological Overview of the Southern Great Plains* (Fayetteville: Arkansas Archaeological Survey, 1989).

21. Dennis J. Stanford, "The Jones-Miller Site: An Example of Hell Gap Bison Procurement Strategy," in *Bison Procurement and Utilization,* ed. L. B. Davis and M. Wilson (*Plains Anthropologist,* Memoir 14, 1978): 90–97.

22. Douglas B. Bamforth, "The Paleoindian Occupation of the Medicine Creek Drainage, Southwestern Nebraska," in *Medicine Creek: Seventy Years of Archaeological Investigations,* ed. Donna C. Roper (Tuscaloosa: University of Alabama Press, 2002), 54–83; Ruthann Knudson, "Medicine Creek is a Paleo Indian Ecotone: The Red Smoke Assemblage," in *Medicine Creek: Seventy Years of Archaeological Investigations,* ed. Donna C. Roper (Tuscaloosa: University of Alabama Press, 2002), 84–141.

23. May, "Holocene Fluvial Landforms."

24. F. W. Albertson and J. E. Weaver, *History of the Native Vegetation of Western*

Kansas during Seven Years of Continuous Drought (Ecological Society of America, 1942).

25. Colleen B. Nicholas, "A Recording of Private Artifact Collections in Morton County, Kansas" (master's thesis, Wichita State University, 2005); Kirk Smith, "The Archaic Period in Southwestern Kansas" (master's thesis, Wichita State University, 2005).

26. Roger T. Grange, Jr., *Salvage Archaeology in the Red Willow Reservoir, Nebraska* (Lincoln: Nebraska State Historical Society, 1980).

27. Mandel, "Effects of Late Quaternary," 24.

28. Cf. sources cited by Mandel, "Effects of Late Quaternary," 37.

29. Cf. Nicholas, "A Recording of Private Artifact Collections"; Smith, "The Archaic Period in Southwestern Kansas."

30. Robert J. Hoard and William E. Banks, "Introduction," *Kansas Archaeology,* ed. Robert J. Hoard and William E. Banks (Lawrence: University Press of Kansas, 2006), 4.

31. Mary J. Adair, "Paleoethnobotanical Research in Kansas," in *Kansas Archaeology,* ed. Robert J. Hoard and William E. Banks (Lawrence: University Press of Kansas, 2006), 252.

32. Adair, "Paleoethnobotanical Research," 254.

33. John Reynolds, "Preliminary Report of Archeological Investigations at 14ML307, the Range Mound, Glen Elder, Kansas," *Kansas Anthropological Association Newsletter* 23, nos.2–3 (1977): 1–11.

33. Mark Latham, personal communication.

35. Jim D. Feagins, "The Other Archaic Burial Mound in Kansas: Sorting the Components at the Range Mound (14ML307)," (paper presented at the 30th annual Flint Hills Conference, Lawrence, Kansas, 2008).

36. Donald J. Blakeslee, "The Marine Shell Artifacts of Kansas," *Central Plains Archaeology* 5, no. 1 (1997): 3–9.

37. Alfred E. Johnson, "Kansas City Hopewell," in *Hopewell Archaeology: The Chillicothe Conference,* ed. David S. Brose and N'omi Greber (Kent, Ohio: Kent State University Press, 1979), 86–93; Alfred E. Johnson, ed., *Hopewellian Archaeology in the Lower Missouri Valley* (Lawrence: University of Kansas, 1976); Brad Logan, "Woodland Adaptations in Eastern Kansas," in *Kansas Archaeology,* ed. Robert J. Hoard and William E. Banks (Lawrence: University of Press of Kansas, 2006), 76–92.

38. Alfred E. Johnson, "Kansas City Hopewell"; Patricia A. O'Brien, "The Ashland Bottom Site (14RY603): A Kansas City Hopewell Site in North Central Kansas," *Plains Anthropologist* 24 (1979): 1–20.

39. J. T. Wasson and S. P. Sedwick, "Possible Sources of Meteoric Material from Hopewell Indian Burial Mounds," *Nature* 222 (1969): 22–24.

40. Donald J. Blakeslee, "A Meteor, A Mirror, A Metaphor," *Wisconsin Archaeologist* 84, nos. 1–2 (2003), 99–106.

41. James B. Griffin, A. A. Gordus, and Gary A. Wright, "Identification of the Sources of Hopewellian Obsidian in the Middle West," *American Antiquity* 34 (1969): 1–14.

42. John R. Bozell, "Plains Woodland Complexes of Western Kansas and Adjacent Portions of Nebraska and Colorado," in *Kansas Archaeology,* ed. Robert J. Hoard and William E. Banks (Lawrence: University of Press of Kansas, 2006), 93–104.

43. Marvin F. Kivett and George Metcalf, *The Prehistoric People of Medicine Creek Reservoir, Frontier County, Nebraska: An Experiment in Mechanical Archaeology, Plains Anthropologist,* Memoir 30 (1997).

44. Blakeslee, *Waconda Lake.*

45. Mark A. Latham, "Sampling Strategies and Site Distribution of the Solomon River Phase of the Glen Elder Locality of North-Central Kansas" (master's thesis, Wichita State University 1996).

46. Donald J. Blakeslee, "Middle Ceramic Period Earthlodges as the Products of Craft Traditions," in *Plains Earthlodges: Ethnographic and Archaeological Perspectives,* ed. Donna C. Roper and Elizabeth P. Pauls (Tuscaloosa: University of Alabama Press, 2005), 83–110.

47. Blakeslee, *Waconda Lake,* 145–47.

48. Blakeslee, *Waconda Lake,* 43–44; Ronald A. Dorsey, "Archaeological Interpretation of Freshwater Mussel Assemblages near the Solomon River, Kansas," *Central Plains Archaeology* 8, no. 1 (1998): 13–24.

49. Blakeslee, *Waconda Lake,* 75–102.

50. Blakeslee, *Waconda Lake,* 97–100, 157–58; Ronald A. Dorsey, "Freshwater Mussel Shells and Archaeological Sites on the Solomon River" (master's thesis, Wichita State University, 1998); Dorsey, "Archaeological Interpretation."

51. Blakeslee, *Waconda Lake,* 97.

52. James O. Marshall, "The Glen Elder Focus: The Cultural Affiliations of Archaeological Material from the Glen Elder Site, 14ML1" (master's thesis, University of Nebraska 1967); Lauren W. Ritterbush, "Late Prehistoric Oneota in the Central Plains," in *Kansas Archaeology,* ed. Robert J. Hoard and William E. Banks (Lawrence: University Press of Kansas, 2006), 151–65.

53. Brad Logan, *Phasing in White Rock: Archaeological Investigation of the White Rock and Warne Sites, Lovewell Reservoir, Jewell County, Kansas, 1994–1995* (Lawrence: Museum of Anthropology, University of Kansas, 1995).

54. Donald J. Blakeslee, Michelle Peck and Ronald A. Dorsey, "Glen Elder: A Western Oneota Bison Hunting Camp," *Midcontinental Journal of Archaeology* 26, no. 1 (2001): 79–104.

55. Edwin James, *An Account of an Expedition from Pittsburgh to the Rock Mountains, Performed in the Years 1819–1820 . . . Under the Command of Major Stephen H. Long* (Philadelphia: H. C. Carey & I. Lea, 1823), 214–15; Tillie Karns Newman, *The Black Dog Trail* (Boston: Christopher Publishing House, 1957), 25.

56. Frank Norall, *Bourgmont: Explorer of the Missouri, 1698–1725* (Lincoln: University of Nebraska Press, 1988), 125–61.

57. Mildred Mott Wedel, "The Wichita Indians in the Arkansas River Basin," in *Plains Indian Studies,* ed. Douglas H. Ubelaker and Herman J. Viola (Washington, D.C.: Smithsonian Institution Press, 1982), 118–34.

58. Richard Flint and Shirley Cushing Flint, *Documents of the Coronado Expedition, 1539–1542* (Dallas: Southern Methodist University Press, 2005), 516.

59. Donald J. Blakeslee and Marlin Hawley, "Great Bend Aspect," in *Handbook of Kansas Archaeology,* ed. Robert Hoard and Will Banks (Lawrence: University Press of Kansas, 2006), 165–79.

60. M. Michelle Peck, "A Study of Great Bend Aspect Hunting Camp Sites within the State of Kansas" (master's thesis, Wichita State University 2003).

61. Steven R. Holen, "Bison Hunting Territories and Lithic Acquisition among the Pawnee: An Ethnohistoric and Archaeological Study," in *Raw Material Economics among Prehistoric Hunter-Gatherers,* ed. Anta Montet-White and Steven R. Holen (Lawrence: University of Kansas, 1991), 399–411.

62. Alice C. Fletcher and Francis La Flesche, *The Omaha Tribe* (Washington, D.C.: Government Printing Office, 1911), 218.

63. Dale R. Henning and Shirley J. Schermer, "Central Siouans in the Northeastern Plains: Oneota Archaeology and the Blood Run Site," in *Dhegihan and Chiwere Siouans in the Plains: Historical and Archaeological Perspectives, Plains Anthropologist,* Memoir 36 (2004).

CHAPTER 3

1. William E. Myer, "Indian Trails of the Southeast," (Washington, D.C.: Bureau of American Ethnology, 42nd Annual Report, 1928), 727–857.

2. Donald J. Blakeslee and Robert Blasing, "Indian Trails in the Central Plains," *Plains Anthropologist* 33 (1988): 17–26; Carling I. Malouf, "On the Trail of the Indian," *Archaeology in Montana* 21, no. 3 (1980): 1.

3. Brian O. K. Reeves, "How Old is the Old North Trail?" *Archaeology in Montana* 31, no. 2 (1990): 1–18.

4. James C. Calder, *The Majorville Cairn and Medicine Wheel,* Mercury Series, Archaeological Survey of Canada, Paper 62 (Ottawa: National Museums of Canada, 1977).

5. Donald J. Blakeslee, Bob Blasing, and Hector Garcia, *Along the Pawnee Trail: Cultural Resource Survey and Testing, Wilson Lake, Kansas* (Kansas City, Mo.: U.S. Army Corps of Engineers, Kansas City District, 1986).

6. Steven R. Holen, "Lithic Procurement at the Gray Site, 25CX1," (master's thesis, University of Nebraska, 1983).

7. Louis F. Burns, *Osage Indian Customs and Myths* (Fallbrook, Calif.: Ciga Press, 1984), 98–101; Francis La Flesche, *A Dictionary of the Osage Language* (Washington, D.C.: Bureau of American Ethnology, 1932), passim.

8. Donald J. Blakeslee, "The Plains Interband Trade System: An Ethnohistoric and Archaeological Investigation" (PhD diss., University of Wisconsin-Milwaukee, 1975).

9. James Mooney, *Calendar History of the Kiowa Indians,* reprint of the 1898

edition, with an introduction by John C. Ewers (Washington, D.C.: Bureau of American Ethnology, 1979), 156.

10. Blakeslee, "Plains Interband Trade System," 150–76.

11. David Anthony, "Migration in Archaeology: the Baby and the Bathwater," *American Anthropologist* 94 (1992): 895–914.

12. Douglas R. Parks and Waldo R. Wedel, "Pawnee Geography: Historical and Sacred," *Great Plains Quarterly* (Summer 1985): 143–76.

13. E.g., James R. Murie, *Ceremonies of the Pawnee,* vol. 2, ed. Douglas R. Park (Washington, D.C.: Smithsonian Institution Press, 1981), 221.

14. Fletcher and La Flesche, *The Omaha Tribe,* 218.

15. Court of Claims, *The Omaha Tribe of Indians v the United States of America. Claim No. 31,002* (Washington, D.C.: Government Printing Office, 1914).

16. Court of Claims, *Omaha Tribe,* 58.

17. Melvin R. Gilmore, "Methods of Indian Buffalo Hunts, with the Itinerary of the Last Tribal Hunt of the Omaha," *Papers of the Michigan Academy of Science, Arts and Letters* 18 (1932), 28.

18. Peter John Powell, *People of the Sacred Mountain: A History of the Northern Cheyenne Chiefs and Warrior Societies, 1830–1879* (San Francisco: Harper & Row, 1981), 167.

19. George P. Hammond, and Agapito Rey, *Narratives of the Coronado Expedition* (Albuquerque: University of New Mexico Press, 1940), 305.

20. Norall, *Bourgmont,* 66.

21. Bob Blasing, personal communication.

22. Murray, *Travels,* 30.

23. Murray, *Travels,* 2: 32.

24. Murray, *Travels,* 2: 30.

25. Col. Richard I. Dodge, *The Plains of the Great West and Their Inhabitants, Being a Description of the Plains, Game, Indians, &c. of the Great North American Desert* (Reprint, New York: Archer House, 1959), 54.

26. James R. Mead, "Trails in Southern Kansas," *Kansas State Historical Society Collections* 5 (1896): 91.

27. Burns, *Osage Indian Customs,* 128–29.

28. Donald J. Blakeslee, and Arthur H. Rohn, *Man and Environment in Northeastern Kansas: The Hillsdale Lake Project,* 6 vols. (Kansas City, Mo.: U. S. Army Corps of Engineers, 1986) 1: 31–33.

29. Robert Blasing, "Prehistoric Geography of the Flint Hills" (master's thesis, Wichita State University, 1986), 19, 83.

30. Cf. Basso, Keith H., *Wisdom Sits in Places: Landscape and Language Among the Western Apache* (Albuquerque: University of New Mexico Press, 1996).

31. Timothy P. McCleary, "Quest for the Morning Star Stone," *North Dakota Quarterly* 67, nos. 3–4 (2000): 132–33.

32. Blasing, "Prehistoric Geography," Figs. 7–8.

33. Wislizenus, *Journey,* 40.

34. James R. Mead, *Hunting and Trading on the Great Plains, 1859–1875,* ed. Schuyler Jones (Norman: University of Oklahoma Press, 1986), 68.

35. Nancy Robertson, personal communication.

36. Court of Claims, *Omaha Tribe,* 53.

37. Blakeslee, Blasing, and Garcia, *Along the Pawnee Trail,* 205–6.

38. Alfred Barnaby Thomas, *After Coronado* (Norman: University of Oklahoma Press, 1935), 66.

39. E.g., Elliott Coues, *The Expedition of Zebulon Montgomery Pike,* vol. 2 (New York: Francis P. Harper, 1895), 420.

40. Blasing, "Prehistoric Geography," 19.

41. Blakeslee, Blasing, and Garcia, *Along the Pawnee Trail,* 205–6.

42. Stephen C. Jett, "Observations Regarding Chartkoff's California 'Rock Feature Complex.'" *American Antiquity* 51, no. 3 (1986): 615–16.

43. Lawrence L. Loendorf, and Joan Louise Brownell, "The Bad Pass Trail," *Archaeology in Montana* 21, no. 3 (1980): 11–102.

44. Harry E. Chrisman, *Lost Trails of the Cimarron* (Denver: Sage Books, 1961), 28; Richard I. Dodge, *Our Wild Indians: Thirty-three Years' Personal Experience among the Red Men of the Great West* (Hartford, Conn.: A. D. Worthington, 1886), 411–12.

45. Court of Claims, *Omaha Tribe,* 58.

46. Blasing, "Prehistoric Geography," Fig 5.

47. Dodge, *Our Wild Indians,* 285.

48. Donald J. Blakeslee, "The Rattlesnake Creek and Walnut Creek Crossings of the Arkansas," *Wagon Tracks* 3, no.1 (1988): 4–5.

49. Wislizenus *Journey,* 48.

50. Wislizenus *Journey,* 40.

51. William P. Clark, *Indian Sign Language* (Philadelphia: L. R. Hamersly, 1885), 153–54.

52. E.g., Dodge, *Our Wild Indians,* 285.

53. Coues, *Expedition,* vol. 2: 420.

54. Alfred E. Bowers, *Mandan Social and Ceremonial Organization* (Chicago: University of Chicago Press, 1950), 85.

55. Alfred E. Bowers, *Hidatsa Social and Ceremonial Organization,* Bureau of American Ethnology Bulletin 194 (Washington, D.C.: Smithsonian Institution Press, 1965), 447.

56. Louis Henry Morgan, *The Indian Journals, 1859–62,* ed. Leslie A. White (Ann Arbor: University of Michigan Press, 1959), 32.

57. Murray, *Travels,* vol. 2: 32.

58. Murray, *Travels,* vol. 2: 37.

59. Elliott Coues, *New Light on the Early History of the Greater Northwest: The Manuscript Journals of Alexander Henry and David Thompson, 1799–1814* (New York: Francis P. Harper, 1897), 376.

60. Gene Weltfish, *The Lost Universe* (New York: Basic Books, 1965), 164–65.

61. Blasing, "Prehistoric Geography," 26, Fig 3.

62. Reeves, "How Old."

63. Mead, *Hunting and Trapping*, 189.

64. Louise Barry, *The Beginning of the West: Annals of the Kansas Gateway to the American West, 1540–1854* (Topeka: Kansas State Historical Society, 1972), 136–37, 139.

65. Weltfish, *Lost Universe*, 186–88.

66. Donald J. Blakeslee, *Along Ancient Trails: The Mallet Expedition of 1739* (Niwot: University Press of Colorado, 1996), 81.

67. Charles C. Osborne, "Adams County: The Early Years," in *Adams County: The Story*, ed. Dorothy Weyer Creigh (Hastings, Neb.: Adams County-Hastings Centennial Commission, 1972), 1.

68. Parks and Wedel, "Pawnee Geography," 160.

69. Blakeslee, *Along Ancient Trails*, 85–86.

70. Blakeslee, Blasing, and Garcia, *Along the Pawnee Trail*, 134.

71. Gilmore, "Methods," 28.

72. Mead, "Trails," 90.

73. Blakeslee, Peck, and Dorsey, "Glen Elder."

74. Reynolds, "Preliminary Report."

75. Russell L. Hall, Amy L. Collett, Timothy A. Hauschild, Lisa A. Hertz and Patricia J. O'Brien, *A Cultural Resource Survey of Lincoln County, Kansas* (Manhattan: Kansas State University, Community Service Project, Kansas Center for Rural Initiatives, 1991).

76. Blakeslee, Blasing, and Garcia, *Along the Pawnee Trail*, Fig. 10.

77. Mead, *Hunting and Trading*, 186.

78. Blakeslee, Blasing, and Garcia, *Along the Pawnee Trail*, 205–6.

79. Blakeslee, *Along Ancient Trails*, 107.

80. Blakeslee, *Along Ancient Trails*, 9; Susan C. Vehik, "Oñate's Expedition to the Southern Plains: Routes, Destinations and Implications for Late Prehistoric Cultural Adaptations," *Plains Anthropologist* 31 (1986): 13–33.

CHAPTER 4

1. Jennings, Francis, *The Invasion of America: Indians, Colonialism, and the Cant of Conquest* (Chapel Hill: University of North Carolina Press, 1975), 173.

2. Thomas, *After Coronado*, 110–33, 141–45.

3. Sheldon, Addison E., "A New Chapter in Nebraska History," *Nebraska History* 6, no. 1 (1927): 13.

4. Hotz, Gottfried, *Indian Skin Paintings from the American Southwest: Two Representations of Border Conflicts between Mexico and the Missouri in the Early Eighteenth Century*, trans. Johannes Malthaner (Norman: University of Oklahoma Press, 1970).

5. Blakeslee, *Ancient Trails.*

6. Douglas Parks cited in Von Del Chamberlain, *When the Stars Came Down to Earth* (Los Altos, Calif.: Ballena Press, 1982), 255.

7. Murray, *Travels,* vol. 1, 319.

8. Parks and Wedel, "Pawnee Geography," 153.

9. Sydney H. Ball, "The Mining of Gems and Ornamental Stones by American Indians," *Bureau of American Ethnology Bulletin* 128, Anthropological Paper No. 13 (Washington, D.C.: Government Printing Office, 1941), 50.

10. Blakeslee, *Ancient Trails,* 108–54.

11. John L. Kessell, *Kiva, Cross, and Crown: The Pecos Indians and New Mexico, 1540–1840* (Washington, D. C.: National Park Service, 1979), 391.

12. Alfred Barnaby Thomas, *The Plains Indians and New Mexico, 1751–1778* (Albuquerque: University of New Mexico Press, 1940), 93–94, 103–6.

13. J. R. Mead collection, Special Collections Department, Ablah Library, Wichita State University.

14. Mildred Wedel, personal communication.

15. Waldo R. Wedel, *An Introduction to Pawnee Archaeology* (Washington, D.C.: Bureau of American Ethnology, 1936), 15.

16. Noel Loomis and Abraham P. Nasatir, *Pedro Vial and the Roads to Santa Fe* (Norman: University of Oklahoma Press, 1967), 401.

17. Republic County Historical Society 1964, 13.

18. Loomis and Nasatir, *Pedro Vial,* 401–402.

19. E.g., C. Robert Haywood, *Trails South: The Wagon Road Economy in the Dodge City Panhandle Region* (Norman: University of Oklahoma Press, 1986).

20. Loomis and Nasatir, *Pedro Vial,* 414–15.

21. Warren L. Cook, *Flood Tide of Empire: Spain and the Pacific Northwest, 1543–1819* (New Haven: Yale University Press, 1973), 462.

22. Loomis and Nasatir, *Pedro Vial,* 415–16.

23. Ruth Steinberg, "José Jarvet, Spanish Scout and Historical Enigma," *New Mexico Historical Review,* July 1992, 227–49.

24. Cook, *Flood Tide,* 446–90.

25. Charles W. Hackett, *Pichardo's Treatise on the Limits of Louisiana and Texas* (Austin: University of Texas Press, 1931–46).

26. Cook, *Flood Tide,* 450.

27. Cook, *Flood Tide,* 453.

28. Cook, *Flood Tide,* 463.

29. Cook, *Flood Tide,* 463.

30. Donald Jackson, ed., *The Journals of Zebulon Montgomery Pike, with Letters and Related Documents,* vol. 2 (Norman: University of Oklahoma Press, 1966), 373, 377n.

31. Loomis and Nasatir, *Pedro Vial,* 412.

32. Coues, *Pike,* vol. 2: 500–502.

33. Abraham P. Nasatir, *Before Lewis and Clark: Documents Illustrating the His-*

tory of the Missouri, 1785–1804, vol. 1 (St. Louis: St. Louis Historical Documents Foundation, 1952), 211, 422.

34. Lansing B. Bloom, "The Death of Jacques d'Eglise," *New Mexico Historical Review* 2 (1927): 369–79.

35. Nasatir, *Before Lewis and Clark,* vol. 2: 742–45.

36. Loomis and Nasatir, *Pedro Vial,* 429.

37. Cook, *Flood Tide,* 472–77.

38. Cook, *Flood Tide,* 482.

39. Coues, *Expedition;* Jackson, *Journals.*

40. Carl Irving Wheat, *Mapping the Transmississippi West, 1540–1861* (San Francisco: Institute of Historical Cartography, 1957), Map 287.

41. Coues, *Expedition,* vol. 2: 394–404.

42. Sheldon, "New Chapter."

43. Bob Blasing, personal communication.

44. Blakeslee, Blasing, and Garcia, *Along the Pawnee Trail;* Coues, *Expedition;* Stephen H. Hart and Archer Butler Hulbert, *Zebulon Pike's Arkansaw Journal: In Search of the Southern Louisiana Purchase Boundary Line* (Westport, Conn.: Greenwood Press, 1972); Jackson *Journals;* Frank J. Munday, "The Record of the Pike Expedition," *Nebraska History Magazine* 10, no. 3 (1927), 168–69.

45. Coues, *Expedition,* vol. 2, 420n.

46. Hart and Hulbert, *Pike's Arkansaw Journal,* 97.

47. E.g., Jackson, *Journals;* Hart and Hulbert, *Pike's Arkansaw Journal.*

48. Martha Royce Blaine, *Pawnee Passage, 1870-1875* (Norman: University of Oklahoma Press, 1990), 240.

49. Hart and Hulbert, *Pike's Arkansaw Journal,* 93n.

50. Coues, *Expedition,* vol. 2, 420.

51. Cook, *Flood Tide,* 477–83.

52. Jackson, *Journals,* vol. 1, 386.

53. Nasatir, *Before Lewis and Clark,* vol. 1, 86–87.

54. Nasatir, *Before Lewis and Clark,* vol. 1, 86.

55. Nasatir, *Before Lewis and Clark,* vol. 1, 109.

56. Nasatir, *Before Lewis and Clark,* vol. 1, 113.

57. Bloom, "Death of Jacques d'Eglise."

58. Loomis and Nasatir, *Pedro Vial,* 248.

59. E.g., Loomis and Nasatir, *Pedro Vial,* 248.

60. Thomas James, *Three Years Among the Indians and Mexicans,* ed. Milo Milton Quaife (Chicago: Lakeside Press, 1953), 101–2; R. F. Strickland, "Robert McKnight," in *The Mountain Men and the Fur Trade of the Far West,* vol. 3, ed. L. R. Hafen (Glendale, Calif.: A. H. Clark, 1972), 27–37.

61. Hiram Chittenden, *The American Fur Trade of the Far West: A History of the Pioneer Trading Posts and Early Fur Companies of the Missouri Valley and the Rocky Mountains and of the Overland Commerce with Santa Fe,* vol. 2 (New York: F. P. Harper, 1902), 495–96; Loomis and Nasatir, *Pedro Vial,* 254.

62. Jacob Fowler, *The Journal of Jacob Fowler,* ed. Elliott Coues (Lincoln: University of Nebraska Press, 1965), 142.

63. Thomas James, *Three Years,* 101–2.

64. Loomis and Nasatir, *Pedro Vial,* 249–50.

65. George Sibley, "Extracts from the Journal of Major George Sibley," *Chronicles of Oklahoma* 5, no. 2 (1927): 196–97.

66. Sibley, "Extracts," 196–97.

67. W. Wedel, *Introduction to Pawnee Archaeology,* 36–37.

68. Sibley, "Extracts," 210.

69. Meriwether, David, *My Life in the Mountains and on the Plains,* ed. R. A. Griffin (Norman: University of Oklahoma Press, 1965).

70. Meriwether, *My Life,* 81.

71. Meriwether, *My Life,* 83.

72. Meriwether, *My Life,* 85–86.

73. Meriwether, *My Life,* 90–93.

74. Two of the classics on this topic are Josiah Gregg, *Commerce of the Pprairies;* ed. Max L. Moorhead (Norman: University of Oklahoma Press, 1954) and Henry Inman, *The Old Santa Fe Trail: The Story of a Great Highway* (Topeka: Crane & Co., 1916).

75. Larry M. Beachum, *William Becknell, Father of the Santa Fe Trade,* Southwestern Studies Monograph 68 (El Paso: Texas Western Press, 1982), 32–33.

76. David J. Weber, *The Taos Trappers: The Fur Trade in the Far Southwest, 1540–1846* (Norman: University of Oklahoma Press, 1971), 60–61.

77. Weber, *Taos Trappers,* 62–63.

78. Weber, *Taos Trappers,* 85.

79. Weber, *Taos Trappers,* 85.

80. Weber, *Taos Trappers,* 86–88.

81. Hispanic merchants quickly became involved in the Santa Fe to Chihuahua portion of the trade and more gradually began making the trip from Santa Fe to Missouri. Cf. Susan Calfonte Boyle, *Los Capitalistas: Hispano Merchants and the Santa Fe Trail Trade* (Albuquerque: University of New Mexico Press, 2000); Sterling Evans, "Eastward, Ho! The Mexican Freighting and Commerce Experience along the Santa Fe Trail," *Kansas History* 19, no. 4 (Winter 1996–97), 242–60; David J. Weber, ed., *The Extranjeros: Selected Documents from the Mexican Side of the Santa Fe Trail, 1825-1828* (Santa Fe: Stagecoach Press, 1967).

82. *St. Louis Enquirer,* May 24, 1824.

83. Barry, *Beginning of the West,* 117–18.

84. James Ohio Pattie, *The Personal Narrative of James Ohio Pattie,* ed. Timothy Flint (Lincoln: University of Nebraska Press, 1984).

85. Gilmore, "Methods," 28.

86. Pattie, *Personal Narrative,* 20.

87. Murray, *Travels,* vol. 1, 259–74.

88. Murray, *Travels,* vol. 1, 378.

89. Murray, *Travels,* vol. 1, 372–73.

90. James Mooney, *Calendar History of the Kiowa Indians,* reprint of the 1898 edition, with an introduction by John C. Ewers (Washington, D.C.: Bureau of American Ethnology, 1979), 407.

91. Donald E. Hattin, *Stratigraphy of the Carlile Shale in Kansas* (Lawrence: State Geological Survey, 1962), 64.

92. Hattin, *Stratigraphy of the Carlile Shale,* 65.

93. Blakeslee, Blasing, and Garcia, *Along the Pawnee Trail,* 205–6.

94. Murray, *Travels,* vol. 2, 25–54.

95. Mooney, *Calendar History,* 294–95.

96. Whit McConnell, "McConnell and the Indians," in *Historical Moments of Mitchell County,* compiled by the Waconda Chapter, Kansas Anthropological Association (Beloit: A. B. D. Printers, 1976), 47.

97. Blaine, *Pawnee Passage,* 234–69.

CHAPTER 5

1. Stanley A. Ahler, Thomas D. Thiessen, and Michael K. Trimble, *People of the Willows: The Prehistory and Early History of the Hidatsa Indians* (Grand Forks: University of North Dakota Press, 1991), 28–29.

2. John Joseph Matthews, *The Osages: Children of the Middle Waters* (Norman: University of Oklahoma Press, 1961), 8.

3. Bowers, *Hidatsa,* 374.

4. E.g., Frank Hamilton Cushing, "Origin Myth from Oraibi," *Journal of American Folklore* 36 (1923): 163–70; Albert S. Gatshet, *Migration Legend of the Creek Indians,* 2 vols. (New York: Kraus Reprint, 1969).

5. Karl H. Schlesier, *The Wolves of Heaven: Cheyenne Shamanism, Ceremonies and Prehistoric Origins* (Norman: University of Oklahoma Press, 1987), 76–80.

6. Gloria J. Fedirchuk and Edward J. McCullough, "Prehistoric Art and Spiritualism: A Perspective from Pine Coulee, Alberta," *Alberta Archaeological Review* 22 (1991), 12.

7. E.g., Kevin Callahan, *The Cupmarked Boulders of Blood Run, Iowa: Death Stones, Baby Rocks, & Vision Questing on the Northern Plains* (Minneapolis: University of Minnesota, 1999); Fedirchuk and McCullough, "Prehistoric Art and Spiritualism."

8. J. Flight (1887), cited in Oliver C. Farrington, *Catalogue of the Meteorites of North America,* Memoirs of the National Academy of Sciences, 13 (Washington, D.C.: Government Printing Office, 1915), 245.

9. Murie, *Ceremonies of the Pawnee,* 40, 442–43.

10. Linea Sundstrom, "Sacred Islands: An Exploration of Religion and Landscape in the Northern Great Plains," in *Islands on the Plains: Ecological, Social and Ritual Use of Landscapes,* ed. Marcel Kornfeld and Alan J. Osborn (Salt Lake City: University of Utah Press, 2003), 264.

11. Gatshet, *Migration Legend.*

12. Sundstrom, "Sacred Islands."

13. Weltfish, *Lost Universe,* 391–94.

14. Parks and Wedel, "Pawnee Geography."

15. Bob Blasing, "Pawnee Animal Lodges Revisited" (Paper Presented at the 13th Flint Hills Conference, Lincoln, Nebraska, 1991); "A Possible Location for the 'Garden of the Gods' Described in Pawnee Stories," paper presented at the 15th Flint Hills Conference, Wichita, Kansas, 1993).

16. Parks and Wedel, "Pawnee Geography," Table 1.

17. Murie, *Ceremonies of the Pawnee,* 323.

18. Blasing, "Possible Location."

19. Parks and Wedel, "Pawnee Geography," 153.

20. Antoine Davis Raudot, "Memoir Concerning the Different Indian Nations of North America," in *The Indians of the Western Great Lakes,* ed. W. Vernon Kinietz (Ann Arbor: Occasional Contributions from the Museum of Anthropology of the University of Michigan, 10, 1940), 404.

21. Parks and Wedel, "Pawnee Geography," 162.

22. Murie, *Ceremonies of the Pawnee,* 281, 395.

23. Bowers, *Hidatsa,* 435.

24. Parks and Wedel, "Pawnee Geography," 153.

25. Murie, *Ceremonies of the Pawnee,* 208.

26. Murie, *Ceremonies of the Pawnee,* 226.

27. Murie, *Ceremonies of the Pawnee,* 233.

28. Murie, *Ceremonies of the Pawnee,* 307.

29. A.L. Graham, A. W. R.Bevan, and R. Hutchison, *Catalogue of Meteorites, with Special Reference to Those Represented in the Collection of the British Museum Natural History* (Tucson: University of Arizona Press, 1985).

30. George Dorsey, *The Mythology of the Wichita* (Washington, D.C.: Carnegie Institution, 1904), 66.

31. E. H. S. Bailey, *Special Report on Mineral Waters* (Topeka: University of Kansas Geological Survey, 1902), 200.

32. Bailey, *Special Report,* 202.

33. Murie, *Ceremonies of the Pawnee,* 223.

34. Murie, *Ceremonies of the Pawnee,* 242.

35. George Bird Grinnell, *Pawnee Hero Stories and Folk Tales* (New York: Forest and Stream, 1889), 359.

36. Murie, *Ceremonies of the Pawnee,* 221–23.

37. Murie, *Ceremonies of the Pawnee,* 100.

38. Oregon Iron Company v. Hughes, 47 OR 313, 82 Pac 572 (1905).

39. G. K. Patrick, "The Great Spirit Spring," *Transactions of the Kansas Academy of Science 7.* (1881), 23.

40. Gregg Dowd, "Waconda Springs," lecture given at Glen Elder State Park, transcript in the Cawker City Public Library (1989); Ava Gentleman, "The History

of Waconda Springs" *Solomon Valley Post, Bicentennial Edition,* 31 (Beloit, 1976); Patrick, "Great Spirit Spring," 23.

41. Patrick, "Great Spirit Spring," 23.

42. Isaac McCoy cited in Parks and Wedel, "Pawnee Geography," 158.

43. Albert S. Gatschet, "A Sacred Well in Kansas," *Journal of American Folklore* 2 (1891), 68.

44. Schlesier, *Wolves of Heaven,* 77.

45. Patrick, "Great Spirit Spring," 25.

46. Wislizenus, *Journey,* 44.

47. John G. Burke, *Cosmic Debris: Meteorites in History* (Berkeley: University of California Press, 1986), 57.

48. E.g., Thomas F. Kehoe and Alice B. Kehoe, "Boulder Effigy Monuments in the Northern Plains," *Journal of American Folklore* 72, no. 284 (1959): 115–27.

49. Donald J. Blakeslee, "The Celestial Mirror: Investigations into Native American Cosmology," manuscript in possession of the author.

50. R. Clark Mallam, *Site of the Serpent: A Prehistoric Life Metaphor in South Central Kansas* (Rice, Kans.: Coronado–Quivira Museum, 1985).

51. Blakeslee and Hawley, "Great Bend Aspect," 168–70.

52. Court of Claims, *Omaha Tribe;* Fletcher and La Flesche *The Omaha Tribe,* 161, 169; George F. Will, *Archaeology of the Missouri Valley,* American Museum of Natural History Anthropological Papers 22, no. 4 (New York: American Museum of Natural History, 1924), 295.

53. May, "Geoarchaeology."

54. P. W. Birkeland, *Pedology, Weathering and Geomorphological Research* (New York: Oxford University Press, 1984).

55. Melvin R. Gilmore, *Uses of Plants by the Indians of the Missouri River Region* (Lincoln: University of Nebraska Press, 1977), 83.

56. Blakeslee and Hawley, "Great Bend Aspect," Fig. 4.

57. Murie, *Ceremonies of the Pawnee,* 242.

CHAPTER 6.

1. Blakeslee, "Waconda Lake," 151–52.

2. Peck, "A Study of Great Bend Aspect Hunting Camp Sites."

3. Mildred Mott Wedel, "The Ethnohistoric Approach to Caddoan Origins," *Nebraska History* 60 (1979): 183–96.

4. Donna C. Roper, "The Central Plains Tradition," in *Kansas Archaeology,* ed. Robert J. Hoard and William E. Banks (Lawrence: University Press of Kansas, 2006), 246–47.

5. Fletcher and La Flesche, *Omaha Tribe,* 74.

6. Court of Claims, *Omaha Tribe.*

7. Elizabeth A. H. John, *Storms Brewed in Other Men's Worlds: The Confronta-

tions of Indians, Spanish and French in the Southwest, 1540–1795 (Lincoln: University of Nebraska Press, 1975), 697 ff.

8. Mooney, *Calendar History,* 156.

9. Morris W. Foster and Martha McCollough, "Plains Apache," in *Handbook of North American Indians, Vol. 13, Part 2, Plains,* ed. Raymond J. DeMaillie (Washington, D.C.: Smithsonian Institution Press, 2001), 926.

10. Thomas W. Kavanaugh, "Comanche," in *Handbook of North American Indians, Vol. 13, Part 2, Plains,* ed. Raymond J. DeMaillie (Washington, D.C.: Smithsonian Institution Press, 2001), 905.

11. Mooney, *Calendar History,* 257–60.

12. Jacob Jablow, *The Cheyenne in Plains Indian Trade Relations, 1795–1840* (Seattle: University of Washington Press, 1950), 6.

13. Mooney, *Calendar History,* 275–76.

14. George E. Hyde, *Spotted Tail's Folk: a History of the Brulé Sioux* (Norman: University of Oklahoma Press, 1961), 20–21.

15. Hyde, *Spotted Tail's Folk,* 29–30.

16. John Y. Nelson, *Fifty Years on the Trail: A True Story of Western Life,* ed. Harrington O'Reilly (Norman: University of Oklahoma Press, 1963), 64.

17. Nelson, *Fifty Years on the Trail,* 51.

18. Connie A. Woodhouse, Jeffrey J. Lukas, and Peter M. Brown, "Drought in the Western Great Plains, 1845–56: Impacts and Implications," *Bulletin of the American Meteorological Society* 83 (2002): 1485–93.

19. Alfred Cuming, "Report Number 27," in *Report of the Office of Indian Affairs, 1854* (Washington, D.C.: A. O. P. Nicholson, 1854), 83; George W. Manypenny, "Report of the Commissioner of Indian Affairs," in *Report of the Office of Indian Affairs, 1854* (Washington, D.C.: A. O. P. Nicholson, 1854), 7–8.

20. Cf., Nathan Boone, "The Nathan Boone Journal manuscript," Special collections manuscript 88–11, Ablah Library, Wichita State University, 1843; John, *Storms Brewed,* 758; La Flesche, *Dictionary of the Osage Language;* Mead, *Hunting and Trading,* 143; Sibley, "Extracts from the Journal."

21. Charles J. Kappler, ed., *Indian Treaties, 1778–1883* (New York: Interland Publishing, 1972), 217.

22. Kappler, *Indian Treaties,* 222.

23. Holen, "Bison Hunting Territories."

24. George A. Schultz, *An Indian Canaan: Isaac McCoy and the Vision of an Indian State* (Norman: University of Oklahoma Press, 1972), 174.

25. Schultz, *Indian Canaan,* 188.

26. Schultz, *Indian Canaan,* 192–93.

27. Schultz, *Indian Canaan,* 117.

28. Alan W. Farley, *The Delaware Indians in Kansas, 1829–1867* (Kansas City, Mo., 1955), 10.

29. E.g., Farley, *Delaware Indians,* 4.

30. Cf. David J. Weber, *The Taos Trappers: The Fur Trade in the Far Southwest, 1540–1846* (Norman: University of Oklahoma Press, 1971).

31. Farley, *Delaware Indians,* 4–5; Schultz, *Indian Canaan,* 174.

32. Kappler, *Indian Treaties,* 416.

33. Kappler, *Indian Treaties,* 417.

34. Farley, *Delaware Indians,* 5–6, 9–10.

35. *Daily Republican, Early Day History of Coffey County, Dating Back to the 1870s, Compiled from Interviews and Articles Written by Old-Timers* (Burlington, Kans.: Daily Republican, 1960), 38–39, 75–79, 100.

36. William E. Connelley, "Prairie Band of Pottawatomie Indians," *Collections of the Kansas State Historical Society* 14 (1918), 493–94, 498.

37. Powell, *People of the Sacred Mountain,* 75.

38. Accounts of this fight can be found in George Bird Grinnell, *The Fighting Cheyennes* (New York: Charles Scribner's Sons, 1915), 75–77; Powell, *People of the Sacred Mountain,* 75–79; and David S. Lavender, *Bent's Fort* (Garden City, N.Y.: Doubleday & Co, 1954), 239–40.

39. Powell, *People of the Sacred Mountain,* 160.

40. Powell, *People of the Sacred Mountain,* 162.

41. Mooney, *Calendar History,* 297.

42. Grinnell, *Fighting Cheyennes,* 103.

43. Mooney, *Calendar History.*

44. Powell, *People of the Sacred Mountain.*

45. Powell, *People of the Sacred Mountain,* 172–73.

46. Mooney, *Calendar History,* 197; Powell, *People of the Sacred Mountain,* 173.

47. Powell, *People of the Sacred Mountain,* 173; John W. Whitfield, "Report Number 29," in *Report of the Office of Indian Affairs, 1854* (Washington, D.C.: A. O. P. Nicholson, 1854), 89.

48. Mooney, *Calendar History,* 297.

49. Powell, *People of the Sacred Mountain,* 173.

50. Mooney, *Calendar History,* 297; Powell, *People of the Sacred Mountain,* 173.

51. Whitfield, "Report Number 29," 89–90.

52. Powell, *People of the Sacred Mountain,* 173–74.

53. Mooney, *Calendar History,* 298; Powell, *People of the Sacred Mountain,* 173.

54. Mooney, *Calendar History,* 299.

55. Powell, *People of the Sacred Mountain,* 190–93, 207–10.

56. Mooney, *Calendar History,* 299–300, 302.

57. Ellen Goodnow, "To My Dear Husband," letter dated August 8, 1857, Isaac Goodnow collection, Kansas State Historical Society, #357, Box 1, Folder 49.

58. Mead, *Hunting and Trading,* 63.

59. Mead, *Hunting and Trading,* 68.

60. Dorothe Tarrence Homan, *Lincoln—That County in Kansas* (Lindsborg, Kans.: Barbos Printing, 1979), 10.

61. James E. Shortridge, *Peopling the Plains: Who Settled Where in Frontier Kansas* (Lawrence: University Press of Kansas, 1995), 72; Manypenny, "Report of the Commissioner," 1.

62. H. Craig Miner and William E. Unrau, *The End of Indian Kansas: A Study of Cultural Revolution, 1854–1871* (Lawrence: Regents Press of Kansas, 1978).

63. M. Winsor and James A. Scarborough, "Jewell County," *Collections of the Kansas State Historical Society* 17 (1928), 4.

64. Republic County Historical Society, *History of Republic County, 1864–1964* (Belleville, Kans.: Belleville Telescope, 1964), 2–3.

65. Darrel Miller, *Waconda Land: The Legends and Pioneers' Accounts of Settling the Land* (Downs, Kans.: Cellar Door Publications, 1989), 16; Lonnie J. White, "Indian Raids on the Kansas Frontier, 1869," *Kansas Historical Quarterly* 38, no. 4 (1972), 387.

66. Homan, *That County in Kansas,* 10–12, 18–19; Miller, *Waconda Land,* 14.

67. White, "Indian Raids"; Miller, *Waconda Land,* 16; Homan, *That County in Kansas,* 22.

68. White, "Indian Raids," 376, 378; Miller, *Waconda Land,* 37–38; Harry E. Ross, *What Price White Rock: A Chronicle of Northwestern Jewell County* (Burr Oak, Kans.: Herald Press, 1937), 25.

69. Alan B. Houghton, *The Frontier Aflame: An Account of the Bell-Bogardus Massacre and Other Indian Raids in Mitchell County and the Solomon Valley in August, 1868* (Beloit, Kans.: Beloit Daily Call, 1958), 9–12.

70. Military Division of the Missouri, *Record of Engagements with Hostile Indians within the Military Division of the Missouri, from 1868 to 1882, Lieutenant General P. H. Sheridan, Commanding. Compiled from Official Records* (Chicago: U.S. Army, Division of the Missouri, 1882), 9.

71. Luther Heddon North, *Man of the Plains: Recollections of Luther North, 1856-1882,* ed. Donald F. Danker (Lincoln: University of Nebraska Press, 1961), 111–19.

72. Houghton, *The Frontier Aflame,* 3.

73. Military Division of the Missouri, *Record of Engagements,* 1882.

74. Houghton, *The Frontier Aflame,* 14, 50.

75. Miller, *Waconda Land,* 53.

76. Anonymous, "A Bit of Mitchell County History," in *Historical Moments of Mitchell County,* compiled by the Waconda Chapter, Kansas Anthropological Association (Beloit: A. B. D. Printers, 1976), 50.

77. Homan, *Lincoln—That County in Kansas,* 40–41.

78. Miller, *Waconda Land,* 44.

79. Miller, *Waconda Land,* 65; Howard Ruede, *Sod-house Days,* ed. John Ise (New York: Cooper Square, 1966), 17.

80. Gilmore, "Methods," 31–32.

81. Ruede, *Sod-house Days,* 19, 168.

82. Ruede, *Sod-house Days,* 124.

83. Mari Sandoz, *Cheyenne Autumn* (New York: McGraw-Hill, 1953).

84. Ruede, *Sod-house Days,* 240.

85. Tom Dillehay, "Late Quaternary Bison Population Changes on the Southern Plains," *Plains Anthropologist* 19 (1974): 180–96.

86. Miller, *Waconda Land,* 12.

87. Kessell, *Kiva, Cross, and Crown,* 180–90; Mildred Mott Wedel, *The Deer Creek Site, Oklahoma: A Wichita Village Sometimes Called Ferdinandina: An Ethnohistorian's View,* Oklahoma Historical Society Series in Anthropology 5 (Norman: Oklahoma Historical Society, 1981).

88. John Ise, *Sod and Stubble* (Lawrence: University of Kansas Press, 1996), 68.

89. Fitzpatrick, J. C., ed., "Land Ordinance of 1785, May 20, 1785," in *Journals of the Continental Congress,* vol. 28, 375 ff.

90. Blakeslee and Rohn, *Man and Environment,* vol. 1: 53–55.

91. Kansas Association of Land Surveyors, *Kansas Survey Plats* (Leavenworth, Kans.: Duke West Intergraphics, 2005).

92. Ruede, *Sod-house Days,* 45.

93. Ruede, *Sod-house Days,* 143.

94. Ise, *Sod and Stubble,* 140.

95. Ruede, *Sod-house Days;* Ise *Sod and Stubble.*

96. Grace Muilenburg and Ada Swineford, *Land of the Post Rock: Its Origins, History, and People* (Lawrence: University Press of Kansas, 1975), 13.

97. Muilenburg and Swineford, *Post Rock,* 13.

98. Muilenburg and Swineford, *Post Rock,* 14.

99. Ise, *Sod and Stubble,* 10, 17.

100. Ruede, *Sod-house Days,* 13.

101. Ruede, *Sod-house Days*, 30–40, 105.

102. Ruede, *Sod-house Days,* 101.

103. Ruede, *Sod-house Days,* 23, 31, 38–39.

104. Ruede, *Sod-house Days,* 23, 130, 135.

105. Ruede, *Sod-house Days,* 49–50, 53.

106. Ise, *Sod and Stubble,* 67, 158–59, 231; Ruede, *Sod-house Days,* 16, 41, 99, 102.

107. Ruede, *Sod-house Days,* 48, 55.

108. Ruede, *Sod-house Days,* 17, 167–68, 178.

109. Ruede, *Sod-house Days,* 35, 47, 52, 63, 66, 76, 93, 153.

110. Ruede, *Sod-house Days,* 171–72.

111. Ruede, *Sod-house Days,* 54, 120.

112. Ise, *Sod and Stubble,* 23, 102, 156.

113. Ise, *Sod and Stubble,* 90.

114. Ruede, *Sod-house Days,* 32–33.

115. Miller, *Waconda Land,* 32.

116. Ruede, *Sod-house Days,* 59.

117. Ise, *Sod and Stubble,* 55.

118.Ise, *Sod and Stubble,* 62–66 Miller, *Waconda Land,* 68–69.

119. Ruede, *Sod-house Days,* 92; Ise, *Sod and Stubble,* 44.

120. Ruede, *Sod-house Days,* 89.

121. Ise, *Sod and Stubble,* 135–36, 141.

122. Muilenburg and Swineford, *Post Rock.*

123. Muilenburg and Swineford, *Post Rock,* 57.

124. Miller, *Waconda Land,* 27.

125. Ise, *Sod and Stubble,* 42.

126. Alonzo Pruitt, "Ancient Glen Elder History," *Glen Elder Sentinel,* April 6, 1933.

127. Muilenburg and Swineford, *Post Rock,* 27–28.

128. Walter Prescott Webb, *The Great Plains* (New York: Grossett & Dunlap, 1931), 280–318; Muilenburg and Swineford, *Post Rock,* 29–30.

129. Muilenburg and Swineford, *Post Rock,* 31.

130. Muilenburg and Swineford, *Post Rock,* 38.

131. Muilenburg and Swineford, *Post Rock,* 31–33, 35, 55.

132. Muilenburg and Swineford, *Post Rock,* 38; Ise, *Sod and Stubble,* 41, 135.

133. Ruede, *Sod-house Days,* 78.

134. Muilenburg and Swineford, *Post Rock,* 35.

135. Muilenburg and Swineford, *Post Rock,* 39–43.

136. Muilenburg and Swineford, *Post Rock,* 46.

137. Muilenburg and Swineford, *Post Rock,* 47–48.

138. Muilenburg and Swineford, *Post Rock,* 50.

139. Muilenburg and Swineford, *Post Rock,* 60.

140. Ruede, *Sod-house Days,* 22.

141. Ruede, *Sod-house Days,* 114.

142. Muilenburg and Swineford, *Post Rock,* 64

143. Ise, *Sod and Stubble,* 163.

144. Muilenburg and Swineford, *Post Rock,* 63.

CHAPTER 7.

1. Dowd, "Waconda Springs;" Inez L. Ernzen, "History of Waconda Springs" in *Historical Moments of Mitchell County,* compiled by the Waconda Chapter, Kansas Anthropological Association (Beloit: A. B. D. Printers, 1976), 2; Gentleman, "History of Waconda Springs," 20.

2. Anonymous cited in Miller, *Waconda Land,* 6.

3. Ambrose Bierce, *The Devil's Dictionary* (New York: Oxford University Press, 1999), 123–24.

4. Patrick, "Great Spirit Spring," 23.

5. Melvin R. Gilmore, "Uses of Plants by the Indians of the Missouri River Region" (PhD diss., University of Nebraska, 1914).

6. Stith Thompson, *The Folktale* (Berkeley: University of California Press, 1977), 8–9.

7. Louise Pound, "Nebraska Legends of Lovers' Leaps," *Western Folklore* 8 (1949): 304–13.

8. Parks and Wedel, "Pawnee Geography," 159.

9. Richard M. Dorson, "A Theory for American Folklore," *Journal of American Folklore* 72, no. 285 (1959), 208.

10. Hutton, "A Lost Bit of Sea," 3.

11. K. K. Landes, *The Geology of Mitchell and Osborne Counties, Kansas,* Kansas Geological Survey, Bulletin 16 (Lawrence: Kansas Geological Survey, 1930), 50.

12. Gentleman, "History of Waconda Springs," 31; Hutton, "A Lost Bit of Sea," 3.

13. Dowd, "Waconda Springs"; Patrick, "Great Spirit Spring," 23.

14. Craig Casey, "The Waconda Story," in *Mitchell County Historical Essays, 1962–1976,* ed. Mitchell County Historical Society (Beloit, Kans.: Mitchell County Historical Society, 1976), 255–56.

15. Gentleman, "History of Waconda Springs," 31.

16. Miller, *Waconda Land,* 7.

17. Hutton, "A Lost Bit of Sea," 3; Wendell, "Waconda, 1871–1971."

18. Bailey, *Special Report,* 200–201.

19. A. van Tubergen and S. van der Linden, "A Brief History of Spa Therapy," *Annals of the Rheumatic Diseases* 61 (2002), 273–75; Křižek, "History of Balneotherapy," in *Medical Hydrology,* ed. Stanley Licht (New Haven: Elizabeth Licht, 1963), 131,149.

20. Křižek, "History of Balneotherapy," 135–36, 140.

21. Křižek, "History of Balneotherapy," 147.

22. Herman L. Kamenetz, "History of American Spas and Hydrotherapy," in *Medical Hydrology,* ed. Sidney Licht (New Haven: Elizabeth Licht, 1963), 165, 167–68.

23. Paul R. Drew, "Sir William Johnson—Indian Superintendent," *Early American Review* 1, no. 2 (1996).

24. Kamenetz, "History of American Spas," 165–67.

25. Kamenetz, "History of American Spas," 165–67.

26. Ise, *Sod and Stubble,* 213; Jane Wendell, "Waconda, 1871–1971," in *Historical Moments of Mitchell County,* compiled by the Waconda Chapter, Kansas Anthropological Association (Beloit: A. B. D. Printers, 1976), 245.

27. Gentleman, "History of Waconda Springs," 21–22; Ise, *Sod and Stubble,* 102; Miller, *Waconda Land,* 72, 74.

28. Dowd, "Waconda Springs;" Inez L. Ernzen, "History of Waconda Springs," in *Historical Moments of Mitchell County,* compiled by the Waconda Chapter, Kansas Anthropological Association (Beloit: A. B. D. Printers, 1976), 2; Parks and Wedel, "Pawnee Geography," 155.

29. Bailey, *Special Report,* 201.

30. Dowd, "Waconda Springs"; Gentleman, "History of Waconda Springs," 31.

31. Křižek, "History of Balneotherapy," 151–52.

32. Křižek, "History of Balneotherapy," 152.

33. Kamenetz, "History of American Spas," 172.

34. Susan E. Cayleff, *Wash and Be Healed: the Water-cure Movement and Women's Health* (Philadelphia: Temple University Press, 1987), 83.

35. Burke cited in Kamenetz, "History of American Spas," 169.

36. Dowd, "Waconda Springs"; Ise, *Sod and Stubble*, 132.

37. Dowd, "Waconda Springs"; Ernzen, "History of Waconda Springs," 2.

38. Gentleman, "History of Waconda Springs," 31.

39. Cayleff, *Wash and Be Healed*, 6.

40. Cayleff, *Wash and Be Healed*, 6–7.

41. Jane B. Donegan, *Hydropathic Highway to Health: Women and Water-cure in Antebellum America* (New York: Greenwood Press, 1986), 10.

42. Cayleff, *Wash and Be Healed*, 7; Donegan, *Hydropathic Highway*, 9.

43. Kamenetz, "History of American Spas," 163–69.

44. Sidney Licht, *Medical Hydrology* (New Haven: Elizabeth Licht, 1963), xvii.

45. Křižek, "History of Balneotherapy," 152.

46. Cayleff, *Wash and Be Healed*, 3.

47. Donegan, *Hydropathic Highway*, 7–8.

48. Alex Berman, "The Thomsonian Movement and Its Relation to American Pharmacy and Medicine," *Bulletin of the History of Medicine* 25 (1951), 519; Cayleff, *Wash and Be Healed*, 12

49. Cayleff, *Wash and Be Healed*, 2, 12; Donegan, *Hydropathic Highway*, 13.

50. Cayleff, *Wash and Be Healed*, 12; Martin Kaufman, *Homeopathy: The Rise and Fall of a Medical Heresy* (Baltimore: Johns Hopkins University Press, 1971).

51. Cayleff, *Wash and Be Healed*, 15.

52. Donegan, *Hydropathic Highway*, xiii, 22.

53. Cayleff, *Wash and Be Healed*, 8, 23; Křižek, "History of Balneotherapy," 141–42.

54. Donegan, *Hydropathic Highway*, xiii,19.

55. Cayleff, *Wash and Be Healed*, 28, 77, 91.

56. Cayleff, *Wash and Be Healed*, 32.

57. Donegan, *Hydropathic Highway*, 135–56.

58. Cayleff, *Wash and Be Healed*, 110.

59. Cayleff, *Wash and Be Healed*, 94. Donegan, *Hydropathic Highway*, 48–50.

60. Cayleff, *Wash and Be Healed*, 94.

61. Cayleff, *Wash and Be Healed*, 13; Donegan, *Hydropathic Highway*, 280.

62. Cayleff, *Wash and Be Healed*, 120–22.

63. Pizzorno, J. E., "Naturopathic Medicine," in *Fundamentals of Complementary and Alternative Medicine*, ed. M. S. Micozzi (New York: Churchill Livingstone, 1996), 163–81.

64. Moore, J. Stuart, *Chiropractic in America: The History of a Medical Alternative* (Baltimore, Johns Hopkins University Press, 1993).

65. Gevitz, Norman, *The DOs: Osteopathic Medicine in America* (Baltimore, Johns Hopkins University Press, 2004).

66. Cayleff, *Wash and Be Healed*, 39.

67. Licht, *Medical Hydrology*, xvi.

68. Donegan, *Hydropathic Highway*, 39; Harry B. Weiss and Howard R. Kemble,

The Great American Water-Cure: A History of Hydropathy in the United States (Trenton, N.J.: Past Times Press, 1967), 68.

69. Dowd, "Waconda Springs"; Gentleman, "History of Waconda Springs," 31.

70. Weston papers, Kansas State Historical Society.

CHAPTER 8.

1. Ise, *Sod and Stubble,* 10, 68, 204, 416–17n.

2. Tula Draher Emigh, *The Story of Lincoln Park, Cawker City, Kansas and the Marvelous Chautauquas Held There at the Turn of the Century* (Cawker City: Cawker City Ledger, n.d.), 1–3.

3. Victoria Case and Raymond Case, *We Called It Culture: The Story of Chautauqua* (Garden City, N.Y.: Doubleday, 1948), 11–14.

4. Case and Case, *We Called It Culture,* 14.

5. Case and Case, *We Called It Culture,* 15–16; Joseph E. Gould, *The Chautauqua Movement: An Episode in the Continuing American Revolution* (New York: State University of New York, 1961. 8–9, 13, 37).

6. Case and Case, *We Called It Culture,* 17.

7. Case and Case, *We Called It Culture,* 14; Gould, *Chautauqua Movement,* 10, 97.

8. Case and Case, *We Called It Culture,* 23.

9. Emigh, *Story of Lincoln Park.*

10. Emigh, *Story of Lincoln Park.*

11. Case and Case, *We Called It Culture,* 149–53.

12. Case and Case, *We Called It Culture,* 152.

13. Harry P. Harrison, as told to Karl Detzer, *Culture under Canvas: The Story of Tent Chautauqua* (Westport, Conn.: Greenwood Press, 1958), 44.

14. Case and Case, *We Called It Culture,* 26–27; Gould, *Chautauqua Movement,* 77.

15. Case and Case, *We Called It Culture,* 31–32.

16. Gould, *Chautauqua Movement,* 85–86.

17. Case and Case, *We Called It Culture,* 222–23.

18. Harrison, *Culture under Canvas,* 257–70.

19. Case and Case, *We Called It Culture,* 16.

20. Gould, *Chautauqua Movement,* 81–82.

21. Harrison, *Culture under Canvas,* 42.

22. Gould, *Chautauqua Movement,* 39–54.

23. John Stephenson, "Lincoln Park and the Years That Were," *Downs News-Times,* January 15–February 26, 1976.

24. U.S. Provost Marshall-General, "Tabulations Containing Information of Prisoners of War and Prisoner of War Camps," U.S. Provost Marshall-General's Bureau, Prisoner of War Operations. National Archives, R.G. 389, File 255, Box 1612, n.d.

25. Cecil Howes, "Prisoners at Work." *Kansas Magazine,* 1944, 57.

26. Patrick G. O'Brien, Thomas D. Isern, and R. Daniel Lumley, "Stalag Sunflower: German Prisoners of War in Kansas," *Kansas History* 7, no. 3 (1977), 188.

27. "German and Italian Prisoners of War Will Be Made Available to Farmers for Group Labor," *Topeka Capital Journal*, August 10, 1943.

28. U.S. Provost Marshall-General, "Tabulations."

29. O'Brien et al., "Stalag Sunflower," 194.

CHAPTER 9

1. James E. Sherow, "Workings of the Geodialectic: High Plains Indians and Their Horses in the Region of the Arkansas River Valley, 1800–1870," *Environmental History Review* 16 (1992): 261–84.

2. Donald J. Blakeslee, "Persistence and Change in the Natural and Cultural Landscapes of the Central Plains," *Transactions of the Kansas Academy of Sciences* 99, nos. 3–4 (1996): 86–94.

3. Dan Flores, "Spirit of Place and the Value of Nature in the American West," *Yellowstone Science* 3 (Spring 1993), 6.

GLOSSARY

Apsáalooke. The Crow nation's name for itself.
Aubrey Crossing. A ford of the Arkansas River on the Cimarron cutoff of the Santa Fe Trail, fifteen miles above Chouteau's Island, Hamilton County, Kansas.

Big Bellies. One of the names by which the Hidatsa were known. The same name was also applied to the unrelated Gros Ventres.
Black Dog Trail. A native trail that ran west near the southern border of Kansas before angling northwest to follow the divide between the Ninnescah and Chicaskia Rivers.
Brule. A subdivision of the Lakota Sioux that moved onto the high plains of Nebraska and Kansas.

Calvi. Pietro Fortunato Calvi (1817–1855) led resistance against the Austrians in defense of the Venetian Republic.
Carlana. An Apache band that lived in southwestern Colorado before being driven into New Mexico by Comanches.
cathartic. A substance that accelerates defecation, as opposed to a laxative, which eases it.
Cheyenne Bottom. An area of internal drainage just north of the Great Bend of the Arkansas River in Barton County, Kansas.
Cimarron River Trail. A native trail along the Cimarron River in southern Kansas.
Clackamas. A Chinookan-speaking band that lived in the Willamette Valley of Oregon.
Council House Fight. An incident in which Texans killed thirty-five Comanches who had gone to San Antonio to negotiate a peace.
cucurbits. The family of plants that includes pumpkins, squashes, and small gourds.

Dhegiha. A linguistic division of the Siouan stock, spoken by the Omahas, Poncas, Kansas, Osages, and Quapaws.
Dodge City–Tascosa Trail. A wagon trail that ran southwest from Dodge City to the Canadian River.

El Cuartelejo. A Spanish name for an Apache settlement in Scott County, Kansas, to which Picuris Indians fled after the reconquest of New Mexico.
emetic. A substance that causes vomiting.

factor. A middle-management-level position in the fur trade.
Fort Cavagnial. A French outpost on the Missouri River near present-day Leavenworth, Kansas, 1744–1764.
Fort Kearney. A military post on the Platte River, along the Oregon Trail, 1848–1871.
Fort Laramie. A fur trade post on the North Platte River, eastern Wyoming, that became a landmark on the Oregon Trail, 1834–1890.
Fort MacPherson. A military post below the forks of the Platte River, 1863–1880.
Fort Supply Trail. A wagon road that ran south from Fort Dodge to the post called Fort Supply on the North Canadian River, Oklahoma.
Fort William. The original name for Fort Laramie on the North Platte, eastern Wyoming, 1834.
Fort Zarah. An army post at the Great Bend of the Arkansas River, 1864–1869.

geomorphology. The science that studies how the surface features of the earth, including sediments, formed.
goosefoot. A weedy plant domesticated during the Archaic period in the eastern United States.
Grand Pawnee. One of the three bands of Pawnee known collectively as the South Band Pawnees, as opposed to the Skidi Pawnees.
Guas. An ethnic name used in the documents of the Coronado expedition for an unidentified group in the vicinity of Quivira.

Harahey. An ethnic name in the documents of the Coronado expedition for an unidentified group that lived somewhere beyond Quivira; often speculated to be Pawnee.
Hidalgo revolution. The unsuccessful Mexican revolution against Spanish rule, 1810–1811, led by Father Manuel Hidalgo.
Hopewell. The term archaeologists use for a period of intense intercultural interaction in the Woodland period that involved acquisition of exotic materials that were fashioned into ceremonial items used in mortuary-related rituals.
Humboldt map. An influential map drawn by Alexander von Humboldt and published in 1803. It mistakenly showed the headwaters of the Red River in the Sangre de Cristo Mountains of New Mexico, leading to decades of cartographic confusion.

Ietan. The Wichita name for the Comanches.
Iturbide revolution. The successful declaration of Mexican independence from Spain, led by Agustín Iturbide in 1821.

Jicarilla. A band of Apaches who were driven by the Comanches from the plains into New Mexico.

Jumano. A term that the Spanish used for any tattooed Indians, such as the Wichitas, and for an ethnic group of the Rio Grande–Concho River area.

Kiowa Apache. An Apache band that remained on the plains, allied to the Kiowa nation.

Lipan Apaches. Apaches who were driven far south into Texas by the Comanches.
Llano Estacado. The southern end of the high plains below the Canadian River—essentially a huge mesa covering much of the Texas panhandle and some of eastern New Mexico.

marsh elder. A plant with oily seeds that was domesticated during the Archaic period in the eastern United States.
Michilimackinac. A fur trade and military post on Michilimacinac Island in the straits that lead from Lake Michigan to Lake Huron.
Morning Star sacrifice. The human sacrifice practiced by the Skidi Pawnees devoted to Morning Star, the deity of warriors.

Oglala. A band of the Lakota Sioux that moved into western Nebraska in the 1820s.
Old Traders' Trail. A trail that ran south from Fort MacPherson on the Platte River to Old Fort Lyon in eastern Colorado.
Oneota tradition. An archaeological tradition of the prairies of the Midwest that spread into the eastern plains in the fourteenth century.

Padouca. A word of Siouan origin that the French used first for the Apaches of the high plains and later for the Comanches.
petroglyph. A form of rock art in which a design is pecked or incised on a rock face.
Pitahawiratas. One of the three bands that comprised the South Band Pawnee, also called Tappage.
placebo effect. The amelioration of medical symptoms that occurs because the patient believes a treatment will be effective.
purge. A laxative.

San Miguel del Vado. A New Mexican settlement on the Pecos River at a ford used by the Santa Fe Trail.
Skidi Pawnee. One of the two main divisions of the Pawnee nation.
South Band. One of the two main divisions of the Pawnee nation.
subluxation. In chiropractic, a syndrome caused by vertebral misalignment.
sutler. A civilian merchant who contracted to sell goods to a military unit in the field.
syndic. A person with standing to represent a corporation in business transactions.

Taovayas. One of the Wichita bands.
Tirawa. In Pawnee religion, the creator of heaven and earth.
travois. A carrying device consisting of two tipi poles crossed over the back of a draft animal and connected by a tray, forming an A-frame, on which goods were packed.

winter count. A mnemonic device consisting of one or two pictures for each year, that allowed a tribal historian to recall significant events.

Yellowstone Expedition. A military expedition led by Col. Henry Atkinson up the Missouri River in 1819–1820, which overwintered in eastern Nebraska. In spite of its name, it never came close to the Yellowstone River.

REFERENCES CITED

Adair, Mary J. "Paleoethnobotanical Research in Kansas." In *Kansas Archaeology,* ed. by Robert J. Hoard and William E. Banks, 248–63. Lawrence: University Press of Kansas, 2006.

Ahler, Stanley A., Thomas D. Thiessen, and Michael K. Trimble. *People of the Willows: The Prehistory and Early History of the Hidatsa Indians.* Grand Forks: University of North Dakota Press, 1991.

Albertson, F. W., and J. E. Weaver. *History of the Native Vegetation of Western Kansas during Seven Years of Continuous Drought.* Ecological Monographs. Ecological Society of America, 1942.

Anonymous. "A Bit of Mitchell County History." In *Historical Moments of Mitchell County,* compiled by the Waconda Chapter, Kansas Anthropological Association, 49–50. Beloit: A.B.D. Printers, 1976.

Anthony, David. "Migration in Archaeology: The Baby and the Bathwater." *American Anthropologist* 94 (1992): 895–914.

Bailey, E. H. S. *Special Report on Mineral Waters.* Topeka: University of Kansas Geological Survey, 1902.

Ball, Sydney H., "The Mining of Gems and Ornamental Stones by American Indians." *Bureau of American Ethnology Bulletin* 128, Anthropological Paper No. 13. Washington, D.C.: Government Printing Office, 1941.

Bamforth, Douglas B. "The PaleoIndian Occupation of the Medicine Creek Drainage, Southwestern Nebraska." In *Medicine Creek: Seventy Years of Archaeological Investigations,* ed. by Donna C. Roper, 54–83. Tuscaloosa: University of Alabama Press, 2002.

Barry, Louise. *The Beginning of the West: Annals of the Kansas Gateway to the American West, 1540–1854.* Topeka: Kansas State Historical Society, 1972.

Basso, Keith H. *Wisdom Sits in Places: Landscape and Language Among the Western Apache.* Albuquerque: University of New Mexico Press, 1996.

Beachum, Larry M. *William Becknell, Father of the Santa Fe Trade.* Southwestern Studies Monograph 68. El Paso: Texas Western Press, 1982.

Bement, L. C., and B. J. Carter. *Bison Hunting at Cooper Site: Where Lightning Bolts Drew Thundering Herds.* Norman: University of Oklahoma Press, 1999.

Berman, Alex, "The Thomsonian Movement and Its Relation to American Pharmacy and Medicine." *Bulletin of the History of Medicine* 25 (1951): 519.

Bierce, Ambrose. *The Devil's Dictionary.* New York: Oxford University Press, 1999.

Birkeland, P. W. *Pedology, Weathering and Geomorphological Research.* New York: Oxford University Press, 1984.

Blaine, Martha Royce. *Pawnee Passage, 1870–1875.* Norman: University of Oklahoma Press, 1990.

Blakeslee, Donald J. *Along Ancient Trails: The Mallet Expedition of 1739.* Niwot: University Press of Colorado, 1996.

———. "The Celestial Mirror: Investigations into Native American Cosmology." Manuscript in possession of the author, n.d.

———. "The Marine Shell Artifacts of Kansas." *Central Plains Archaeology* 5, no. 1 (1997): 3–9.

———. "A Meteor, A Mirror, A Metaphor." *Wisconsin Archaeologist* 84, nos. 1–2 (2003): 99–106.

———. "Middle Ceramic Period Earthlodges as the Products of Craft Traditions." In *Plains Earthlodges: Ethnographic and Archaeological Perspectives,* ed. Donna C. Roper and Elizabeth P. Pauls, 83–110. Tuscaloosa: University of Alabama Press, 2005.

———. "Persistence and Change in the Natural and Cultural Landscapes of the Central Plains." *Transactions of the Kansas Academy of Science* 99, nos. 3–4 (1996): 86–94.

———. *The Plains Interband Trade System: An Ethnohistoric and Archaeological Investigation.* Ann Arbor: University Microfilms, 1975.

———. "The Rattlesnake Creek and Walnut Creek Crossings of the Arkansas." *Wagon Tracks* 3 no.1 (1988): 4–5.

———. "Waconda Lake: Prehistoric Swidden-Foragers in the Central Plains." *Central Plains Archaeology* 7, no. 1 (1999).

Blakeslee, Donald J., and Robert Blasing. "Indian Trails in the Central Plains." *Plains Anthropologist* 33 (1988): 17–26.

Blakeslee, Donald J., Bob Blasing, and Hector Garcia. *Along the Pawnee Trail: Cultural Resource Survey and Testing, Wilson Lake, Kansas.* Kansas City, Mo.: U.S. Army Corps of Engineers, Kansas City District, 1986.

Blakeslee, Donald J., and Marlin Hawley. "Great Bend Aspect." In *Handbook of Kansas Archaeology,* ed. Robert Hoard and Will Banks, 165–79. Lawrence: University Press of Kansas, 2006.

Blakeslee, Donald J., Michelle Peck, and Ronald A. Dorsey. "Glen Elder: A Western Oneota Bison Hunting Camp." *Midcontinental Journal of Archaeology* 26, no. 1 (2001): 79–104.

Blakeslee, Donald J., and Arthur H. Rohn. *Man and Environment in Northeastern*

Kansas: The Hillsdale Lake Project. Kansas City: U. S. Army Corps of Engineers, 1986.

Blasing, Robert. "Pawnee Animal Lodges Revisited." Paper presented at the 13th Flint Hills Conference, Lincoln, Nebraska, 1991.

———. "A Possible Location for the 'Garden of the Gods' Described in Pawnee Stories." Paper presented at the 15th Flint Hills Conference, Wichita, Kansas, 1993.

———. "Prehistoric Geography of the Flint Hills." Master's thesis, Wichita State University, 1986.

Bloom, Lansing B. "The Death of Jacques d'Eglise." *New Mexico Historical Review* 2 (1927): 369–79.

Bolton, Herbert E. "French Intrusions into New Mexico, 1749–1752." In *Bolton and the Spanish Borderlands,* ed. John Francis Bannon, 150–71. Norman: University of Oklahoma Press, 1964.

Boone, Nathan. The Nathan Boone Journal manuscript. Special collections manuscript 88–11, Ablah Library, Wichita State University, 1843.

Bowers, Alfred W. *Hidatsa Social and Ceremonial Organization.* Bureau of American Ethnology Bulletin 194. Washington, D.C.: Smithsonian Contributions to Anthropology Institution Press, 1965.

———. *Mandan Social and Ceremonial Organization.* Chicago: University of Chicago Press, 1950.

Boyle, Susan Calfonte. *Los Capitalistas: Hispano Merchants and the Santa Fe Trail Trade.* Albuquerque: University of New Mexico Press, 2000.

Bozell, John R. "Plains Woodland Complexes of Western Kansas and Adjacent Portions of Nebraska and Colorado." In *Kansas Archaeology,* ed. Robert J. Hoard and William E. Banks, 93–104. Lawrence: University of Press of Kansas, 2006.

Bray, Edmund C., and Martha Coleman Bray. *Joseph N. Nicollet on the Plains and Prairies: The Expedition of 1838–39 with Journals, Letters, and Notes on the Dakota Indians.* St. Paul: Minnesota Historical Society Press, 1976.

Burke, John G. *Cosmic Debris: Meteorites in History.* Berkeley: University of California Press, 1986.

Burns, Louis F. *Osage Indian Customs and Myths.* Fallbrook, CA: Ciga Press, 1984.

Calder, James C. *The Majorville Cairn and Medicine Wheel.* Mercury Series, Archaeological Survey of Canada, Paper 62. Ottawa: National Museums of Canada, 1977.

Callahan, Kevin. *The Cupmarked Boulders of Blood Run, Iowa: Death Stones, Baby Rocks, & Vision Questing on the Northern Plains.* Upper Midwest Rock Art Papers. Minneapolis: University of Minnesota, 1999.

Carroll, John M., ed. *The Grand Duke Alexis in the United States of America.* New York: Interland Publishing, 1972.

Case, Victoria, and Raymond Case. *We Called It Culture: The Story of Chautauqua.* Garden City, N.Y.: Doubleday, 1948.

Casey, Craig. "The Waconda Story." In *Mitchell County Historical Essays, 1962–1976,* ed. Mitchell County Historical Society, 255–56. Beloit, Kans.: Mitchell County Historical Society, 1976.

Catlin, George. *Letters and Notes on the North American Indians.* New York: Clarkson N. Potter, 1975.

Cayleff, Susan E. *Wash and Be Healed: The Water-cure Movement and Women's Health.* Philadelphia: Temple University Press, 1987.

Chamberlain, Von Del. *When the Stars Came Down to Earth.* Los Altos, CA: Ballena Press, 1982.

Chittenden, Hiram. *The American Fur Trade of the Far West: A History of the Pioneer Trading Posts and Early Fur Companies of the Missouri Valley and the Rocky Mountains and of the Overland Commerce with Santa Fe.* New York: F. P. Harper, 1902.

Chrisman, Harry E. *Lost Trails of the Cimarron.* Denver: Sage Books, 1961.

Clark, W. P. *Indian Sign Language.* Philadelphia: L. R. Hamersly, 1885.

Connelley, William E. "Prairie Band of Pottawatomie Indians." *Collections of the Kansas State Historical Society* 14 (1918): 488–570.

Cook, Warren L. *Flood Tide of Empire: Spain and the Pacific Northwest, 1543–1819.* New Haven: Yale University Press, 1973.

Coues, Elliott. *The Expedition of Zebulon Montgomery Pike.* New York: Francis P. Harper, 1895.

———. *New Light on the Early History of the Greater Northwest: The Manuscript Journals of Alexander Henry and David Thompson, 1799–1814.* New York: Francis P. Harper, 1897.

Court of Claims, *The Omaha Tribe of Indians v the United States of America. Claim No. 31,002.* Washington, D.C., 1914.

Cuming, Alfred. "Report Number 27." In *Report of the Office of Indian Affairs, 1854.* Washington, D.C.: A. O. P. Nicholson, 1854.

Cushing, Frank Hamilton. "Origin Myth from Oraibi." *Journal of American Folklore* 36 (1923): 163–70.

Cutler, William G. *History of the State of Kansas.* Chicago: A. T. Andreas, 1883.

Daily Republican. Early Day History of Coffey County, Dating Back to the 1870s, Compiled from Interviews and Articles Written by Old-Timers. Burlington, Kans.: Daily Republican, 1960.

Dillehay, Tom. "Late Quaternary Bison Population Changes on the Southern Plains." *Plains Anthropologist* 19 (1974): 180–96.

Dodge, Richard I. *Our Wild Indians: Thirty-three Years' Personal Experience among the Red Men of the Great West.* Hartford, CT: A. D. Worthington, 1886.

———. *The Plains of the Great West and their Inhabitants, Being a Description of the Plains, Game, Indians, &c. of the Great North American Desert.* Reprint. New York: Archer House, 1959.

Donahue, R. L., R. W. Miller and J. C. Shickluna. *Soils: An Introduction to Soils and Plant Growth.* Englewood Cliffs, N.J.: Prentice-Hall, 1983.

Donegan, Jane B. *Hydropathic Highway to Health: Women and Water-cure in Antebellum America.* New York: Greenwood Press, 1986.

Dorsey, George. *The Mythology of the Wichita.* Washington, D.C.: Carnegie Institution, 1904.

Dorsey, Ronald A. "Archaeological Interpretation of Freshwater Mussel Assemblages near the Solomon River, Kansas." *Central Plains Archaeology* 8, no. 1 (1998): 13–24.

———. "Freshwater Mussel Shells and Archaeological Sites on the Solomon River." Master's thesis, Wichita State University, 1998.

Dorson, Richard M. "A Theory for American Folklore." *Journal of American Folklore* 72, no. 285 (1959): 197–215.

Dowd, Gregg. "Waconda Springs." Lecture given at Glen Elder State Park. Transcript in the Cawker City Public Library, 1989.

Drew, Paul R. "Sir William Johnson—Indian Superintendent." *Early American Review* 1, no. 2 (1996), www.earlyamerica.com/review/fall96/johnson.html.

Eighmy, Jeffry L., and Jason M. LaBelle. "Radiocarbon Dating of Twenty-Seven Plains Complexes and Phases." *Plains Anthropologist* 41 (1996): 53–70.

Emigh, Tula Draher. *The Story of Lincoln Park, Cawker City, Kansas and the Marvelous Chautauquas Held There at the Turn of the Century.* Cawker City: Cawker City Ledger, n.d.

Ernzen, Inez L. "History of Waconda Springs." In *Historical Moments of Mitchell County,* compiled by the Waconda Chapter, Kansas Anthropological Association, 2. Beloit: A. B. D. Printers, 1976.

Evans, Sterling, "Eastward, Ho! The Mexican Freighting and Commerce Experience along the Santa Fe Trail." *Kansas History* 19, no. 4 (Winter 1996–97): 242–60.

Farley, Alan W. *The Delaware Indians in Kansas, 1829–1867.* Kansas City, Mo., 1955.

Farrington, Oliver C. *Catalogue of the Meteorites of North America.* Memoirs of the National Academy of Sciences, 13. Washington, D.C., 1915.

Feagins, Jim D. "The Other Archaic Burial Mound in Kansas: Sorting the Components at the Range Mound (14ML307)." Paper presented at the 30th annual Flint Hills Conference, Lawrence, Kansas, 2008.

Fedirchuk, Gloria J., and Edward J. McCullough. "Prehistoric Art and Spiritualism: A Perspective from Pine Coulee, Alberta." *Alberta Archaeological Review* 22 (1991): 11–19.

Fitzpatrick, J. C., ed. "Land Ordinance of 1785, May 20, 1785." *Journals of the Continental Congress,* vol. 28: 375 ff.

Fletcher, Alice C., and Francis La Flesche. *The Omaha Tribe.* Twenty-seventh Annual Report, Smithsonian Institution. Washington, D.C.: Government Printing Office, 1911.

Flint, Richard, and Shirley Cushing Flint. *Documents of the Coronado Expedition, 1539–1542.* Dallas: Southern Methodist University Press, 2005.

Flores, Dan. "Bison Ecology and Bison Diplomacy: The Southern Plains from 1800 to 1850." *Journal of American History* 78, no. 2 (1991), 465–85.

———. "Spirit of Place and the Value of Nature in the American West." *Yellowstone Science* 3 (Spring 1993), 6–10.

Foster, Morris W., and Martha McCollough. "Plains Apache." In *Handbook of North American Indians, Volume 13, Part 2, Plains,* ed. Raymond J. DeMaillie, 926–40. Washington, D.C.: Smithsonian Institution Press, 2001.

Fowler, Jacob. *The Journal of Jacob Fowler.* Ed. Elliott Coues. Lincoln: University of Nebraska Press, 1965.

Frison, George C. *The Mill Iron Site.* Albuquerque: University of New Mexico Press, 1996.

Frison, George C., and Bruce A. Bradley. *Folsom Tools and Technology at the Hanson Site.* Albuquerque: University of New Mexico Press, 1980.

Frison, George C., and Dennis J. Stanford, ed. *The Agate Basin Site: A Record of the Paleoindian Occupation of the Northwestern High Plains.* New York: Academic Press, 1982.

Frison, George C., and Lawrence C. Todd. *The Colby Mammoth Site: Taphonomy and Archaeology of a Clovis Kill in Northern Wyoming.* Albuquerque: University of New Mexico Press, 1986.

Gatschet, Albert S. *Migration Legend of the Creek Indians.* 2 vols. Reprint. New York: Kraus Reprint, 1969.

———. "A sacred well in Kansas." *Journal of American Folklore* 2 (1891): 68–70.

Gentleman, Ava. "The History of Waconda Springs." *Solomon Valley Post, Bicentennial Edition,* 31. Beloit, Kans., 1976.

Gevitz , Norman. *The DOs: Osteopathic Medicine in America.* Baltimore, Johns Hopkins University Press, 2004.

Gilmore, Melvin R. "Methods of Indian Buffalo Hunts, with the Itinerary of the Last Tribal Hunt of the Omaha." *Papers of the Michigan Academy of Science, Arts and Letters* 18 (1932): 17–32.

———. "Uses of Plants by the Indians of the Missouri River Region." PhD diss., University of Nebraska, 1914.

———. *Uses of Plants by the Indians of the Missouri River Region.* Lincoln: University of Nebraska Press, 1977.

Goodman, George J., and Cheryl A. Lawson. *Retracing Major Stephen H. Long's 1820 Expedition: The Itinerary and Botany.* Norman: University of Oklahoma Press, 1995.

Goodnow, Ellen. "To My Dear Husband." Letter dated August 8, 1857. Isaac Goodnow collection, Kansas State Historical Society, #357, Box 1, Folder 49.

Gould, Joseph E. *The Chautauqua Movement: An Episode in the Continuing American Revolution.* New York: State University of New York, 1961.

Graham, A. L., A. W. R. Bevan, and R. Hutchison. *Catalogue of Meteorites, with Special Reference to Those Represented in the Collection of the British Museum (Natural History).* Tucson: University of Arizona Press, 1985.

Grange, Roger T., Jr. *Salvage Archaeology in the Red Willow Reservoir, Nebraska.* Nebraska State Historical Society Publications in Anthropology 9. Lincoln: Nebraska State Historical Society, 1980.

Grayson, Donald K., and David Meltzer. "A Requiem for North American Overkill." *Journal of Archaeological Science* 30 (2003): 585–93.

Gregg, Josiah. *Commerce of the Prairies.* Ed. Max L. Moorhead. Norman: University of Oklahoma Press, 1954.

Griffin, J. B., A. A. Gordus, and G. A. Wright. "Identification of the Sources of Hopewellian Obsidian in the Middle West." *American Antiquity* 34 (1969): 1–14.

Grinnell, George Bird. *The Fighting Cheyennes.* New York: Charles Scribner's Sons, 1915.

———. *Pawnee Hero Stories and Folk Tales.* New York: Forest and Stream, 1889.

Hackett, Charles W. *Pichardo's Treatise on the Limits of Louisiana and Texas.* Austin: University of Texas Press, 1931–46.

Hall, Russell L., Amy L. Collett, Timothy A. Hauschild, Lisa A. Hertz, and Patricia J. O' Brien. A *Cultural Resource Survey of Lincoln County, Kansas.* Manhattan: Kansas State University, Community Service Project, Kansas Center for Rural Initiatives, 1991.

Hammond, George Peter, and Agapito Rey. *Narratives of the Coronado Expedition.* Albuquerque: University of New Mexico Press, 1940.

Harrison, B. R., and K. L. Killen. *Lake Theo: A Stratified Early Man Bison Butchering and Camp Site, Briscoe County, Texas.* Panhandle-Plains Historical Museum, Special Archaeological Report 1. Canyon, Tex.: Panhandle-Plains Historical Museum, 1978.

Harrison, Harry P., as told to Karl Detzer. *Culture under Canvas: The Story of Tent Chautauqua.* Westport, Conn.: Greenwood Press, 1958.

Hart, Stephen H., and Archer Butler Hulbert. *Zebulon Pike's Arkansaw Journal: In Search of the Southern Louisiana Purchase Boundary Line.* Westport, Conn.: Greenwood Press, 1972.

Hattin, Donald E. *Stratigraphy of the Carlile Shale in Kansas.* State Geological Survey of Kansas Bulletin 156. Lawrence: State Geological Survey, 1962.

Haynes, Gary. *The Early Settlement of North America: The Clovis Era.* Cambridge: Cambridge University Press, 1980.

Haywood, C. Robert. *Trails South: The Wagon Road Economy in the Dodge City Panhandle Region.* Norman: University of Oklahoma Press, 1986.

Henning, Dale R., and Shirley J. Schermer. "Central Siouans in the Northeastern Plains: Oneota Archaeology and the Blood Run Site." In *Dhegihan and Chiwere Siouans in the Plains: Historical and Archaeological Perspectives. Plains Anthropologi*st, Memoir 36, 2004.

Hoard, Robert J., and William E. Banks. "Introduction." In *Kansas Archaeology,* ed. Robert J. Hoard and William E. Banks, 1–9. Lawrence: University Press of Kansas, 2006.

Hofman, Jack L., R. L. Brooks, D. W. Owsley, R. L. Jantz, M. K. Marks, and M. H. Manheim. *From Clovis to Comanchero: An Archaeological Overview of the Southern Great Plains.* Research Report No. 35. Fayetteville: Arkansas Archaeological Survey, 1989.

Holen, Steven R. "Bison Hunting Territories and Lithic Acquisition among the Pawnee: An Ethnohistoric and Archaeological Study." In *Raw Material Economics anong Prehistoric Hunter-Gatherers,* ed. Anta Montet-White and Steven R. Holen, 399–411. University of Kansas Publications in Anthropology No. 19. Lawrence: University of Kansas, 1991.

———. "Lithic Procurement at the Gray Site, 25CX1." Master's thesis, University of Nebraska, 1983.

Holen, Steven R., and David W. May. "The La Sena and Shaffert Mammoth Sites: History of Investigations, 1987–1998." In *Medicine Creek: Seventy Years of Archaeological Investigations,* ed. Donna C. Roper, 20–36. Tuscaloosa: University of Alabama Press, 2002.

Homan, Dorothe Tarrence. *Lincoln—That County in Kansas.* Lindsborg, Kans.: Barbos Printing, 1979.

Hotz, Gottfried. *Indian Skin Paintings from the American Southwest: Two Representations of Border Conflicts between Mexico and the Missouri in the Early Eighteenth Century.* Translated Johannes Malthaner. Norman: University of Oklahoma Press, 1970.

Houghton, Alan B. *The Frontier Aflame: An Account of the Bell-Bogardus Massacre and Other Indian Raids in Mitchell County and the Solomon Valley in August, 1868.* Beloit, Kans.: Beloit Daily Call, 1958.

Howes, Cecil. "Prisoners at Work." *Kansas Magazine,* 1944: 57–62.

Hutton, Marjorie. "A Lost Bit of Sea." In *Mitchell County Historical Moments County,* compiled by the Waconda Chapter, Kansas Anthropological Association, 3. Beloit: A. B. D. Printers, 1976.

Hyde, George E. *Spotted Tail's Folk: A History of the Brulé Sioux.* Norman: University of Oklahoma Press, 1961.

Inman, Henry. *The Old Santa Fe Trail; The Story of a Great Highway.* Topeka: Crane & Co., 1916.

Irving, John Treat. *Indian Sketches Taken During an Expedition to the Pawnee Tribes.* Norman: University of Oklahoma Press, 1955.

Irving, Washington. *A Tour on the Prairies.* Ed. John Francis McDermott. Norman: University of Oklahoma Press, 1956.

Irwin-Williams, Cynthia, Henry T. Irwin, George A. Agogino, and C. Vance Haynes, Jr. "Hell Gap: Paleo-Indian Occupation on the High Plains." *Plains Anthropologist* 18 (1973): 40–53.

Ise, John. *Sod and Stubble.* Lawrence: University of Kansas Press, 1996.

Jablow, Jacob. *The Cheyenne in Plains Indian Trade Relations, 1795–1840.* Seattle: University of Washington Press, 1950.

Jackson, Donald, ed. *The Journals of Zebulon Montgomery Pike, with Letters and Related Documents.* Norman: University of Oklahoma Press, 1966.

James, Edwin. *An Account of an Expedition from Pittsburgh to the Rock Mountains, Performed in the Years 1819–1820 . . . Under the Command of Major Stephen H. Long.* Philadelphia: H. C. Carey & I. Lea, 1823.

James, Thomas. *Three Years Among the Indians and Mexicans.* Ed. Milo Milton Quaife. Chicago: Lakeside Press, 1953.

Jennings, Francis. *The Invasion of America: Indians, Colonialism, and the Cant of Conquest.* Chapel Hill: University of North Carolina Press, 1975.

Jett, Stephen C. "Observations Regarding Chartkoff's California 'Rock Feature Complex.'" *American Antiquity* 51, no. 3 (1986): 615–16.

John, Elizabeth A. H. *Storms Brewed in Other Men's Worlds: The Confrontations of Indians, Spanish and French in the Southwest, 1540–1795.* Lincoln: University of Nebraska Press, 1975.

Johnson, Alfred E., ed. *Hopewellian Archaeology in the Lower Missouri Valley.* University of Kansas Publications in Anthropology 8. Lawrence: University of Kansas, 1976.

———. "Kansas City Hopewell." In *Hopewell Archaeology: The Chillicothe Conference,* ed. David S. Brose and N'omi Greber, 86–93. Kent, Ohio: Kent State University Press, 1979.

Johnson, Eileen. "The Lubbock Lake PaleoIndian Record." In *Guidebook to the Central Llano Estacado,* ed. Vance T. Holliday, 81–105. Lubbock: Friends of the Pleistocene, South-Central Field Trip, ICASALS and the Museum, Texas Tech University, 1983.

Kamenetz, Herman L., "History of American Spas and Hydrotherapy." In *Medical Hydrology,* ed. Sidney Licht, 160–88. New Haven: Elizabeth Licht, 1963.

Kansas Association of Land Surveyors. *Kansas Survey Plats.* [Digitized maps and notes]. Leavenworth, Kans.: Duke West Intergraphics, 2005.

Kappler, Charles J., ed. *Indian Treaties, 1778–1883.* With a new foreword by Brantley Blue. New York: Interland Publishing, 1972.

Kaufman, Martin. *Homeopathy: The Rise and Fall of a Medical Heresy.* Baltimore: Johns Hopkins University Press, 1971.

Kavanaugh, Thomas W. "Comanche." In *Handbook of North American Indians, Vol. 13, Part 2, Plains,* ed. Raymond J. DeMaillie, 886–906. Washington, D.C.: Smithsonian Institution Press, 2001.

Kehoe, Thomas F., and Alice B. Kehoe. "Boulder Effigy Monuments in the Northern Plains." *Journal of American Folklore* 72, no. 284 (1959): 115–27.

Kelley, Robert L., and Lawrence C. Todd. "Coming into the Country: Early PaleoIndian Hunting and Mobility." *American Antiquity* 53 (1998): 231–44.

Kessell, John L. *Kiva, Cross, and Crown: The Pecos Indians and New Mexico, 1540–1840.* Washington, D.C.: National Park Service, 1979.

Kivett, Marvin F., and George Metcalf. *The Prehistoric People of Medicine Creek Reservoir, Frontier County, Nebraska: An Experiment in Mechanical Archaeology. Plains Anthropologist,* Memoir 30, 1997.

Knudson, Ruthann. "Medicine Creek is a PaleoIndian Ecotone: The Red Smoke Assemblage." In *Medicine Creek: Seventy Years of Archaeological Investigations,* ed. Donna C. Roper, 84–141. Tuscaloosa: University of Alabama Press, 2002.

Křižek, Vladimír. "History of Balneotherapy." In *Medical Hydrology,* ed. Stanley Licht, 131–59. New Haven: Elizabeth Licht, 1963.

La Flesche, Francis. *A Dictionary of the Osage Language.* Bureau of American Ethnology Bulletin 109. Washington, D.C.: Bureau of American Ethnology, 1932.

Landes, K. K. *The Geology of Mitchell and Osborne Counties, Kansas.* Lawrence: Kansas Geological Survey, Bulletin 16, 1930.

Latham, Mark A. "Sampling Strategies and Site Distribution of the Solomon River Phase of the Glen Elder Locality of North-Central Kansas." Master's thesis, Wichita State University, 1996.

Lavender, David S. *Bent's Fort.* Garden City, N.Y.: Doubleday, 1954.

Licht, Sidney. *Medical Hydrology.* New Haven: Elizabeth Licht, 1963.

Loendorf, Lawrence L., and Joan Louise Brownell. "The Bad Pass Trail." *Archaeology in Montana* 21, no. 3 (1980): 11–102.

Logan, Brad. *Phasing in White Rock: Archaeological Investigation of the White Rock and Warne Sites, Lovewell Reservoir, Jewell County, Kansas, 1994–1995.* Museum of Anthropology University of Kansas Project Completion Series 90. Lawrence: Museum of Anthropology, University of Kansas, 1995.

———. "Woodland Adaptations in Eastern Kansas." In *Kansas Archaeology,* ed. Robert J. Hoard and William E. Banks, 76–92. Lawrence: University of Press of Kansas, 2006.

Loomis, Noel, and Abraham P. Nasatir. *Pedro Vial and the Roads to Santa Fe.* Norman: University of Oklahoma Press, 1967.

Mallam, R. Clark. *Site of the Serpent: A Prehistoric Life Metaphor in South Central Kansas.* Occasional Publications of the Coronado–Quivira Museum 1. Rice, Kans.: Coronado–Quivira Museum, 1985.

Malouf, Carling I. "On the Trail of the Indian." *Archaeology in Montana* 21, no. 3 (1980): 1.

Mandel, Rolfe D. "The Effects of Late Quaternary Landscape Evolution on the Archaeological Record of Kansas." In *Kansas Archaeology,* ed. Robert J. Hoard and William E. Banks, 28–45. Lawrence: University Press of Kansas, 2006.

Manypenny, George W. "Report of the Commissioner of Indian Affairs." In *Report of the Office of Indian Affairs, 1854.* Washington, D.C.: A. O. P. Nicholson, 1854.

Marino, Cesare, and Ken Comery. "Carlo deRudio: A Survivor of the Little Bighorn." www.derudio.co.uk.

Marshall, James O. "The Glen Elder Focus: The Cultural Affiliations of Archaeological Material from the Glen Elder Site, 14ML1." Master's thesis, University of Nebraska, 1967.

Martin, Paul S. "Prehistoric Overkill." In *Pleistocene Extinctions: The Search for a Cause,* ed. Paul S. Martin and H. E. Wright, Jr., 75–120. New Haven: Yale University Press, 1967.

———. "Prehistoric Overkill: The Global Model." In *Quaternary Extinctions: A Prehistoric Revolution,* ed. Paul S. Martin and Richard G. Klein, 354–403. Tucson: University of Arizona Press, 1984.

Matthews, John Joseph, *The Osages: Children of the Middle Waters.* Norman: University of Oklahoma Press, 1961.

May, David W. "Geoarchaeology of Four Sites at Lake Waconda, Kansas." Report submitted to Bureau of Reclamation, Grand Island, Nebraska, 1991.

———. "Holocene Fluvial Landforms and Alluvial Stratigraphy in the Solomon River Valley, Lake Waconda, Kansas." Report to the Bureau of Reclamation, Grand Island, Nebraska, 1991.

Mayewski , Paul A., and Michael Bender. "The GISP2 Ice Core Record—Paleoclimate Highlights." In *U.S. National Report to IUGG, 1991–1994. Review of Geophysics* 33 suppl. (1995).

McCleary, Timothy P. "Quest for the Morning Star Stone." *North Dakota Quarterly* 67, nos. 3–4 (2000): 127–34.

McConnell, Whit. "McConnell and the Indians." In *Historical Moments of Mitchell County,* compiled by the Waconda Chapter, Kansas Anthropological Association, 46–48. Beloit: A. B. D. Printers, 1976.

Mead, James R. *Hunting and Trading on the Great Plains, 1859–1875.* Ed. Schuyler Jones. Norman: University of Oklahoma Press, 1986.

———. J. R. Mead collection, Special Collections Department, Ablah Library, Wichita State University.

———. "Trails in Southern Kansas." *Kansas State Historical Society Collections* 5: (1896): 88–93.

Meriwether, David. *My Life in the Mountains and on the Plains.* Ed. R. A. Griffin. Norman: University of Oklahoma Press, 1965.

Military Division of the Missouri. *Record of Engagements with Hostile Indians within the Military Division of the Missouri, from 1868 to 1882, Lieutenant General P. H. Sheridan, Commanding, Compiled from Official Records.* Chicago: U.S. Army, Division of the Missouri, 1882.

Miller, Alfred Jacob. *The West of Alfred Jacob Miller (1837), from the Notes and Water Colors in the Walters Art Gallery.* Norman: University of Oklahoma Press, 1951.

Miller, Darrel. *Waconda Land: The Legends and Pioneers' Accounts of Settling the Land.* Downs, Kans.: Cellar Door Publications, 1989.

Miner, H. Craig, and William E. Unrau. *The End of Indian Kansas: A Study of Cultural Revolution, 1854–1871.* Lawrence: Regents Press of Kansas, 1978.

Mooney, James. *Calendar History of the Kiowa Indians.* Reprint of the 1898 edition, with an introduction by John C. Ewers. Bureau of American Ethnology 17th Annual Report. Washington, D.C.: Bureau of American Ethnology, 1979.

Moore, J. Stuart. *Chiropractic in America: The History of a Medical Alternative.* Baltimore: Johns Hopkins University Press, 1993.

Moore, Robert J. *Native Americans: A Portrait: The Art and Travels of Charles Bird King, George Catlin, and Karl Bodmer.* New York: Stewart, Tabori & Chang, 1997.

Morgan, Louis Henry. *The Indian Journals, 1859–62.* Ed. Leslie A.White. Ann Arbor: University of Michigan Press, 1959.

Muilenburg, Grace, and Ada Swineford. *Land of the Post Rock: Its Origins, History, and People.* Lawrence: University Press of Kansas, 1975.

Munday, Frank J. "The Record of the Pike Expedition." *Nebraska History Magazine* 10, no. 3 (1927), 168–69.

Murie, James R. *Ceremonies of the Pawnee.* Ed. Douglas R. Parks. Smithsonian Contributions to Anthropology. Washington, D.C.: Smithsonian Institution Press, 1981.

Murray, Charles Augustus. *Travels in North America during the Years 1834, 1835, & 1836.* London: Richard Bentley, 1839.

Myer, William E. "Indian Trails of the Southeast." Washington, D.C.: Bureau of American Ethnology, 42nd Annual Report (1928): 727–857.

Nasatir, Abraham P. *Before Lewis and Clark: Documents Illustrating the History of the Missouri, 1785–1804.* 2 Vols. St. Louis: St. Louis Historical Documents Foundation, 1952.

Nelson, John Y. *Fifty Years on the Trail: A True Story of Western Life.* Ed. Harrington O'Reilly. Norman: University of Oklahoma Press, 1963.

Newman, Tillie Karns. *The Black Dog Trail.* Boston: Christopher Publishing House, 1957.

Nicholas, Colleen B. "A Recording of Private Artifact Collections in Morton County, Kansas." Master's thesis, Wichita State University, 2005.

Nickerson, Colin. "Cosmic Blast May Have Killed Off Megafauna." *Boston Globe,* September 25, 2007.

Norall, Frank. *Bourgmont: Explorer of the Missouri, 1698–1725.* Lincoln: University of Nebraska Press, 1988.

North, Luther Heddon. *Man of the Plains: Recollections of Luther North, 1856-1882.* Ed. Donald F. Danker. Lincoln: University of Nebraska Press, 1961.

O'Brien, Patricia A. "The Ashland Bottom Site (14RY603): A Kansas City Hopewell Site in North Central Kansas." *Plains Anthropologist* 24 (1979): 1–20.

O'Brien, Patrick G., Thomas D. Isern, and R. Daniel Lumley. "Stalag Sunflower: German Prisoners of War in Kansas." *Kansas History* 7, no. 3 (1977): 182–98.

Osborne, Charles C. "Adams County: The Early Years." In *Adams County: The Story,* ed. Dorothy Weyer Creigh, 1–5. Hastings, Neb.: Adams County-Hastings Centennial Commission, 1972.

Owsley, Douglas W., and David R. Hunt. "Clovis and Early Archaic Period Crania from the Anzick Site (24PA506), Park County, Montana." *Plains Anthropologist* 46 (2001): 125–48.

Parks, Douglas R., and Waldo R. Wedel. "Pawnee Geography: Historical and Sacred.'" *Great Plains Quarterly,* Summer 1985, 143–76.

Patrick, G. K. "The Great Spirit Spring." *Transactions of the Kansas Academy of Science* 7 (1881): 22–26.

Pattie, James Ohio. *The Personal Narrative of James Ohio Pattie.* Ed. Timothy Flint. Lincoln: University of Nebraska Press, 1984.

Peck, M. Michelle. "A Study of Great Bend Aspect Hunting Camp Sites within the State of Kansas." Master's thesis, Wichita State University, 2003.

Pizzorno, J. E. "Naturopathic Medicine." In *Fundamentals of Complementary and Alternative Medicine,* ed. M. S. Micozzi, 163–81. New York: Churchill Livingstone, 1996.

Pound, Louise. "Nebraska Legends of Lovers' Leaps." *Western Folklore* 8 (1949): 304–13.

Powell, Peter John. *People of the Sacred Mountain: A History of the Northern Cheyenne Chiefs and Warrior Societies, 1830–1879.* San Francisco: Harper & Row, 1981.

Pruitt, Alonzo. "Ancient Glen Elder History." *Glen Elder Sentinel,* April 6, 1933.

Raudot, Antoine Davis. "Memoir Concerning the Different Indian Nations of North America." In *The Indians of the Western Great Lakes,* ed. W. Vernon Kinietz. Occasional Contributions from the Museum of Anthropology of the University of Michigan, 10 (1940): 341–410.

Reeves, Brian. "How Old is the Old North Trail?" *Archaeology in Montana* 31, no. 2 (1990): 1–18.

Republic County Historical Society. *History of Republic County, 1864–1964.* Belleville, Kans.: Belleville Telescope, 1964.

Reynolds, John. "Preliminary Report of Archeological Investigations at 14ML307, the Range Mound, Glen Elder, Kansas." *Kansas Anthropological Association Newsletter* 23, nos. 2–3 (1977): 1–11.

Ritterbush, Lauren W. "Late Prehistoric Oneota in the Central Plains." In *Kansas Archaeology,* ed. Robert J. Hoard and William E. Banks, 151–65. Lawrence: University Press of Kansas, 2006.

Roper, Donna C. "The Central Plains Tradition." In *Kansas Archaeology,* ed. Robert J. Hoard and William E. Banks, 105–32. Lawrence: University Press of Kansas, 2006.

Ross, Harry E. *What Price White Rock: A Chronicle of Northwestern Jewell County.* Burr Oak, Kans.: Herald Press, 1937.

Ruede, Howard. *Sod-house Days.* Ed. John Ise. New York: Cooper Square, 1966.

San Francisco Call. "De Rudio Served with Gen. Custer." *The San Francisco Call,* September 30, 1908.

Sandoz, Mari. *Cheyenne Autumn.* New York: McGraw-Hill, 1953.

Schindler, Hal. "Sir George, the Buffalo Slayer." *Salt Lake Tribune,* February 16, 1997.

Schlesier, Karl H., *The Wolves of Heaven: Cheyenne Shamanism, Ceremonies and Prehistoric Origins.* Norman: University of Oklahoma Press, 1987.

Schultz, George A. *An Indian Canaan: Isaac McCoy and the Vision of an Indian State.* Norman: University of Oklahoma Press, 1972.

Sheldon, Addison E. "A New Chapter in Nebraska History." *Nebraska History* 6, no. 1 (1927): 1–31.

Sherow, James E. "Workings of the Geodialectic: High Plains Indians and Their Horses in the Region of the Arkansas River Valley, 1800–1870." *Environmental History Review* 16 (1992): 261–84.

Shortridge, James R. *Peopling the Plains: Who Settled Where in Frontier Kansas.* Lawrence: University Press of Kansas, 1995.

Sibley, George. "Extracts from the Journal of Major George Sibley." *Chronicles of Oklahoma* 5, no. 2 (1927): 196–220.

Smith, Kirk. "The Archaic Period in Southwestern Kansas." Master's thesis, Wichita State University, 2005.

Stafford, Michael D. "The Powars II Site (48PL330): A PaleoIndian Red Ocher Mine in Eastern Wyoming." Master's thesis, Department of Anthropology, University of Wyoming, 1990.

Stanford, Dennis J. "The Jones-Miller Site: An Example of Hell Gap Bison Procurement Strategy." In *Bison Procurement and Utilization,* ed. L. B. Davis and M. Wilson, 90–97. *Plains Anthropologist,* Memoir 14, 1978.

Steinberg, Ruth. "José Jarvet, Spanish Scout and Historical Enigma." *New Mexico Historical Review,* July 1992, 227–49.

Stephenson, John, "Lincoln Park and the Years that Were." *Downs News-Times,* Jan 15–Feb 26, 1976.

Strickland, R. F. "Robert McKnight." In *The Mountain Men and the Fur Trade of the Far West,* vol. 3, ed. L. R. Hafen, 27–37. Glendale, Calif.: A. H. Clark, 1972.

Sundstrom, Linea. "Sacred Islands: An Exploration of Religion and Landscape in the Northern Great Plains." In *Islands on the Plains: Ecological, Social and Ritual Use of Landscapes,* ed. by Marcel Kornfeld and Alan J. Osborn, 258–300. Salt Lake City: University of Utah Press, 2003.

Thomas, Alfred Barnaby. *After Coronado.* Norman: University of Oklahoma Press, 1935.

———. *The Plains Indians and New Mexico, 1751–1778.* Albuquerque: University of New Mexico Press, 1940.

Thompson, Stith. *The Folktale.* Berkeley: University of California Press, 1977.

Topeka Capital Journal. "German and Italian Prisoners of War Will Be Made Available to Farmers for Group Labor." *Topeka Capital Journal,* August 10, 1943.

U.S. Provost Marshall-General. "Tabulations Containing Information of Prisoners of War and Prisoner of War Camps." U.S. Provost Marshall-General's Bureau, Prisoner of War Operations. National Archives, R.G. 389, File 255, Box 1612, n.d.

van Tubergen, A., and S. van der Linden. "A Brief History of Spa Therapy." *Annals of the Rheumatic Diseases* 61 (2002): 273–75.

Vehik, Susan C. "Oñate's Expedition to the Southern Plains: Routes, Destinations and Implications for Late Prehistoric Cultural Adaptations." *Plains Anthropologist* 31 (1986): 13–33.

Wasson, J. T. and S. P. Sedwick. "Possible Sources of Meteoric Material from Hopewell Indian Burial Mounds." *Nature* 222 (1969): 22–24.

Webb, Walter Prescott. *The Great Plains.* New York: Grossett & Dunlap, 1931.

Weber, David J., ed. *The Extranjeros: Selected Documents from the Mexican Side of the Santa Fe Trail, 1825-1828.* Santa Fe: Stagecoach Press, 1967.

———. *The Taos Trappers: The Fur Trade in the Far Southwest, 1540–1846*. Norman: University of Oklahoma Press, 1971.

Wedel, Mildred Mott. *The Deer Creek Site, Oklahoma: A Wichita Village Sometimes Called Ferdinandina: An Ethnohistorian's View.* Oklahoma Historical Society Series in Anthropology 5, 1981.

———. "The Ethnohistoric Approach to Caddoan Origins." *Nebraska History* 60 (1979): 183–96.

———. "The Wichita Indians in the Arkansas River Basin." In *Plains Indian Studies,* ed. Douglas H. Ubelaker and Herman J. Viola, 118–34. Smithsonian Contributions to Anthropology 30. Washington, D.C., Smithsonian Institution Press, 1982.

Wedel, Waldo R. *An Introduction to Pawnee Archaeology.* Bureau of American Ethnology Bulletin 112. Washington, D.C.: Bureau of American Ethnology, 1936.

Weiss, Harry B., and Howard R. Kemble. *The Great American Water-Cure: A History of Hydropathy in the United States.* Trenton, N.J.: Past Times Press, 1967.

Wells, P. V., and J. D. Stewart. "Spruce Charcoal, Conifer Macrofossils, and Landsnail and Small Vertebrate Fauna in Wisconsinan Sedimentation in the High Plains of Kansas." In *Quaternary Environments of Kansas,* ed. W. C. Johnson, 129–40. Kansas Biological Survey Guidebook Series 5. Lawrence: Kansas Geological Survey, University of Kansas, 1987.

Weltfish, Gene. *The Lost Universe.* New York: Basic Books, 1965.

Wendell, Jane. "Waconda, 1871–1971." In *Historical Moments of Mitchell County,* compiled by the Waconda Chapter, Kansas Anthropological Association, 245–46. Beloit: A. B. D. Printers, 1976.

West, Frederick H. "The Antiquity of Man in America." In *Late Quaternary Environments of the United States, Vol. 1: The Late Pleistocene,* ed. S. C. Porter, 364–82. Minneapolis: University of Minnesota Press, 1983.

Wheat, Carl Irving. *Mapping the Transmississippi West, 1540–1861.* San Francisco: Institute of Historical Cartography, 1957.

White, Lonnie J. "Indian Raids on the Kansas Frontier, 1869." *Kansas Historical Quarterly* 38, no. 4 (1972): 369–88.

Whitfield, John W. "Report Number 29." In *Report of the Office of Indian Affairs, 1854.* Washington, D.C.: A. O. P. Nicholson, 1854.

Wied, Maximillian. *Maximilian, Prince of Wied's Travels in the Interior of North America, 1832–1834.* New York: AMS Press, 1966.

Wilhelm, Paul, Duke of Württemberg. *Travels in North America, 1822–1824,* trans. W. Robert Nitske, ed. Savoie Lottinville. Norman: University of Oklahoma Press, 1973.

Will, George F. *Archaeology of the Missouri Valley.* American Museum of Natural History Anthropological Papers 22, no. 4. New York, 1924.

Wilmsen, Edwin N., and Frank H. H. Roberts, Jr. *Lindenmeier: 1934–1974: Concluding Report on Investigations.* Washington, D.C.: Smithsonian Institution Press, 1978.

Winsor, M., and James A. Scarborough. "Jewell County." *Collections of the Kansas State Historical Society* 17 (1928): 389–409.

Wislizenus, Frederick A. *A Journey to the Rocky Mountains, 1839*. Glorieta, N.M.: Rio Grande Press, 1969.

Woodhouse, Connie A., Jeffrey J. Lukas, and Peter M. Brown. "Drought in the Western Great Plains, 1845–56: Impacts and Implications." *Bulletin of the American Meteorological Society* 83 (2002): 1485–93.

INDEX